STRUGGLING
WITH SUCCESS

Challenges Facing the
International Economy

Anne O Krueger

Johns Hopkins University, USA

STRUGGLING WITH SUCCESS

Challenges Facing the International Economy

World Scientific

NEW JERSEY • LONDON • SINGAPORE • BEIJING • SHANGHAI • HONG KONG • TAIPEI • CHENNAI

Published by

World Scientific Publishing Co. Pte. Ltd.

5 Toh Tuck Link, Singapore 596224

USA office: 27 Warren Street, Suite 401-402, Hackensack, NJ 07601

UK office: 57 Shelton Street, Covent Garden, London WC2H 9HE

British Library Cataloguing-in-Publication Data
A catalogue record for this book is available from the British Library.

STRUGGLING WITH SUCCESS
Challenges Facing the International Economy

ISBN-13 978-981-4374-31-6
ISBN-10 981-4374-31-8

In-house Editor: Ms. Sandhya Venkatesh

Typeset by Stallion Press
Email: enquiries@stallionpress.com

Printed in Singapore by B & Jo Enterprise Pte Ltd

PREFACE

Since the outset of the financial crisis in 2007, it has become fashionable to assert that globalization was an, if not the, underlying cause of the crisis. From that assertion, some have concluded that globalization had gone too far, and needed to be reversed in one or more critical dimensions.

It is certainly true that some lessons have been learned and more will be learned from the crisis. Policy makers will adjust domestic and international policies and procedures in response, and doubtless many of the changes will strengthen the international economic system.

But it often seems forgotten how great the benefits of globalization have been. The past half century has seen huge progress in living standards of the vast majority of the world's population. This progress has translated into increases in life expectancy, greater literacy, improved health and nutritional status, especially in the places which were regarded as "underdeveloped" in the 1950s.

When Zvi Ruder of World Scientific Publishers approached me to put together some of the papers I had done, I thought that I could assemble material that might remind the critics of the successes of globalization, and simultaneously point to some of the challenges that must be addressed if we are to improve on the functioning of the system.

Focus should not be on reversing globalization; rather, it should be on finding ways to strengthen domestic and international economic policies to reduce the costs, including the costs of crises. There will be future crises, but if the lessons learned from the past half decade can be translated into appropriate policies, the severity of future crises will be reduced. The economic history of the world is one of progress, often enabled through adaptation to the changing structure of economies, but sometimes precipitated by crises when adaptation has been absent or insufficient.

The chapters in this book are intended to contribute to the discussion of needed changes, while simultaneously reminding all of the enormous benefits most have realized by progress to date. It is to be hoped that policy makers will confront the issues and lessons learned constructively and adapt, rather than waiting for the next crisis to force needed changes.

Anne O. Krueger
Washington DC
September 2011

ACKNOWLEDGEMENTS

As indicated in the Preface, this volume contains revised versions of papers most of which were initially written for conferences or for parts of books. I owe thanks for support to a number of individuals who helped with individual chapters; they are acknowledged at the beginning of the relevant chapters.

Others, however, were helpful over a longer time period. Many of the chapters were originally presented while I was at the IMF, and I owe a major debt of thanks to Graham Ingham, who supported me for most of my tenure there. Chapters 2, 5, and 13 were ones in which he played an especially large role as wordsmith and more. Ernest Parham was also invaluable in preparation of the manuscripts for those chapters and chapters 9 and 10.

Woan Foong Wong, now a graduate student at the University of Wisconsin, provided valuable research assistance in putting together the various parts of the manuscript. Sherry Russo was my assistant and gave valuable support in assembling the volume.

Some of the chapters were previously published and have been edited for inclusion here. I am indebted to the following publishers for permission to include the papers indicated:

Chapter 3: Published in *American Economic Review*, "Trade policy and Economic Development: How We Learn". This was originally published in the May 1997 American Economic Review Papers and Proceedings.

Chapter 4: Reserve Bank of Australia, "Increased Understanding of Supply Side Economics", Christopher Kent and Michael Robson, editors, *Reserve Bank of Australia, 50th Anniversary Symposium*, Sydney, Australia, 2010.

Chapter 5: John Wiley, publishers of the *World Economy*, in which an earlier version of "The Importance of Getting Reforms Right" was published, Vol. 28, No. 6, June 2005, pp. 749–763.

Chapter 6: Initially presented as a talk to a conference in Brazil entitled "International Derivatives and Financial Market conference" and was published in Portuguese. A short section on events post 2007 events has been added and much of the material specific to Brazil has been deleted. The sponsors of the conference, the Brazilian Financial and gave their permission for it to be reproduced.

Chapter 7: Published by the Federal Reserve Bank of San Francisco in Reuven Glick and Mark M. Speigel, editors, *Asia and the Global Financial Crisis*, pp. 93–110, December 2010.

Chapter 9: International Monetary Fund, published in 2002, under the same title as the chapter.

Chapter 10: (with Sean Hagan) Published in the *Chicago Journal of International Law*, Vol. 6, 2005, No. 1, pp. 203–218.

Chapter 11: Published in Gustav Ranis, S. C. Hu and Y.P. Chu, editors *Development into the Twenty First Century*, pp. 335–354, Edward Elgar, 1999.

Chapter 12: First published in the *Journal of International Trade and Diplomacy*, Volume 3, (1), Spring 2009, pp. 33–62. The journal is no longer published. Anyone claiming copyright should write to World Scientific Publishing at editor@wspc.com.

Chapter 13: Talk given at the 18th Australasian Finance and Banking Conference, Sydney, 2005.

Chapters 1 (Introduction), 8 and 15 were written for this volume and have not previously been published:

Chapter 14 has not previously been published. I presented it as a talk at the Annual Meetings of the World Bank and the International Monetary Fund in Singapore in October 2006 as my "farewell" address.

LIST OF ABBREVIATIONS

AD	Antidumping
AIDS	Acquired Immune Deficiency Syndrome
AMS	Aggregate Measure of Support
BRIC	Brazil Russia India China
BRSA	Banking Regulation and Supervision Agency
CACs	Collective Action Clauses
CVD	Countervailing Duty
DRF	Dispute Resolution Forum
DSP	Dispute Settlement Procedures
ECA	Economic Cooperation Administration
ECB	European Central Bank
EU	European Union
FDI	Foreign Direct Investment
FSA	Financial Services Agency
FSAP	Financial Sector Assessment Program
FTA	Free Trade Agreement or Area
GATS	General Agreement on Trade in Services
GATT	General Agreement on Tariffs and Trade
GDP	Gross Domestic Product
GNP	Gross National Product
HCI	Heavy and Chemicals Industry
IBRD	International Bank for Reconstruction and Development
IFIs	International Financial Institutions
IMF	International Monetary Fund
IPO	Initial Public Offering
ITA	Information Technology Agreement
ITO	International Trade Organisation
LDCs	Less Developed Countries
LICs	Low Income Countries
MAP	Mutual Assessment Process
MDGs	Millennium Development Goals

MFN	Most Favoured Nation
MTNs	Multilateral Trade Negotiations
NAFTA	North America Free Trade Agreement
NPL	Nonperforming Loans
NSC	National Security Council
OECD	Organisation for Economic Co-operation and Development
PPP	Public-Private Partnership
PSE	Producer Subsidy Equivalent
PTAs	Preferential Trading Arrangements
ROA	Return on Assets
ROE	Return on Equity
ROO	Rules of Origin
ROSCs	Reports on Standards and Codes
S&D	Special and Differential
SDIF	Savings Deposit Insurance Fund
SDRM	Sovereign Debt Restructuring Mechanism
SMEs	Small and Medium Enterprises
SOEs	State Owned Enterprises
SRF	Supplemental Reserve Facility
TA	Technical Assistance
TL	Turkish Lira
TPR	Trade Policy Review
UCLA	University of California, Los Angeles
UNCITRAL	United Nation Commission on International Trade Law
WTO	World Trade Organisation

CONTENTS

Chapter 1

OVERVIEW

To anyone with knowledge of economic history, attacks on globalization and politicians' expressed desires to reverse it are astonishing. Globalization has been going on for centuries. Its consequences have greatly increased life expectancies, the quality of life, and standards of living. As seen in Chapter 2, even in 1900 in the United States, only about 6 percent of Americans lived above what is now the poverty line! Until the 1950s, per capita incomes were low throughout the developing world, malnutrition and hunger were widespread, and life expectancies and literacy rates were very low. As documented later in this volume, progress in the past half century has been enormous.

Globalization, by which is meant the increasing economic inter-dependence among nations, has been a critical ingredient in enabling this enormous improvement in mankind's condition. While progress has not always been smooth, and has not come without dislocation for some, the economic policy challenge has been, and is, to enable the realization of the large potential benefits of globalization while simultaneously reducing the negative side effects and providing safety nets for those whose lives are disrupted in the process.

This volume focuses on the successes of globalization, and some of the main economic policy challenges and solutions that arise to enhance the benefits and lower the costs. It contains reprints of several articles published earlier on various aspects of globalization, as well as revised versions of papers previously not published and an essay written for this volume.

A first Part contains three chapters centering on different aspects of the status of globalization and its achievements at the beginning of the twenty first century. The following four chapters center on the crucial role that economic policies play in enabling the benefits of globalization and the reasons why policy reform is important when the existing economic structure and policy framework constrains positive outcomes.

In the third Part, there are two chapters on sovereign debt and sovereign debt restructuring, one of the issues about which the international community has had great difficulty in agreeing a process for instances when sovereign debt is truly unsustainable. In Part IV, focus is on the multilateral economic institutions, the International Monetary Fund, the World Bank and the World Trade Organization. As interdependence has increased, the need for international economic understandings and agreements to provide an appropriate framework for global economic activity has intensified. Three chapters examine various aspects of the governance of the international economy.

A final chapter, in Part V, addresses the future, outlining some of the challenges that the international community can address to improve the performance of the international economy.

The chapters in Part I are intended to set the stage for what comes later, focusing on the benefits of globalization. But as the benefits have increased, and more and more countries have adopted economic policies conducive to attaining those benefits, the critics of globalization have centered their attention on some of the side effects. While policies need to be adopted to buffer some of the consequences, it is important not to lose sight of the tremendous progress mankind has made in the past several centuries. Chapter 2, "Be Careful What You Wish For", documents some of these benefits and the role that the international economy has played in achieving them. It also refutes some of the criticisms of globalization that have been made, showing how life expectancies and other indicators of the quality of life have improved dramatically. Finally, it addresses the link between those improvements and the increasing integration of the international economy, especially the expanding role of international trade.

Whereas international merchandise trade is estimated to have accounted for only 2 percent of world GDP in 1800 and 5 percent in 1950, it accounted for more than 20 percent in 2000, having grown at about 8 times the rate of world GDP. Moreover, services trade has been growing even more rapidly than trade in goods, and is estimated to have risen to more than 30 percent of all trade in goods and services. Trade has grown more rapidly than world GDP in all but a few years since the Second World War, providing an "engine of growth".

Until the 1970s, most of the developing countries (which were in many cases newly independent) did not avail themselves of opportunities to grow through expansion of trade, and rather chose to encourage new developments of industry by extending high walls of protection for domestic production. That was a major reason why those countries did not grow as rapidly as might have been hoped, but even they, as seen in Chapter 2, grew at rates higher than those that had earlier prevailed. But by the 1970s, a few developing countries had shifted away from "import-substitution" development strategies toward an "outer-oriented" one (in which incentives for producing import-competing goods were generally no greater than incentives for exportable production). The acceleration in their growth rates was spectacular. Other developing countries, including especially China and India, followed their lead later on.

The experience of those countries, and much other evidence, shows the importance of an open and growing international economy for the prospects of those countries whose policies still insulate them from the world economy. It is also one manifestation of the importance of economic policy for enabling the growth rates that can result in rapid growth and poverty reduction.

Hence, Chapter 3 describes and analyzes the shift in thinking about trade policy, and how it came about, in the decades after 1970. After the adoption of import substitution policies in so many countries, experience mounted demonstrating the limitations of these policies. As is seen in Chapter 3, research analyzing those policies and their effects interacted with experience in the countries themselves. Moreover, the success of the countries that changed their policies to integrate with the international economy was remarkable. Chapter 3 shows how, in a social science, learning comes about. That learning takes place and interacts with research to show the drawbacks of old ways and the potential of new ones is an especially important lesson as the academic and policy communities struggle to understand the factors leading up to the Great Recession of 2007–09 and to use the lessons learned to find policies that can prevent a repetition of the mistakes leading up to 2008–09, or at least reduce the magnitude of any future financial crisis.

Part II then proceeds to focus on economic policy reform itself. One of the lessons of the past sixty years for all economies is the importance of economic policies that promote a stable macroeconomic framework, an open economy, and appropriate domestic incentives. Chapter 4 expands on this theme. In "Increased Understanding of Supply Side Economics", the increased appreciation of the role of economic policies over the past sixty years (including but not limited to trade policy) is shown. One of the ways in which an open trade policy is supportive of economic growth is that policy makers are constrained in the extent to which they can intervene counter-productively in economic activity.

Understanding of the overall role of economic policy (governing macroeconomic and microeconomic issues, as well as trade) has been greatly improved. Evaluation and comparison of the experience of different countries with their different policy regimes and outcomes, analysis of the ways in which policy changes have worked, and other research tools have all contributed to better understanding. This same combination is now at work with regard to the lessons that may be learned from the Great Recession, a subject to which attention returns in the final chapter.

As is elaborated in Chapter 4, appreciation of the importance of incentives (in both the public and the private sector) has increased markedly, while there is significantly greater awareness of the political economy of economic policy formulation and implementation.

The papers in Part I are designed to demonstrate the huge contribution globalization has made to human welfare. They also indicate the role of appropriate economic policies in bringing about increased prosperity. While no country has ever had "perfect" policies, sufficiently ill-chosen policies can greatly retard growth potential and, on occasion, even result in falling per capita incomes.[1]

In Part II, the difficult questions associated with economic policy reform are addressed. For it is one thing to know what appropriate and realistic economic policies are, and it is quite another for policy makers to formulate and implement economic policy reforms. Yet those countries that have succeeded in sufficient economic reforms have usually been able to achieve much higher rates of economic growth. All the successful countries have reformed in ways that have opened their economies and increased their integration with the international economy.

The perils in the reform process are many: there are always some who are benefitting from existing policies, no matter how costly they are; there are always some who believe they will be harmed by change; and there are some who will be harmed, at least in the short run. Moreover, there may be doubt or even disbelief that things could ever improve significantly, and some may therefore question whether the effort at reform is worth it.

These sources of resistance have sometimes resulted in reforms being reversed before they have had a chance to take effect. In some cases, the "reforms" are sufficiently watered down before being introduced that they could not be expected to accomplish much. And in some instances, policies not being considered for reforms prevent realization of the gains that might otherwise have been had from reforms that are enacted. Moreover, when reformers promise large benefits from reform and then reforms "fail" (or are reversed before they have a chance to succeed or are sufficiently weak so as to change little), skepticism about the potential for great gains from reforms

---

[1] In recent years, the most prominent examples of falling incomes have come from Africa where a number of countries entered the 1990s with lower per capita incomes than they had twenty or thirty years earlier.

increases, resistance to reforms mounts, and the next set of efforts to achieve reforms is even more difficult to inaugurate and implement.

The challenges confronting would-be reformers are the subject of Chapter 5. Very often, change is resisted until there is a crisis, at which time decision-makers must act quickly. Moreover, there is always considerable uncertainty about the outcome, both because it is difficult to predict how quickly economic units will believe that the altered economic policy frame-work will be sustained and because it is not possible to know how the external environment will evolve and how large responses will be.

Any given reform has more impact when other economic policies are appropriate. If, for example, there are domestic price controls on agricultural products, moving toward a more realistic exchange rate will have less impact than if price controls are relaxed at the same time as the exchange rate is per-mitted to move to an appropriate level. But the more reforms are undertaken simultaneously, the more thinly policy makers and those implementing reforms are stretched, and the more difficult it is to communicate clearly what the objectives are. Moreover, some reforms may need to be phased in more quickly (as, for example, the exchange rate), while for others it may be desirable to move more gradually to allow time for firms and individuals to adjust (as with lowering and removal of high tariffs). When gradual changes are contemplated, it is of course essential that they be preannounced and credible. An important task of the reformer is to evaluate which reforms are critical at early stages, how much can be undertaken at once, and what the timing of additional reforms should be. These, and other, considerations are set forth in Chapter 5, with examples of some major reform efforts, includ-ing Argentina, New Zealand, South Korea, and Turkey.

Chapter 6 then addresses the crucial role of the financial sector and the importance of its liberalization in the process of economic growth. It was written in 2007, prior to the financial crisis.[2] It focused, as the title suggests, on the importance of financial sector development for economic growth, starting with the need for financial intermediation and then proceeding to focus on the lessons from the Asian financial crises in the 1990s.

Despite the questions that have arisen about the financial system in light of the events of the Great Recession of 2007–09, there is ample evidence that financial development (both the broadening and the deepening of financial markets) has been an important component in all countries that have developed

---

[2] The paper was delivered at a conference in Brazil in August 2007 and subsequently published as "The Crucial Role of Financial Intermediation in Economic Growth." The portion included in this volume omits the discussion specific to the Brazilian financial situation.

successfully. Rudimentary banking can suffice in a poor, mostly rural subsistence, economy, but bankers must develop capabilities to evaluate risk-reward trade-offs to lend to new and expanding activities; equity markets become important, especially to finance large-scale undertakings; and bond markets, venture capitalists, and other forms of finance become increasingly needed as development progresses.

This does not negate the need for financial regulation, as incentives can be perverse if financial institutions lose their equity: "gambling for resurrection" may result as the firms' managers take on high yield-high risk portfolios: if their bets are wrong, they are wiped out anyway, and if their bets pay off, they are rescued. Regulation, however, must balance the need to align financial incentives and the need for innovation and risk assessment capabilities within the system.

Whereas Chapter 6 focuses on the financial system and its importance, Chapter 7 contains an analysis of the Asian crises of the late 1990s. Attention is paid primarily to the circumstances surrounding Japan, for whom a protracted period of stagnation started in the early 1990s, and South Korea in the Asian crisis of 1997, which also impacted many other Asian countries. Japan's floating exchange rate, strong international reserve position, and current account surpluses meant that the authorities did not seek support from the IMF or the international financial community. But the failure to address the difficulties of the banking system, and especially to remove the bad loans from banks' portfolios to enable them to resume normal lending, led to extremely low growth and even deflation for part of the period.

The South Korean crisis, already touched upon in Chapter 6, demonstrated the importance of addressing issues in the banking system rapidly, as the South Koreans removed nonperforming loans (NPLs) from the banks into a "bad bank", and rapidly undertook other needed reforms, including allowing the Korean won to float freely, imposing restrictions on connected lending, and improvements in corporate governance. The IMF played a key role in South Korea (and Thailand and Indonesia) in providing funding to enable economic activity to return gradually to normalcy and in supporting much needed economic policy forms in economic governance and the financial sector. South Korean authorities moved very rapidly to implement the needed reforms, and were the first of the crisis-afflicted Asian countries to reattain their pre-crisis levels of real GDP and to resume growth.

The Asian crises were called by some "the first crises of the twenty-first century", by which was meant that the role of an open capital account was much greater than in earlier, "balance-of-payments" crises, where capital controls had meant that difficulties were primarily in the current account.

But two other crises after the Asian crises demonstrated exhibited another set of ways in which economies could get into difficulty, and also showed another facet of the IMF's role in crisis resolution. In Chapter 8, the histories of the Brazilian and Turkish crises and their aftermaths are recounted. Both countries' economies were in severe economic difficulties in the late 1990s, and both entered into IMF programs that were designed to curb inflation and correct fundamental imbalances.

In Turkey's case, the authorities were unable to implement the program, and there were in any case doubts as to whether the contemplated changes were sufficient to enable a return to normalcy. Turkey had very high inflation rates for a number of years, with high volatility in rates of growth and inflation. In Brazil's case, the 1999 program had seemed to be taking hold, but a forthcoming election in 2002 raised questions as to whether the policies would be maintained. In both cases, IMF programs were adopted which addressed key issues. In Turkey's case, these issues included the control of inflation, the restructuring of the banking system, and sustainability of fiscal policy. In Brazil's case, emphasis was on sustaining a reasonable fiscal balance, controlling inflation, and enabling growth.

These programs were both eminently successful. Turkish inflation fell to single digits within a few years, and the banking system was sufficiently healthy to withstand the challenges of the 2007–09 Great Recession. Turkish growth rates were above even those envisioned in the IMF programs, and Turkish foreign debt was brought down to manageable levels. Brazil's inflation rate was also low, and economic growth picked up after the program began. At the time of writing (early 2011), the Brazilian economy is seen, if anything, to be overheating as growth has accelerated, and foreign capital has flowed in. As in Turkey, Brazil's public indebtedness has dropped markedly. Interestingly, these countries represent two cases in which moves toward tighter fiscal policies enabled an acceleration of growth. The usual association of fiscal cutbacks with austerity did not hold in these cases.

One of the issues that has plagued the international economic system has been how to judge countries' levels of indebtedness, and how to deal with debt, especially sovereign. Until the 1990s, most indebtedness of developing countries was to official lenders, and various measures were adopted through the "Paris Club" to reduce the debt and debt-servicing obligations. This was done in a number of ways: reducing the face value of official debt, postponing payments coming due and providing for several years' grace before debt servicing obligations resumed, lowering the interest rate, and, ultimately, debt forgiveness. At the same time, an unofficial "London Club" of creditors met to decide upon relief for low-income countries.

But as private capital flows to emerging sovereigns and markets increased, difficulties with debt service to private creditors inevitably arose. In some cases, policy changes (especially including adjusting fiscal balances) were sufficient to enable countries to maintain voluntary debt servicing. This was usually in the context of IMF programs in which official money from the IMF enabled sufficient liquidity for debt servicing until reforms took hold. That was certainly the case in the Asian crises, Brazil, and Turkey.

But in some other countries, the situation differed. The most publicized was that of Argentina, where abandonment of the quasi-currency board (which linked the peso to the U.S. dollar at a one to one ratio) and devaluation to three pesos to the dollar rendered Argentine debt unsustainable. The authorities suspended service on their international obligations to private creditors for over two years before unilaterally offering a restructuring to creditors. As of 2011, some of Argentina debt, which was not restructured, is still outstanding and not serviced.

While the Argentina situation appeared at the time to be extreme, other countries had had difficulties earlier.[3] The international community confronted this issue in the 1990s, as it seemed that "bailouts" were substituting official monies for private monies so that private creditors were repaid. The outcome in the Asian crisis was that both official creditors and private creditors were paid in full.

The issue was raised again at the beginning of the 21st century. There were concerns that long delays before debt restructuring in cases where debt was truly unsustainable imposed a higher than necessary costs on both borrowers and creditors. A sovereign debt restructuring mechanism (SDRM) was proposed by the IMF, and Chapters 9 and 10 are articles from 2002 and 2003 (the latter written jointly with Sean Hagan) as the possibility of an SDRM was being discussed.

Ultimately, the Governors of the IMF decided that Collective Action Clauses (CACs) should be used in sovereign bond issues, to insure that holdout creditors could not undermine a restructuring being negotiated between creditors and debtors. During the global economy's boom years from 2003 to 2006, the issue was dormant, as few countries were confronted with economic crises. With the Great Recession, however, difficulties with debt servicing have emerged, especially in the Euro area with Greece, Ireland, and Portugal (at the

---

[3] See Sturzenegger and Zettlemeyer (2007) for an analysis and examination of the historical record.

time of writing) negotiating and adopting IMF programs and observers questioning the sustainability of their debts. Chapters 9 and 10 outline the considerations that led to the SDRM proposal.

Chapter 9 is the proposal as it was set forth at a conference early in 2002. By that time, some modifications to the original proposal had been made in response to objections that the IMF might have too much power. The proposal was further modified after subsequent discussions, and Chapter 10 gives a perspective after it was clear that there would be no adoption of the mechanism at that time.[4] In many discussions of sovereign debt, it is often forgotten that there is some level of debt that is absolutely not repayable. That level is never reached, of course, because potential creditors become concerned at a much earlier point as to the ability of the country (politically as well as economically) to service their debt and roll over debt as it comes due. When that happens and roll overs and new debt can take place only at ever-higher interest rates, the point of crisis is reached. In some instances, a country's economic prospects are sufficiently bright that a temporary loan for liquidity purposes can enable resumption of voluntary debt-servicing relatively quickly. That was the case, for example, in South Korea. In other cases, however, the ability to resume voluntary debt service seems much more questionable. When it is agreed that the debt level is unsustainable, the question arises as to how much of a debt reduction is needed. The SDRM mechanism, as outlined in Chapters 9 and 10, was intended to facilitate and speed up that resolution.

Because of the enormous gains from a well-functioning international economic system, global economic prospects depend in significant part on how well the international understandings and institutions underpinning international economic transactions perform. Just as a well-functioning judicial system (to enforce contracts, property rights, etc.) is important for a domestic economy, so too there must be international institutions that can underpin the international economic system. Part IV contains four chapters covering the World Trade Organization and the International Monetary Fund, which along with the World Bank are the global organizations designed to promote the smooth operation of the international economy.

The open multilateral system, as we know, was established during and immediately after the Second World War. The United States was economically dominant, with 80 percent of the world's gold reserves, more than 40 percent of the world's GDP and over 25 percent of international trade. But

---

[4] See Roubini and Setser (2004). Chapter 8 contains an account of the international politics of the SDRM discussion.

enlightened leadership in the U.S. supported the development of the postwar framework even as the war was still proceeding.

Multilateralism was seen as key to postwar economic prospects. The grim experience of the 1930s had shown what could happen with discriminatory trade relations and in the absence of any international understandings about exchange rate regimes and the circumstances under which exchange rates could be altered. "Beggar thy neighbor" policies had certainly intensified the Great Depression and led to a resolve that it should not happen again.

The postwar international economic arrangements were devised against this background. The World Bank was intended to enable international capital flows (as it was assumed that private capital flows would not resume, as they did not for a long time). The International Monetary Fund was intended to foster international trade by creating clear rules for exchange rate regimes, enabling predictable and orderly exchange rate changes when these were deemed necessary, and provide a for a stable and well-functioning international monetary system. Initially, the system was supposed to operate under a "gold-exchange" standard, under which exchange rates would be fixed in terms of either dollars or gold, and the dollar would be pegged in terms of gold. That system lasted until the 1970s when the major currencies were moved to a flexible exchange rate regime. Under the aegis of the IMF, exchange controls on current account transactions were removed, and currency convertibility increased. This, in turn, further facilitated the flow of trade and underpinned economic growth, as seen in Chapter 2.

The third major institution established at the end of the war was one to govern international trade. As explained in Chapter 11, the original intent was that there should be an International Trade Organization. Its articles were drafted, but consisted of two parts, a first part setting forth the underlying arrangements for times when the world economy was at full employment. These covered nondiscrimination in trade, agreement to eschew quantitative restrictions on trade (except in specified special circumstances), provisions for a dispute settlement mechanism and mutual multilateral negotiations for tariff reductions. A second part, however, in effect let countries pursue whatever protectionist measures they deemed suitable in cases where unemployment was deemed to be higher than desirable.

Although the International Trade Organization's charter was never ratified (because of objections that the second part would permit countries to do whatever they wanted to anyway), the first half of the charter was adopted as the General Agreement on Tariffs and Trade (the GATT), and underpinned the tremendous liberalization of trade in the postwar years. It was the only one of the three bodies that was not initially an international organization. But by

1994, the GATT had proved its worth sufficiently so that it was decided to transform it into the World Trade Organization (WTO) it is today. Chapter 11 traces the history of the founding of the GATT and its evolution into the WTO analyzing the reasons for its effectiveness.

Interestingly, it can be argued that the rapid expansion of trade (in goods and services) has been the most spectacular and crucial phenomenon accounting for the rapid growth of the world economy in the past sixty years. Yet the GATT was the weakest of the three international entities established.

The first fifty years of the GATT/WTO were marked by success, both in terms of the expansion and liberalization of international trade and in terms of development of protocols governing dispute settlement, and a host of items such as customs valuation procedures where uniformity and simplification lowered the costs of trade. Successive rounds of multilateral trade negotiations resulted in greatly reduced tariff rates, while simultaneously almost all quantitative restrictions on trade were removed.

After the conclusion of the Uruguay Round of trade negotiations in 1992 (the round in which the GATT was transformed into the WTO), however, it was nine years before agreement to launch a new round, the Doha Round, was reached. Much of the easy trade liberalization had been accomplished. Issues such as trade in agricultural commodities (where domestic interventions are a major distortion to international trade in agricultural commodities) and trade in services had become increasingly important as tariffs and other barriers to trade in manufactures had fallen.

These issues are difficult, and there are many more countries now actively involved in the negotiations. Partly because of these factors, and perhaps also because support for multilateralism seems to have diminished, the Doha Round of trade negotiations has yet to be completed. Chapter 12 suggests reasons why the round should be quickly wound up, and a possible set of issues that might be handled outside the framework of multilateral trade negotiations. That, however, is not to say that multilateralism is unimportant — on the contrary, with economic growth, it is more important than ever. But finding ways to facilitate trade is important for the entire global economy, and especially for low income countries that have yet to move very far in their policy reforms to achieve more rapid growth. For them, a healthy expanding international trading system will be a key determinant of the payoff for their reforms.

Chapter 13 then turns to the IMF. It is an abridged version of a speech given in 2005 focusing on the role of the IMF. While earlier chapters on the Asian crises, and on Brazilian and Turkey showed the Fund's role in those crises, the Fund has many other functions. Many of these are important in improving economic policy and implementation in small and big ways, but are not the stuff of headlines. Chapter 13 focuses, not on recipient countries, but on the Fund's activities as a whole.

The fact that the Fund's membership covers 187 countries enables a comparative perspective that has provided data, analysis and insights that have enabled learning throughout the global policy and academic community. The Fund's technical assistance has enabled countries to improve tax administration, track public expenditures, and undertake many other public functions more efficiently than would otherwise have been possible. This has included support for strengthening the financial sector through special programs described in Chapter 13. And the Fund's surveillance work continues to be important to member countries in many ways.

Chapter 14 then raises questions about the future of the international economy. The earlier chapters in the volume demonstrated the importance of increasing international integration for raising living standards and reducing poverty throughout most of the world. However, despite the importance of the multilateral economic institutions in enabling progress in a multilateral context, support for multilateralism seems to have diminished in recent years. Chapter 14 focuses on some of the key concerns for the international economy going forward and shows how they can best be addressed in a multilateral context.

REFERENCES

Roubini, N and B Setser (2004). *Bailouts or Bail-ins?* Institute for International Economics, Washington, DC.

Sturzennegger, F and J Zettelmeyer (2007). *Debt Defaults and Lessons from a Decade of Crisis.* Cambridge, MA: MIT Press.

Part I

SUCCESSES OF GLOBALIZATION

Chapter 2

BE CAREFUL WHAT YOU WISH FOR*

There is, in economic discussions today, a huge puzzle: as I shall attempt to demonstrate (as others have also done), there has been enormous progress in improving the opportunities and material conditions for much of mankind. That progress has been in significant part been a result of globalization. Given that, the puzzle is why there are so many critics of globalization when in fact most of the critics' goals would have been even more remote and unachievable had it not taken place. The critics should be on the defensive: yet somehow, the supporters of globalization have found the critics on the offensive and they have let themselves be on the defense.

I shall start by considering what is meant by globalization, and then provide evidence on the factual issue: there have been huge gains in economic well-being, first for industrial countries starting around 1800, and then for almost all countries after the Second World War. The next step will be to show that globalization has been a necessary background for these enormous gains. Over the past two centuries, mankind's well-being has advanced enormously, by any measure. Life expectancies have risen dramatically, the incidence of debilitating illness has greatly diminished, literacy and educational attainments have increased remarkably, and, of course, real incomes have risen greatly. It is no exaggeration to say that the nature of life itself has changed qualitatively as well as quantitatively.

Moreover, the rate of improvement in these and other measures of well-being has accelerated in the sixty years since the Second World War. This is true not only of countries that did not significantly participate in the improvements prior to 1945, but even of the industrial countries.

No observer of the economic scene can contend that all is perfection, and clearly there remain economic problems — including the abject poverty that

---

* This is a slightly edited version of a paper presented at the Conference of Australian Economic Society, Conference of Economists, Hobart, Tasmania, on September 24, 2007.

still exists in parts of the world — but equally, it would be difficult to contend seriously that things have not improved. Indeed, as I shall argue later, it is possible if not probable that the changes have been so great that many in the current bodies politic simply take current well being and living standards for granted without recognition of the fact that life has not always been this way or of the factors that enabled the transformation of life for so many.

One of the key contributors to economic progress has been globalization. The increasing integration of the global economy been a necessary underpinning for much of the progress, but, sadly, many observers have blamed globalization for some of the world's remaining ills, rather than recognizing its role in enabling the advances that have been made to date. So, after sketching some of the key indicators of progress in economic well-being, I will address the role of globalization in enabling it.

After addressing these factual issues, I will turn (defensively, regrettably) to some of the criticisms of globalization, arguing that some of the complaints are simply false — in the sense that the facts do not support the assertions — and that others are correctly pointing to issues that require addressing, but that those issues would not be resolved, nor would conditions be made better, by attempting to stem the tide of globalization; the appropriate policy responses are otherwise. I will conclude by sketching some of the policy responses that can meet the legitimate objectives of some of globalization's critics and simultaneously be consistent with further progress.

A first step is to define what is meant by globalization for present purposes. In a meaningful sense, globalization has been occurring throughout recorded history, if by globalization is meant the increasing interaction and integration of economic activity over ever-longer distances. On that definition, which I shall use, the Romans were great globalizers, as they built roads and shipped goods by sea (especially from North Africa to Italy) to a much greater degree than had earlier been done. One might even nominate Alexander as an important globalizer!

But, in fact, after the Romans there appears to have been little progress in improving transport routes or in further integration. While there appear to have been some productivity increases starting around 1200 in manufacturing in northern Europe, population changes (both positive and negative) seem to have absorbed them, and it is quite possible that there was less integration in 1600 than there had been in Roman times.[1] Roman roads were often not maintained. Blanning reports that roads built by the Romans had in fact deteriorated over the centuries, and that in consequence times and

---

[1] Blanning (2007), p. 3.

costs of transport were probably higher in 1600 than they had been fifteen or more centuries earlier. Thus, there was little further globalization for the next fifteen or so centuries.

Integration, in the sense of increasing economic interaction and integration over distances, started once again as transport and communications costs (both time and resources) began falling. Most travel was by road. In England, where road travel was apparently at least somewhat better than on the continent, Blanning estimates that travel time from London to Manchester in 1700 was 90 hours; by 1750 it had fallen to 65 hours, and by 1800 it was 33 hours. While 33 hours looks incredibly long by today's standards (and the journey was arduous as it was mostly by foot or, at best, by coaches without springs), the improvements in earlier years must have seemed huge to contemporary travelers. It is estimated that most people never were more than 5–6 miles from their places of birth during their lifetimes.

Evidently, travel on the continent was even more arduous than in England. While water routes (the Rhine, in particular) were an alternative for much of what did move between places barge animals dictated the pace of travel inland, and prevailing winds set the pace for seagoing vessels. Even then, tolls were a heavy burden on river traffic, as Eli Hecksher so well documented.

Because the costs and difficulties of moving between places were so high, and because most productivity of persons engaged in agriculture (probably more than 90 percent of the population) was so low, there was very little interdependence. Most goods consumed had been produced within a short distance of the consumption point. We all know about the spice trade: but spices were among the few goods with a sufficiently high value-to-weight ratio to be economic for trade at longer distances. For the average person, what went on even a hundred miles away was probably of little relevance to their everyday life. In that sense, we can conclude that integration, and hence globalization, was minimal between Roman times and 1700 or thereabouts.

It is also worth noting that economic historians estimate that living standards in 1700 are thought to have been little, if at all, better than they were two thousand or more years before. Indeed, Clark reports that for England (for which the best data are available), "Real wages in England showed remarkably little gain in the six hundred years from 1200 to 1800. The fluctuations over that period are much more dramatic than any long-run upward trend. Thus in thirty-nine of the sixty decades between 1200 and 1800 real wages for farm workers are estimated to be above their level in 1800. The highest real wages are found in the interval 1400–1549..."[2] (p. 42) I should

---

[2] Clark (2007), p. 42.

mention in passing that he also concludes that "there is no sign of any improvement in material conditions for settled agrarian societies as we approach 1800. There was no gain between 1800BC and AD1800 — a period of 3600 years."(p. 49)

By 1800, however, transport costs were falling, and trade between Europe and the western hemisphere had started. But, starting about 1870 — the date now chosen by most economic historians — the decline in transport costs became precipitous. Data given by Mohammed and Williamson[3] indicate that the decline varied between routes and cargoes. But overall, their real ocean freight rate index shows a decline of 78 percent between 1870–74, a date by which there had already been substantial declines for more than a century, and 1975–79 (after which they rose somewhat). While declining costs surely reflected in part the smaller wage bill associated with faster trips, the benefits of more rapid transit no doubt also enabled shipment of goods that earlier could not be transported over given distances.

Meanwhile, many observers credit containerization, and later the ability to ship at least some high value and/or perishable goods by air, as providing an equally important reduction in transport costs.

As well as transport, the cost, timeliness, and ease of communications is also crucial for many economic transactions, and, if anything, the drop in costs and pickup in speed has been even more dramatic than in transport. It was 84 days after the Treaty of Nanjing before the report reached London in 1842, and 46 days before the Indian Mutiny of 1857 was reported. By contrast, news of Lincoln's assassination reached London in 12 days in 1865. And only 17 years later, the assassination of Alexander II in St. Petersburg was news in London in 1881 a half a day later; the Japanese earthquake of 1891 was reported within a day. This sharp change was of course attributable to the introduction of the telegraph and the telephone. It constituted a major revolution in communications. But costs were still high, especially overseas.[4] One frequently cited and dramatic number is that a New York-to-London three minute telephone call cost $290 (in 2000 prices) in 1930 and cost only a few cents by 2000. Currently, of course, the price is even lower and the internet makes instantaneous communications virtually cost-free.

It should be noted that falling costs of transport and communications enabled increased integration of domestic economies as well as of the global economy. Transactions between distant parts of individual countries

---

[3] Mohammed and Williamson (2004), pp. 172–173.
[4] Clark (2007), p. 306.

obviously became more economic as the costs and difficulties of doing business at a distance fell.

Until the Second World War, though, transport and communications costs were so high that increasing economic integration — globalization — was primarily the result of the technological and other changes that enabled transport and communications costs to fall so dramatically. With very high transport costs, tariff barriers did not constitute the biggest obstacle to trade: with a 20 percent tariff and transport costs of 50 percent, a reduction of the tariff to 10 percent — halving it, that is — would have resulted in a reduction in the imported price of a good of only about 6 percent. At the end of the Second World War, however, high barriers to trade imposed by governments constituted the more important deterrent for people in most countries. Removal of quantitative restrictions under the GATT, the WTO, and self-interest of countries, combined with multilateral and unilateral tariff reduction, brought about large reductions in costs of doing business across borders.

In the mid 1940s, it is estimated that the average tariff on manufactured goods among the industrial countries was between 45 and 50 percent, while transport costs for manufactured goods averaged around 20 percent. The calculus had changed, but with it, international political economy. Successive rounds of trade liberalization under the GATT brought the average tariff among industrial countries on manufactures down to around 2 percent. Simultaneously, many developing countries, which had (and still have) much higher trade barriers than the industrial countries, recognized the harm those measures inflicted on their economies and were dismantling their restrictions (both tariffs and quantitative restrictions on imports).

As a result of all these factors, the costs of trading at any given distance have fallen dramatically over the past two centuries. Whether that fall was greater in the twentieth century with the development of transport and communications via the internet, airplanes and containerization, or in the 19th century with the telegraph, telephone, and steam engine, is an open question. But the economics of doing business at a distance certainly changed.

As a result, there has been increased economic integration worldwide. Whereas farmers and people in villages doing farm-related activities were constituted over 90 percent of populations almost everywhere and were relatively self-sufficient in 1700, in advanced countries today fewer than three percent of the population is engaged in agricultural activities and, even then, they rely on goods produced at considerable distances both for consumption and for inputs (such as fertilizers and farm machinery) into production. Clark presents estimates that, prior to 1800, laborers (in England, a country for which the most reliable data seem to be available) are estimated to have spent 75 percent of their incomes on food and drink, 10 percent on clothing and bedding, and 25 percent on housing. Today, less than 20 percent of income is spent on food in industrial countries, and much of that 20 percent consists of services such as processing and restaurant-provided meals. Obviously, much of the 80 percent of nonfood expenditures (as well as the nonfood) originates from much greater distances, and has much greater variety than 200 years ago.

In consequence, the degree to which workers and employers in a city such as Manchester are integrated into the world economy is much, much greater. Not only is the share of goods and services entering international trade much greater now than it was earlier, but in addition, the speed with which events in far-flung parts of the world affects each economy has greatly accelerated. Interdependence has increased not only through the exchange of goods and services, but also because economic shifts anywhere in the world affect others much more directly and more quickly.

The trend has been almost unrelentingly for increased global integration. The exception was the period from 1914 to 1945, when there was a degree of global disintegration. It started with World War 1, which raised the costs of shipping dramatically. While there was some recovery to prewar levels in the 1920s, the Great Depression of the 1930s and the policy measures associated with it (especially competitive devaluations and rising tariff barriers) again reversed the trend. But since the end of the Second World War, economic integration has increased continuously.

There is little doubt that globalization will continue, barring a major geopolitical event or severe policy reversals. But one can question whether the pace of change, and the degree to which perceptions of interdependence have increased over the past several decades, will be sustained. Either way, it is clear, as I shall now argue, that there have been huge benefits to mankind from the economic changes over the past several decades.

Let me then turn to the changes that have taken place over the past two centuries. That these improvements have been huge is unquestionable, but they are now so often taken for granted that it is worth pausing and reflecting on them. Then, the crucial role of economic integration in enabling the attainment of these benefits can readily be shown.

It is difficult to know where to start. One dramatic and telling statistic is that economic historians[5] estimate that, as late as in 1900, only about 6–7 percent

---

[5] Fogel (2007).

of the American population had incomes sufficient so that they would have been classified as above the poverty line by today's American standards. And real incomes in the richest industrial countries are estimated to be 10–20 times higher than they were in 1800.[6] And, over that long time period, those whose incomes rose most rapidly were the unskilled workers.[7]

But if there are claims that that is "just material", there are other indicators. Life expectancies have increased enormously, and those increases have come about as real incomes have risen. A first point to be made is that people with similar income levels have, by and large, similar life expectancies and similar lifestyles in other important dimensions of well-being.[8] Life expectancies at birth in the United Kingdom are estimated to have been 38 years in the last half of the 16th century, 35 years in the last half of the 17th century, and 38 years in the last half of the 18th century.[9] This was not significantly different from estimates for other countries in those and other eras: French life expectancy at birth is estimated to have been 28 years in the second half of the 18th century, the same as China's over the five centuries after 1300 and rural Egypt's over the period 11–257 (urban life expectancy is estimated to have been lower). Much of this low life expectancy resulted from high infant mortality rates, as well as deaths of those surviving birth but dying before the age of 15. By contrast, life expectancies in the rich countries today are approximately double those of earlier years, and continued to rise throughout the 20th century.

But few would argue with the proposition that those in the industrial countries are better off today than were their parents, who in turn were better off than their parents, and so on. More observers question, or fail to recognize, the improvements in quality of life that have occurred in most other countries. And it is worth spending a few moments pointing to the enormous achievements in those countries that were identified as "developing" in the 1950s.

It should first be noted that the achievements of developing countries, even in the first twenty-five years of development, were significantly greater than had been thought attainable. In surveying the first twenty-five years of development for the World Bank, Morawetz concluded that "On average per capita income the developing countries grew more rapidly between 1950 and 1975 — 3.4 percent a year — than either they or the developed

---

[6] Clark (2007), pp. 2–3.
[7] Clark (2007), p. 3.
[8] Clark (2007), p. 3.
[9] Clark (2007), p. 94.

countries had done in any comparable period in the past. They thereby exceeded both official goals and private expectation. Increases in life expectancy that required a century of economic development in the industrialized countries have been achieved in the developing world in two or three decades. Progress has been made in the eradication of communicable diseases. And the proportion of adults in developing countries who are literate has increased substantially."[10]

And that was up to 1975. Economic growth has proceeded at even higher rates among the developing countries since 1975, while the rate of population growth has fallen. Indeed, over the past several years, developing countries as a group have achieved an average rate of economic growth well over 5 percent, contrasted with 2 percent in high income countries.[11]

Per capita incomes have risen rapidly in most, but not all, developing countries over the past several decades. The story of the East Asian "tigers" — Hong Kong, Singapore, South Korea, and Taiwan, all experienced sustained rates of growth of real GDP and per capita incomes well above any the world had earlier witnessed, doubling per capita income every decade from 1960 into the 1990s. In so doing, their economies and the quality of their peoples' lives were transformed. South Korea went from being one of the poorest countries in Asia (and the world) as late as 1960, to its current classification as a rich country by the World Bank. And other countries in southeast Asia began growing rapidly in the 1970s. China followed suit in the 1980s and India began growing at accelerated rates in the 1990s. In these and other emerging economies, even those failing to experience such rapid rates of growth, real incomes have risen at far higher rates than had been experienced in earlier years.

These higher incomes have been accompanied by dramatic changes in life expectancy. Life expectancy in India, for example, is estimated to have been around 30 years in the late 1940s and was 64 years in 2005. And in Korea, which as already mentioned was the 3rd poorest country in Asia in the late 1950s with a life expectancy similar to India's, life expectancy (with per capita income at around $20,000) in 2005 was estimated at 78 years, the same as the United States and one year less than the United Kingdom.[12]

Two things should be noted: life expectancies have risen not only proportionately but absolutely more in developing countries than in developed countries; and those countries that have grown more rapidly have achieved

---

[10] Morawetz (1977), p. 67.
[11] World Bank, WDR (2007), p. 289, Appendix Table 1.
[12] World Development Indicators (2007), Table 2.20.

even greater increases in life expectancies. Even in developing countries where growth rates were discouragingly low, life expectancies and other health indicators were increasing until the AIDS epidemic began taking its toll in the 1990s. For many, where the toll from the AIDS epidemic is not so high, life expectancies have risen even when per capita income growth has been anemic of virtually nonexistent.

Poverty reduction within individual developing countries has by and large been greatest with more rapid per capita income growth. That poverty in China has been reduced by 300 million people is a widely-repeated statistic; poverty in India has begun dropping more rapidly as economic growth has accelerated. It is widely expected that the global millennium development goals with respect to poverty reduction will have been met by 2015 because of the successes of China and India.

Literacy rates have also increased substantially, and more so in countries with higher growth rates of per capita income over sustained periods. Whereas many poor countries had literacy rates of 20–30 percent in the late 1940s, those same countries now report rates between 60 and 80 percent. While there are still many educational deficiencies including both the failure to provide universal primary education and the low quality of education in many cases, there can be little question that rising real incomes have contributed significantly to this result.

Most developing countries (weighted by population) have experienced rising living standards and improving conditions, with a falling fraction of people in poverty, longer life expectancies, better nutritional status, improved health, and so on. In a moment, I will turn to the proposition that much of that progress would not have been possible without globalization, the increasing integration of those economies into the global economy. But before doing that, I must note that there are a number of countries where the evidence is strong that living standards now are no higher, and in some instances are lower, than they were several decades ago.

The countries that have failed to experience rising per capita incomes are largely, but not exclusively, in Africa. I shall return later to some of the reasons for their failure, but at this juncture I want simply to point out the changing relative global landscape. One dramatic statistic that highlights change is the relative positions of South Korea, a dramatic success story, and Ghana, a country which has experienced much greater economic difficulties. In the 1950s, estimates of per capita incomes put that of Ghana more than two and a half times that of South Korea. By 2005, South Korean per capita income was estimated to be almost seven times that of Ghana! When discussions of poverty were held in the 1950s, most observers regarded Asia as the poorest continent: South Asia's 1950 average per capita income was estimate to have been $85, and East Asia's $130 (not including Japan), while Africa's was $170. Now, most East and many South Asian countries have living standards and life expectancies well above those of most Sub-Saharan African countries.

Let me summarize the argument to this point. First, global economic integration, or globalization, has proceeded at a rapid pace since about 1800, and the degree of interdependence has greatly increased. The only interruption in this trend was from the outbreak of the First World War to the end of the Second. Second, whereas the vast majority of the world's population lived at very low living standards until about 1800, thereafter there was rapid growth in the quality of life in many dimensions in the industrial countries — referred to by some as "the Great Divergence". By the middle of the twentieth century, the industrial countries had real incomes a large multiple of that of the poorer countries.

But, starting after the Second World War, many of the poor countries began experiencing more rapid per capita income growth, in some cases very rapid. Most of the population of the world's poor countries now has a much improved quality of life contrasted with a half century ago. In the most rapidly growing countries, lifestyles more closely resemble those of other industrialized countries than those of people in those countries two hundred years ago. Gains in life expectancies, health and nutritional status, literacy, and other measures are larger in countries where real output and incomes grew more rapidly, but they took place in virtually all countries.

Those propositions take us immediately to the question of the role of globalization in achieving the enormous material progress, and accompanying improvements in economic well being, of the past two centuries. There is no question but that economic integration took place; and there is equally little question but that material well-being improved and, with it, the quality of life for the vast majority. The only possible question is the link between these two phenomena. Association, after all, does not prove causation.

Three lines of argument, or proof, all point to the central role of increasing integration as a component of, and indeed, even as a necessary — if not sufficient — condition for the tremendous increase in the efficiency, or productivity, of the global economy. The first is that no country, or group of countries, has for any considerable period of time sustained reasonable (or faster) rates of growth of real per capita incomes without integrating into the international economy as they did so. The second has to do with the economics of productivity gains, as first noted by Adam Smith: the size of the market is an important determinant of productivity. The third is the record of within-country growth performance wherein the same countries experienced slow growth, if not stagnation, while maintaining barriers to integration, while achieving much more satisfactory economic performances once they had liberalized and opened up their economies.

Let me elaborate briefly on each of these, only pausing first to note that, quite clearly, other factors such as innovation also contributed to growth and enabled the integration that took place. Without the introduction of the steam engine and many other productivity-enhancing innovations, there would have been no opportunity for integration. But, had authorities fought the technical changes that were occurring, as for example, by prohibiting imports of now-cheaper goods, increases in economic well being would have fallen far short of the major accomplishments of the past two centuries.

Turning then to the first line of argument as to the role of economic integration, every country that has grown rapidly has been increasingly integrated with the world economy as it did so. That trade has been an "engine of growth" has been recognized by all for the past half century. To be sure, integration with the rest of the world has generally been more crucial the smaller the domestic economy. But even among economies with large populations, trade in goods and services has generally increased as a percentage of GDP as the economy has grown. Indeed, as already mentioned, for the world as a whole, trade as a percentage of world GDP has increased over the entire postwar period, and had been growing during the 19th century until 1913. It is estimated that trade volumes (the sum of imports plus exports) in 1800 were about 2 percent of output,[13] and about 22 percent in 1913. By 1938, that figure had fallen to 9 percent (below even the level of 1870). But since 1945, the importance of trade has increased dramatically. It is estimated that trade (again, exports plus imports of goods and services) as a percentage of world GDP was 40.1 percent in 1990 and 58.3 percent in 2005.[14]

This upward trend was shared by all groups of countries. Low income countries' trade was equal to 29.8 percent of GDP in 1990 and 50.9 percent in 2005; middle income countries' trade was 41.6 percent in 1990 and 72.6 percent in 2005; and industrial countries' shares were 40.2 and 55.0 percent in those same years.

Moreover, the growth of trade relative to real GDP has generally been most rapid for those growing most rapidly. This has been true of both industrial and of developing countries. During the European Union's period of

---

[13] Estevadeordal, Frantz and Taylor (2003), p. 4.
[14] World Bank, World Development Indicators (2007), Table 6.1, 'Merchandise trade plus trade in services'.

rapid growth, trade increased sharply as a proportion of GDP. The same has happened in the United States since growth rates accelerated in the mid-1990s. And, of course it has happened for the world as a whole.

But in developing countries where trade barriers were even higher, the association has been even stronger. When South Korea embarked upon the export-oriented growth strategy, for example, exports were three percent of GDP. Less than thirty years later, during which time incomes had doubled every seven years, exports constituted almost 40 percent of GDP. Taiwan, Singapore, and Hong Kong recorded the same sorts of sharp increases in the role of trade. And countries that later accelerated growth, most notably India and China, have experienced share increases in the importance of trade for their economies. In the case of China, trade rose from almost zero in 1980 to 63.5 percent of GDP in 1995 and 70.7 percent in 2005; in India, over the 1990-to-2005 period, trade rose from 16.5 percent of GDP to 36.7 percent.

The association between more openness and trade holds over the developing world as a whole. The World Bank reports that during the decade starting in 1995, the first decade in which growth rates were significantly higher in developing than in industrial countries, countries that opened up trade less rapidly "recorded much lower per capita GDP growth".[15] For the worst performers in terms of trade opening, per capita GDP growth was minus one percent; for the best, it was plus 0.4 percent. The Bank notes, of course, that some domestic policy changes result in increased competitiveness in ways that affect both per capita income growth and also trade share, and as such, the statistic does not prove causation.

That shares of trade in GDP were growing rapidly is part of the phenomenon of globalization, or global integration. That the relative growth of shares in the more rapidly growing countries was increasing more rapidly is a telling statistic for suggesting, at a minimum, a strong association between trade integration and more rapid improvements in well-being. It should, of course, be pointed out that a high share of trade in GDP may not reflect openness in a poor economy where only one or two primary commodities constitute the vast bulk of exports. In those cases, policies have rendered the export of all but a few primary commodities with high rents from being profitable for export. That is why focus is on the changing share in GDP, rather than the share itself: differences in per capita income levels, location, factor endowments, and size all affect the "optimal" share of exports in GDP.

The second set of linkages between growth of the relative importance of trade and economic well being of people, especially the poor, has to do with

---

[15] World Development Indicators (2007), p. 3.

the effects of trade. In all countries, growth is faster when there is more competition; when trade barriers are reduced, competition is increased. For many developing countries, high barriers to trade conferred monopoly positions on the elite few, and kept the majority of the labor force in agriculture or the informal sector. Opening up to trade meant that entrepreneurs had to compete for business, often with dramatic increases in productivity. Often, new exports were manufactures, employing considerable unskilled labor where there was comparative advantage. At the same time, having the world for a market enabled producers to take advantage of economies of scale; especially in poor countries, the size of markets for virtually any nonstaple food commodity was extremely small; producing behind a highly protective trade barrier enabled domestic producers to have monopoly positions in their home markets, but left them high-cost not only because of their monopoly positions, but because of their short production runs and uneconomically small scales of production.

Another consequence of falling trade barriers was that domestic producers who had previously been forced to rely on domestic (often high-cost, low-quality) sources of supply for their intermediate goods and raw materials were enabled to obtain needed quality and precise specifications from international markets; as such, they were enabled in many cases to become competitive internationally, no longer handicapped in their suppliers. Needless to say, many of those finding exporting attractive were those using factors of production which were relatively abundant in their countries, generally unskilled labor. That in itself enhanced growth prospects, as shortages of scarce factors arose only more slowly, while real wages for unskilled labor, in particular, could rise as productivity increased. Again using Korea as an example, it is estimated that, when the policy reforms were undertaken, about 25 percent of the small urban labor force was unemployed. Within four years, however, unemployment had fallen to less than 5 percent. Meanwhile, real wages for manufacturing workers rose at an average annual rate of 8 percent over a period of 30 years, while the migration of farm labor to the cities permitted rapid expansion in urban employment: by the 1990s, more than 90 percent of Korea's labor force was in the urban sector, whereas in 1960, more than 60 percent had been rural.

While cross-country comparisons are useful, it is always wise to check the results against evidence provided by changes in the same country over time. Here, too, the evidence is overwhelming that the increased integration into the international economy was an important component of improved economic performance and well being. The Korean, Chinese, and Indian dramatic cases have already been mentioned. South Korea's rapid economic growth started after a policy change in which the authorities switched from an import-substitution regime to an outer-oriented regime. Likewise, China's rapid growth has been accompanied by a dramatic opening of the economy to trade with the rest of the world, and India, too, reduced trade barriers dramatically after reforms started in 1991. Chile, whose economic performance since reforms has transformed its economy, started with very high protection levels, and reduced trade barriers until now, when there is a uniform tariff of 5 percent on all imports, except for those originating from countries with which the country has free trade agreements.

Next, consider some of the major allegations of the critics of globalization. There are four broad groups of criticisms that are widely heard. Three relate to developing countries and one to the impact on developed countries. The three concern the use of child labor, volatility arising from terms of trade fluctuations or other disturbances in the international economy, and immiserization of the poor in low-income countries including the absence of labor standards. The allegation regarding developed countries has been that globalization has harmed workers.

That there is child labor in many poor countries is beyond dispute. It is quite obviously a tragedy that these practices exist. And certainly some of the child workers are employed in activities that will result in exports. Not only is the fact of child labor to be deplored, but those children who are working are usually being deprived of any educational opportunities, as well, thus building in a future generation of poor people.

A first point to be made is that child labor has been a necessary and unhappy fact of life for the poor for many centuries. For that reason alone, it is hard to accept the argument that globalization has brought it about, although there are surely instances when the incentives to employ child labor have increased, although there is an offset as populations become more urban with growth, and urbanites have higher rates of school enrollment. Secondly, as real incomes have risen, use of child labor has diminished. Economic growth itself has been part of the solution to the problem, not the cause. One careful study of child labor in Vietnam, where about 33 percent of children work, examined what happened when the price of rice rose by about 30 percent as a result of trade liberalization. Researchers found that households earning higher incomes from rice were enabled to remove their children from the labor force.[16]

The second point to raise is to consider what the alternatives are. Simply outlawing child labor and leaving all else unaltered is not necessarily a solution.

---

[16] Bhagwati (2004), pp. 71–72.

Some alternatives to child labor — infanticide when struggling parents do not believe they can feed more children or otherwise cope, early forced marriages for girls (again depriving them of education), starvation, and begging — may be worse. The real problem is low incomes. Historically, child labor was a factor throughout the world; the practice diminished and finally ceased as living standards improved. Accelerating the growth of per capita incomes is certainly a partial palliative. And, since globalization enables more rapid growth and generally raises real wages of unskilled workers, it contributes to the reduction in the use of child labor. Other measures, targeted at enabling parents to send their children to school (such as school lunches), can also contribute. But the main message for present purposes is that globalization contributes to the solution to the problem and is not its cause. Rejection of globalization leaves countries with much slower, if any, rate of increase in real incomes and living standards, which in turn is likely to perpetuate more child labor for a longer period of time.

Critics of globalization have also argued that developing countries' increasing integration to the global economy exposes those countries to greater fluctuations than they would experience if trading and other ties were weaker. That there are fluctuations in the international economy is certainly true, although there is hope that as policy makers are learning more, the extent of volatility has been reduced.

Fluctuations are of two types. On one hand, individual countries experience marked and often abrupt changes in their terms of trade. On the other hand, some countries with strong linkages to the international economy have experienced major financial crises. Both of these sorts of fluctuations obviously have sharp economic costs in individual countries experiencing them. While domestic policy measures, such as being prudent and adopting countercyclical fiscal stances, have the potential to offset much more of these fluctuations than has happened historically (when the afflicted economies' governments have run procyclical fiscal policies), there is no doubt that fluctuations in the terms of trade make macroeconomic management more difficult than it would be were international prices constant. But international prices are not, and never will be, constant. So the relevant question is whether people in low and middle-income countries are better off integrating with the global economy and managing fluctuations as well as possible, or whether the fluctuations are severe enough so that some degree of delinkage is warranted.

The answer is clearly on the side of globalization. First of all, in countries in which subsistence agriculture is a large component of GDP, weather fluctuations domestically can be as large, if not larger, than the fluctuations brought about by changes in the terms of trade. It is not true that there are no sources of fluctuation domestically. In an open economy, increasing imports can compensate significantly from a poor harvest; in a closed economy, offsetting domestic supply fluctuations is much more costly or difficult.

Moreover, the gains from trade are so large (especially when the terms of trade are an issue as they are with primary commodities) that the costs of terms of trade fluctuations take away at most a small part of the gains. Even for countries with high tariff barriers that have rejected integration with the world economy, there has been no effort to reduce exports of the primary commodities (and it is primarily primary commodities) whose prices are subject to large fluctuations. Indeed, there could be a great deal more mitigation of the ill effects of fluctuations through domestic economic policies than in fact takes place.

As to financial crises, these appear to be largely the domain of middle-income countries, such as Korea and Brazil. Obviously these countries experienced sharp changes in real incomes because of the crises and there was great hardship for many individuals. There has been learning, and it is to be hoped that there will be fewer such crises in the future. But even if that is not the case, if one contrasts the rate of economic growth and level of per capita income in the Asian crisis countries (all of which were closely integrated into the international economy) with that of countries that remained much more inner-oriented, there can be little doubt that the costs of fluctuation were smaller than the costs of remaining inner oriented. Korean real GDP fell for about 18 months and at its trough was less than 10 percent below its peak. The previous peak was reattained within two years, and Korean economic growth since that time has exceeded 5 percent on average. But even at its trough, Korean per capita incomes were about seven times what they had been in 1960. Had per capita incomes grown over those decades at an average annual rate of three percent — a relatively high number for an inner-oriented economy — and there been no crises, average per capita incomes would have been less than half of what they actually were. One could, in addition, point to policies that could have averted or at least diminished the magnitude of the crises. But even given the magnitude of past crises, the point is that the globally integrated countries were far better off than those in relatively similar countries where integration was eschewed.

But those considerations still leave open the last item to be considered. It is argued by many antiglobalists that higher rates of growth of real income do not translate into rising living standards for the poor. That is just plain wrong. Throughout economic history, and across developing countries at the present, higher rates of per capita economic growth are associated with higher rates of growth of real incomes of the poor. Conversely, those countries where real incomes of the poor have grown most slowly (or even fallen) have been, by and large, those countries where inner-oriented, antiglobalization policies have been followed.

It is certainly not true that every single poor individual benefits as real incomes rises, but the vast majority do. And it is certainly not necessarily true that the income distribution becomes more equal as real incomes rise, at least at early stages of development. But increasing income inequality is sometimes a necessary concomitant of rapid economic growth: witness China, where rapid economic growth has removed several hundred million from poverty but simultaneously increased inequality. Income distribution generally changes only slowly over time; as such, when real incomes rise, most benefit, although some more than others. To be sure, development policies — such as improving access to health services and educational opportunities — can affect income distribution and the extent to which the poor gain regardless of the rate of growth of real incomes. But it has been amply documented that higher rates of growth of per capita incomes are associated with more rapid improvement in living standards for the poor.[17]

The World Bank reports that in only one country (out of 60) was poverty reduced over the 1990–2004 period despite negative income growth. In 17 countries, income distribution became more unequal but the poor became better off because of rising real incomes; in another 11 countries, reduced inequality accentuated the effect of rising real incomes. Statistically, the relationship between poverty reduction and growth was positive and significant. The same has been found in other studies.

Globalization has clearly not made things worse. As already seen, globalizing countries have grown more rapidly on average than others. As such, real incomes have risen more rapidly. In a survey done with Andrew Berg[18] in 2002, we showed that the preponderance of evidence suggested that trade liberalization accelerated growth and reduced poverty; the impact on income distribution was less clear-cut but was certainly not more likely negative than positive.

The fourth major concern of antiglobalists concerns the impact of increasing integration internationally on workers, and especially unskilled workers, in industrial countries. That jobs are "lost" seems to be a difficult argument to make, given the relatively low rates of unemployment in industrial countries. Indeed, at least in the United States, it is arguable that the noninflationary rate of unemployment is lower than it used to be because of

---

[17] World Development Indicators (2007), p. 5 says much of this.
[18] Berg and Krueger (2003).

the availability of more goods intensive in the use of unskilled labor from developing countries. Certainly, many observers associate the lower rates of inflation (which themselves bring gains to the poor even more than the rich) with the increased availability of imports from lower income countries. And there is a wider variety of goods consumed by the majority of workers, at a lower price, as a consequence of increased production in low-income countries. Both of these, considerable, benefits seem to be ignored in discussions of the impact of globalization.

But the more telling argument concerns not the impact on employment, but on real wages. Labor economists attribute much of the increased differential between compensation of skilled and unskilled workers (whose real wages have risen, but less rapidly) to biased technical change: information technology and other innovations have shifted the demand for labor from relatively less skilled workers to those with more skills. While trade may have played a role, it is likely secondary to that of innovation.

But there is another, more serious, argument. The costs of trying to (probably unsuccessfully) protect workers from competition with imports would be exceptionally high in terms of their own real living standards over the long run. Appropriate policy responses to any difficulties experienced by the less skilled in the labor force need to find ways in which those individuals can be more productive through more education and training, fostering greater mobility, and other measures. The need for these responses within any modern society originates in the plight of those with few skills and low incomes, not only from trade. Attempting to use trade protection measures as a means of fighting any impact of economic growth on the less-skilled would be a cure worse than the disease. It is hard to estimate how high the trade barriers would have to be to have a significant impact on the wages of the unskilled in industrial countries, if trade protection would have a positive impact at all. And the costs within industrial countries would be enormous relative to alternative ways of achieving the same objectives.

Moreover, efforts to thwart trade on the part of industrial countries would doom countries — especially those that have not yet opened up their economy — to much poorer economic prospects than could exist were they to alter their policy frameworks in the context of a healthy, growing, world economy. While increased protection in the industrial world would reduce growth rates and possibly result in recession and even stagnation in real incomes, the negative impact on developing countries would be even larger.

Hence, some of the criticisms of the antiglobalizers are simply wrong: developing countries and workers in those countries benefit from globalization if other policies are appropriate. Globalization and integration of emerging markets has not caused child labor — it was already there, and rising real incomes tend to reduce its incidence. Even when there is an element of truth — as with financial crises and other fluctuations — the appropriate policy responses would keep globalization and adopt policies to mitigate side effects. The same surely holds true of industrial countries in efforts to improve the lot of lower-wage workers: domestic policy measures to improve productivity and efficiency through education, training, and other means, can enable surer gains for low-skilled workers and simultaneously avoid the great harm that would otherwise be inflicted upon the prospects for improvement in living standards in developing countries.

To conclude, the world is a very imperfect place. Millions of people live in miserable conditions, with poor health, poor nutrition, and little hope. But in that dimension, the world is a much better place than it was two centuries ago. Much has been learned about the process of economic growth and rising living standards, and policies needed to achieve them, over the past half century, and many have escaped poverty. The world is thus a much less imperfect place than it was. The now-industrial countries have living standards that would have been beyond recognition two hundred years ago. Globalization has been a major contributor and there is every prospect that integration, and with it, rising living standards and attainable economic welfare will continue to improve.

Most of the very poor countries have still to embrace globalization, although they are less insulated than they were fifty years ago. Policies in individual countries aiming at rising living standards can do much to improve prospects for the poor, but growth rates will be far below those potentially achievable unless globalization is further embraced. Globalization by itself cannot do the job; but in the absence of globalization, the job cannot be done.

Today's antiglobalizers recognize the many challenges that remain, but appear not to recognize the progress of the past two centuries for the world and the past half century for some poor countries. In decrying the continued existence of poverty, they blame globalization, failing to recognize that poverty and its associated evils existed long before globalization. Efforts to reverse globalization, or to discourage those still-inner-oriented countries from embracing it, will diminish the prospects for those countries to accelerate their growth. For the world as a whole, a setback to globalization of the sort advocated by the antiglobalizers might succeed in reversing rising living standards in developing countries and reducing trade flows. While that would disadvantage the relatively poor in the now-rich countries, and could result in worldwide recession, even more seriously it would dash the prospects of those countries whose governments are now recognizing the need for faster growth and trade liberalization. Quite likely, many of those who recently escaped from poverty might once again slip into that catastrophic state.

Without a healthy and growing international economy, the outlook for continued economic progress in the industrial countries would greatly diminish, and world economic growth would surely slow, if not grind to a halt. Once that happens, the growth rates of poor countries would certainly fall. With those events, the prospects for future progress in poverty reduction would be greatly diminished.

Globalization is not a cure-all. But it is a necessary condition. Attention needs to turn to finding policies to mitigate those undesirable accompaniments while simultaneously maintaining and strengthening the healthy and sustainable growth of the international economy.

REFERENCES

Berg, A and A Krueger (2003). Trade, Growth, and Poverty — A Selective Survey. In *The New Reform Agenda*, B Pleskovic and N Stern (eds.), pp. 47–90. Annual World Bank Conference on Development Economics.

Bhagwati, J (2004). *In Defense of Globalization*. New York: Oxford University Press.

Blanning, T (2007). *The Pursuit of Glory: Europe 1648–1815*. New York: Viking Press.

Clark, G (2007). *A Farewell to Alms*. Princeton: Princeton University Press.

Estevadeordal, A, B Frantz and AM Taylor. (2003). The Rise and Fall of World Trade, 1870–1939. *Quarterly Journal of Economics*, 118(2), 359–407.

Fogel, R (2007). Interview, by T. Taylor. *Journal of Economic Perspectives*, 21(3), 245–246.

Harley, CK (1988). Ocean Freight Rates and Productivity, 1740–1913: The Primacy of Mechanical Invention Reaffirmed. *Journal of Economic History*, XLVIII(4), 851–876.

Maddison, A (2003). *The World Economy: Historical Statistics*. Organization for Economic Cooperation and Development (OECD) Development Centre Studies.

Mohammed, S and JG Williamson (2004). Freight Rates and Productivity Gains in British Tramp Shipping 1869–1950. *Explorations in Economic History*, 41, 172–203.

Morawetz, D (1977). *Twenty Five Years of Economic Development 1950 to 1975*. World Bank, Washington DC.

Chapter 3

TRADE POLICY AND ECONOMIC DEVELOPMENT: HOW WE LEARN†

The improvement in living standards, life expectancy, and economic growth prospects in developing countries ranks among the most important economic success stories since the Second World War. Growth in some has been dramatic, and while progress has been far from uniform, there are grounds for optimism that future growth prospects can be even better than performance to date.

One factor accounting for that success has been improved understanding and adoption of economic policies much more conducive to satisfactory economic growth than was the case in the 1950's and 1960's. That better understanding, in turn, resulted from a combination and interaction of research and experience with development and development policy.

Ideas with regard to trade policy and economic development are among those that have changed radically. Then and now, it was recognized that trade policy was central to the overall design of policies for economic development. But in the early days, there was a broad consensus that trade policy for development should be based on "import substitution." By this was meant that domestic production of import-competing goods should be started and increased to satisfy the domestic market under incentives provided through whatever level of protection against imports, or even import prohibition, was

† Presidential Address delivered at the 109th meeting of the American Economic Association, January 5, 1997, New Orleans, LA.

* Herald L. and Carolyn L. Ritch Professor of Humanities and Sciences, Department of Economics, and Senior Fellow, Hoover Institution, Stanford University, Stanford, CA 94305.1 am grateful to Ronald McKinnon and Richard Snape for very helpful discussions on an earlier draft of this manuscript. My thanks also go to Chonira Aturupane and Evren Ergin for valuable research assistance. An earlier version of this paper was presented as the Chris Higgins Memorial Lecture at the Economic Society of Australia.

necessary to achieve it. It was thought that import substitution in manufactures would be synonymous with industrialization, which in turn was seen as
the key to development.

The contrast with views today is striking. It is now widely accepted that
growth prospects for developing countries are greatly enhanced through an
outer-oriented trade regime and fairly uniform incentives (primarily through
the exchange rate) for production across exporting and import-competing
goods.[1] Some countries have achieved high rates of growth with outer-
oriented trade strategies. Policy reform efforts removing protection and shifting
to an outer-oriented trade strategy are under way in a number of countries.
It is generally believed that import substitution at a minimum outlived its usefulness and that liberalization of trade and payments is crucial for both
industrialization and economic development. While other policy changes also
are necessary, changing trade policy is among the essential ingredients if there
is to be hope for improved economic performance.

And, while there are still some disagreements over particular aspects of
trade policy both among academic researchers and policy makers,[2] the current
consensus represents a distinct advance over the old one, in terms both of
knowledge and of the prospects it offers for rapid economic growth. While it
will no doubt be further refined in light of experience, a changing world
economy, and research, there is no question of "going back" to the earlier
thinking and understanding of the process.

A number of interesting questions arise about this change in thought and
policy. How could it happen that a profession, for which the principle of comparative advantage was one of its key tenets, embraced such protectionist
policies? What was the contribution of economic research to the sea change
in thinking, policy prescriptions, and politicians' acceptance of the need for
policy reform? What sorts of economic research best informed the policy
process? In a nutshell, how did we learn? And what was the contribution of
economists and their research to the process?

---

[1] John Williamson (1994 pp. 26–28) summarized the set of policy prescriptions he believed
most policy makers and academics concerned with development subscribed to. An outer-
oriented trade policy is prominent on his list. He dubbed this set of views "the Washington
consensus."

[2] Perhaps the key issue on which there remains disagreement regarding appropriate trade policy
is whether there is a role for the state in "picking the winners," or selectivity in incentives confronting different industries. Even those advocating such selectivity, however, would be far less
protectionist than were advocates of import substitution in the 1950's, while those advocating
uniformity of incentives nonetheless point to key roles for appropriate incentives through macroeconomic policy, provision of infrastructure, enforcement of contract, and other public goods.

Attempting to answer these questions is the subject of this lecture. Even with a focus limited to trade and development, analysis of the role of research and its usefulness is at least somewhat conjectural. The issue, however, of what types of research inform good policy is an important one. I suspect that the tentative conclusions I draw here may be relevant for other areas of research-informing policy, but leave that to others to demonstrate or refute.[3]

In what follows, I first sketch the initial approach to trade policy in early development research and thought. Next, consideration is given to the evolution of thought, research, and experience with respect to trade and development over the next several decades, and to the "conventional wisdom" of the 1990's. Thereafter, I consider the role of research and the sorts of research that proved most fruitful in guiding policy and changing the consensus.

Before proceeding, two caveats are necessary. First, it is very difficult to disentangle views of the proper role for trade policy in development from views about the appropriate role for the state. Partly as a legacy of the Great Depression, partly because of the belief that the Soviet Union had succeeded in its developmental and industrial aspirations through central planning, and partly because of the perceived success of wartime controls, there was widespread agreement — in developed and developing countries alike — that the state should play a major role in economic activity, not only in affecting aggregate demand, but also in regulating private markets and indeed augmenting or supplanting them with state-owned enterprise production of manufactured and other goods. Quite clearly, early views about the necessity for a leading role for the state in guiding resource allocation were incompatible with an open trade policy or outer-oriented trade strategy. Yet to attempt to consider the evolution of both views is well beyond the scope of this paper, and focus here is confined to trade policy.

Second, to focus on research that influenced thinking about economic policy is not to denigrate the importance of research that does not appear to have had immediate policy relevance. First of all, basic research often informs more applied research. Second, in some cases of research that provided little of lasting value, that outcome could not be known at the time, Perhaps some

---

[3] To name just one example from another field, consider the pioneering work of Theodore W. Schultz (1964), challenging the view that irrational peasants were unresponsive to incentives. Once his work was accepted, it was no longer possible to maintain low prices for agricultural commodities and believe that there would be little or no output effects.

of that research served to demonstrate the infeasibility of certain policy paths,[4] or to demonstrate the futility of further explorations.

Nonetheless, *ex post* it is clear that some lines of research served to hasten the day when policy makers would accept the desirability of removing high walls of protection, while others were irrelevant or served largely to reinforce prejudices and perpetuate the "old wisdom." Perhaps that is inevitable in the "marketplace of ideas" as new paradigms are brought forth to replace old ones.

I. EVOLUTION OF THEORY, UNDERSTANDING, AND POLICY

A. The Early Years

As developing countries gained independence from their former colonial rulers,[5] their leaders had a political mandate to achieve higher living standards and rapid economic growth.[6] It is difficult in the 1990's to recall the extent to which it was then plausible to view the world economy as split into the industrialized countries and the underdeveloped countries, or "first world" and "third world," as they were often called. Underdeveloped countries had markedly lower average educational attainments (including a great deal of illiteracy and a high fraction of the population with no schooling), poor health conditions, and very little infrastructure. They were heavily specialized in the production and export of primary commodities and imported most of their manufactured goods. While differences among the

---

[4] An example is the line of research, which continued into the 1970's, improving methodology for planning models. This research certainly contributed greatly to understanding both the functioning of the economy and also to one aspect of what would be necessary in order for the planning approach to succeed. Without those research contributions, it is possible that many would claim that planning failed because it was incorrectly done (rather than, as most would now believe, it was misconceived).

[5] Latin America and a few other countries (including China, Thailand, and Turkey), then deemed "underdeveloped," were not formally colonies prior to the Second World War. However, it was widely believed that they had been "economically dependent." The leaders and elite in most poor countries shared the perception that their economies were "different" from industrialized countries and like other developing countries. The G-77 (77 countries), or nonaligned nations, were all developing countries whose leaders perceived themselves to be in a similar economic situation with similar goals of rapid growth and improved living standards.

[6] As was then conventional, I shall assume here that higher living standards, more rapid growth, and economic development were/are synonymous for purposes of analyzing trade policy.

underdeveloped countries were acknowledged, these seemed minor contrasted with the overwhelming realities of their common attributes and
widespread poverty.

The new field of development economics was regarded by many as covering underdevelopment because "conventional economics" did not apply
(see Albert Hirschman, 1982). Focus on how the developing countries
should shape policies for accelerating growth and raising living standards was
the central issue.[7]

B. Accepted Stylized Facts and Premises

Early trade and development theories and policy prescriptions were based on
some widely accepted stylized facts and premises about the underdeveloped
countries. These were a mixture of touristic impressions, half-truths, and mis-
applied policy inferences. In hindsight, it is surprising how some then-accepted
stylized "facts" were so uncritically accepted and held sway for so long.
However, it is not possible to understand what thinking about trade and
development was except in light of those premises. Indeed, it can be argued
that improved understanding of trade and development came about in large
part through research which effectively demonstrated the falsity of these
premises.

A first premise was based on the fact — then certainly true — that developing economies' production structures were heavily oriented toward
primary commodity production. The dependence on foreign trade was
believed to be extreme, as there was virtually no production capacity for manufactured goods outside a few light mass-consumed commodities. However,
many observers went further and *attributed* the low living standards in developing countries to dependence on primary commodity production and
export.

A second "fact," or premise, was that if developing countries adopted
policies of free trade, their comparative advantage would forever lie in primary commodity production. It followed that industrialization and, hence,
development would not take place if free trade policies were adopted.

A third premise — termed "export pessimism" — was that both the
global income and price elasticities of demand for primary commodities were

---

[7] There was, to be sure, a growing literature on the contribution of technical change and factor accumulation to growth in the industrialized countries. But most development economists
saw that research as irrelevant for developing countries.

low. Consequently, it was anticipated that export earnings would not grow very rapidly, if at all.[8]

A fourth premise was that the labor force in developing countries, predominantly engaged in agricultural activities as it was, had a marginal product of labor that was "negligible, zero, or even negative," to quote W. Arthur Lewis (1954 p. 141). The stylized "fact" that there was "surplus" labor, or disguised unemployment in less developed countries (LDCs) was widely accepted.[9] In many analytical formulations, it was explicitly or implicitly assumed that labor was a free good while capital was the scarce factor of production.[10]

Related to the fourth premise was a fifth premise: that capital accumulation was crucial for growth, and in early stages of development it could occur only with the importation of capital goods. Since it was expected that the demand for capital goods imports, and imports of other products used in the production process, would grow rapidly while foreign exchange earnings would not, it appeared that growth could follow only if domestic production of import-competing goods could expand rapidly.

Yet a sixth widely accepted premise was that there was very little response to price incentives in developing countries: peasants were "traditional" in their behavior, and there were "structural" problems within the economy.[11]

Based on these stylized facts and premises, it was a straightforward step to believe that the process of development was that of industrialization, by which was essentially meant the accumulation of capital for investment in manufacturing industry and related infrastructure. Moreover, since most manufactured goods were imported, it seemed to follow logically that, as

---

[8] Another widely held view, closely related to export pessimism, was the proposition that the terms of trade had inexorably deteriorated against primary commodities and would continue to do so. Investigation of this proposition tended to demonstrate that at the very least the deterioration had been much less than was believed. John Spraos (1980) provided a classic review of the evidence.

[9] A modern interpretation would be that there are many people in developing countries with very low marginal products of labor. While they are too poor to remain unemployed, the process of development entails equipping people with the capabilities (partly through education) and opportunities to increase their productivity.

[10] To be sure, all analysts recognized the importance of increased provision of education and health services. But for purposes of analyzing trade policy, emphasis was almost exclusively on investment.

[11] This gave rise to a great deal of literature based on "structuralism." According to some, it was the absence of responsiveness to price that made developing countries "different." Structuralism was also used as an argument that inflation was necessary in order to achieve growth. See Hollis B. Chenery (1975) for a fuller description.

stated by Chenery (1958 p. 463) among many others: "Industrialization consists primarily in the substitution of domestic production of manufactured goods for imports."

C. Initial Policies

Policy prescriptions were derived from these propositions, or stylized facts. Since it was thought that industrialization was necessary for development and that free trade would leave underdeveloped countries specialized in primary commodity production, it followed that there had to be investment in new manufacturing industries whose output would substitute for imports. Further, it was widely believed that new industries in poor countries could not possibly compete with their established counterparts in the developed world. Therefore, industry would have to be protected during its initial phase. Import-substitution policies therefore became the hallmark of development strategies for manufacturing and the underlying rationale for trade policy.[12]

The case for import substitution was based both on the premises outlined above and also on received doctrine: the infant industry argument. The notion that dynamic considerations and externalities might imply that an industry, although economic, would not be established by private agents had been accepted by economists as a legitimate exception to the case for free trade since Hamilton and List.[13]

It was stipulated that a low-cost producer or producers were already in operation abroad; then, the argument proceeded, a potential entrant in a developing country would be faced with an initial period of high costs, but could in the longer run compete. However, in the presence of dynamic externalities (presumably internal to the industry), it was believed that no

---

[12] There were many important subthemes that are not elaborated here, since they are not essential to the main argument. It should, however, be noted that there were many who believed that the situation of developing countries was "structural" and that marginal changes would not matter. It was then concluded that a "big push" was needed, with many new investments simultaneously generating additional demand and then becoming profitable. Ragnar Nurkse's (1958) "balanced growth" prescription reflected the same viewpoint.

[13] See Robert E. Baldwin's (1969) classic analysis of the argument, which not only sets up the conditions under which there might be an infant industry, but also carefully and critically scrutinizes the various circumstances in which those conditions might hold. Baldwin's article was an important contribution to better understanding of the empirical relevance of the theory, as I shall argue below.

individual producer would find it profitable to start production. In these circumstances, the infant industry argument could justify temporary intervention to make entry into the new industry privately profitable provided that, over the longer term, its costs would decline *below* the imported cost by enough to yield an economic return on the intervening loss, which could be viewed as an investment.

Although the infant industry argument was, in a first-best world, an argument for a production subsidy (which would presumably equal the unit value of the externality and might apply as well for production for exports as for the domestic market), it was combined with the appeal for import substitution[14] to yield a justification for protection of newly established manufacturing industries in developing countries.

However, combining the assumptions that industrialization would have to take place through substituting for imports, that there were infant industries requiring initial intervention, and that export earnings were unlikely to increase, the stage was set for trade and industrialization policies.

The premises underlying import-substitution policies were so widely accepted that developing country exceptions were even incorporated into the General Agreement on Tariffs and Trade (GATT) articles. Article XVIII explicitly protected the developing countries from the "obligations" of industrialized countries and permitted them to adopt tariffs and quantitative restrictions. They also were entitled to "special and differential treatment" in other regards under GATT. That the GATT, the upholder of an open international trading system, would accept an "exception" for developing countries shows how deeply entrenched the views supporting import substitution were. It is arguable that the very existence of this exception not only legitimized developing countries' inner-oriented trade policies, but also removed pressures that might otherwise have been brought to bear earlier for them to adopt trade and payments regimes more conducive to economic growth.[15]

D. Resulting Evolution of Policies

In one way or another, provision was made in country after country that, once domestic production became feasible, imports would be restricted. In

---

[14] It was also believed that there was a revenue constraint, making the first-best production subsidy infeasible. More recent analyses would also point to the greater potential for corruption inherent in production subsidies as yet another reason why protection might be preferable.

[15] See Kenneth Dam (1970 Ch. 14) for a full discussion.

Brazil, a "Law of Similars" provided that firms importing goods that were similar to those available domestically would lose their government privileges, which included not only access to credit and tax treatment, but also eligibility to bid on government contracts and a variety of other valuable rights. In India, imports were licensed, and in the event that there was domestic production, any would-be importer was required to obtain letters from any supplier government officials thought might be capable of producing the good to the effect that the supplier could not meet the specifications. In Turkey, goods were removed from the list of items for which import licenses could be granted once domestic production capacity was available. Similar provisions, or very high tariffs, were used to encourage import substitution in most developing countries.[16]

In some countries and industries, the trade regime was used as the key policy instrument to provide incentives for import-substituting investment and production by private firms. In other circumstances, state-owned enterprises were established, and investments were made directly by the state sector in new manufacturing activities. In that case, the trade regime provided protection to the state-owned enterprises, although their budget constraints were, in any event, very soft, None of these policies, as adopted, provided means of identifying where dynamic externalities were largest, nor was there any provision for reduction of protection after an initial period. Indeed, protection was virtually automatic for any new import-substitution industry.

A final aspect of early policies also contributed to high and indiscriminate levels of protection. That is, as countries embarked on ambitious development plans, inflation rates rose to levels significantly above those in industrial countries (although far below inflation rates prevailing in many developing countries today). Demand for foreign exchange was rising rapidly in response to the development plans, rising incomes, and domestic inflation. Nonetheless, policy makers in most developing countries chose to maintain their fixed nominal exchange rates. In part, this reflected the perception, noted above, that there was little response to prices and that, indeed, maintaining the nominal exchange rate "taxed" agriculture while simultaneously subsidizing capital goods imports. In part, exchange rates were held fixed because it was believed that so doing made imports of capital goods cheaper

---

[16] In Argentina, an effort was made to liberalize the trade regime by lowering tariffs in the late 1970's. To the surprise of officials, there was no apparent effect of the first round of tariff cuts. Subsequent investigation revealed that the tariffs in question had been between 500 and 1.000 percent, and that they had been above the rates at which domestic producers could compete.

and thus increased investment. The net result was, of course, real appreciation of the exchange rate, which further intensified *ex ante* payments
imbalances, reduced foreign exchange availability, and induced greater restrictiveness in import licensing.

It will be recalled that the 1950's and 1960's were a time of unprecedented economic growth for the industrial countries and for world trade.
Buoyed in part by international markets, and in part by the stimuli of
increased investment and other aspects of development programs, the rates of
growth of per capita incomes rose markedly relative to historical levels in most
developing countries, although they remained below those in industrial countries with few exceptions. Even the growth of industry itself was fairly rapid,
as the "easy" import-substitution opportunities were by and large undertaken
first.[17]

However, with real exchange rate appreciation and the pull of resources
into newly profitable, import-competing industries, the growth of foreign
exchange earnings inevitably slowed. It is not widely appreciated that developing countries, which had a 44 percent share of world exports of agricultural
commodities in 1955, lost share to the point where they had only 31 percent
by 1970.[18]

With acceleration in the growth of demand for foreign exchange, and
deceleration in the growth of supply, foreign exchange difficulties were
inevitable. The export pessimism premise had been self-fulfilling, given the
policies that were followed. The drop in primary commodity prices in the
early 1950's accentuated the phenomenon, but affected the timing more than
the actuality of the result. The initial response by most policy makers was to
impose rationing of scarce foreign exchange (and require the surrender of
foreign exchange from exports) on imports, and the resulting system had little to do with encouraging infant industries.

---

[17] See Raul Prebisch (1984) for the argument. It can be argued that, with uniform incentives,
import substitution would have taken place first in those industries with least comparative disadvantage. In fact, the use of import licensing and prohibitions meant that rates of protection
were not uniform even across import-competing activities. In addition, monopoly power in the
domestic market was conferred to domestic producers, so that profitability hinged more on the
price elasticity of the demand curve than on producers' abilities to reduce costs and compete
with imports.

[18] Agricultural protection in Japan, Europe, and the United States may have contributed somewhat to this result. But in most developing countries, the demand for food was growing more
rapidly than the supply (as producer prices were suppressed relative to the prices of industrial
goods,) and, thus, the supply (demand) curve for exports (imports) of agricultural commodities was shifting down (up) (see Krueger, 1990 p. 95).

Although initial rationing of imports was usually on a relatively uniform and across-the-board procedure, controls over foreign trade generally became more restrictive and complex over the next two decades, both in response to growing "foreign exchange shortage," in reaction to the "unfairness" of the undifferentiated controls, and in response to evasion of the regimes.[19] Periodic balance of payments crises arose in reaction to overvaluation of the real exchange rate, increased indebtedness, and the failure of export earnings to grow.

International Monetary Fund (IMF) "stabilization" programs were undertaken, under which import regimes were simplified and rationalized (as import licensing was, in those years, not abolished). The nominal exchange rate was normally altered (but usually to a new fixed exchange rate in the face of continuing inflation).[20] Even in IMF programs, however, it was seldom intended that the underlying trade policies related to import substitution be changed: the intent, rather, was to rationalize the trade regime and find ways to induce more foreign exchange earnings to finance the capital goods that would be imported to undertake additional import-substitution investments. Growth proceeded in "stop-go" fashion, as periods of foreign exchange crisis were followed by tight(er) monetary and fiscal policies, a consequent reduction in excess demand for imports, and an increase in foreign exchange earnings. When the trade regime was again relaxed, growth resumed and the demand for imports again mushroomed until the next crisis.[21]

E. Research Directions and Contributions

Most research in the 1950's and 1960's was based on the premises outlined above, and supported the basic thrusts of policy. It needs only brief mention here. Some focussed on the possible existence of externalities and the need for "balanced growth," as it was assumed that expansion of any one industry alone would not be feasible because of the limited size of the market.[22] This prescription, of course, was based on the premise that development of manufactured exports was not feasible. Another line of supportive research

---

[19] For a description, see Jagdish N. Bhagwati (1978).

[20] See William R. Cline and Sydney Weintraub (1981) for analyses of some of these episodes.

[21] See Carlos Diaz-Alejandro (1976) for an analysis of the "stop-go" cycle in Colombia.

[22] For a modern presentation of the "big push" need for balanced growth, see Kevin M. Murphy *et al.* (1989). The notion of balanced growth and "big push" in the 1940's and 1950's was associated with such analysts as Paul Rosenstein-Rodan (1943) and Nurkse (1958), among others.

focussed on planning models, concentrating in large part on interindustry flows and linkages.[23] Empirical research on patterns of development began, focussing on the structure of economies and their growth performance. For more than a decade, the growing disparity between theory and practice was all but ignored.

There was also research providing a rationale for protection of new industries and import substitution. These results demonstrated that domestic distortions could warrant trade intervention[24] in a number of situations. Everett E. Hagen (1958), in perhaps the best known of these, set up a model assuming that urban wages exceeded rural wages exogenously, and demonstrated that a tariff could improve welfare by inducing resources into the (artificially) higher-cost urban industries.

Work also continued on structuralist models, as a number of authors found reasons why developing countries' economic structures were "different" and why, therefore, the usual economic analysis would not apply.[25] Chenery and Michael Bruno (1962), Chenery and Alan Strout (1966), and Chenery and many other coauthors developed the "two-gap" model, using the stylized fact that foreign exchange was "scarce" in developing countries. In this model, export earnings were exogenously given and growing more slowly than the demand for foreign exchange.

Investment was limited by the more binding of two linear constraints: the available savings and the available foreign exchange. There were thus two "gaps" — between savings and investment, and between demand for, and supply of, foreign exchange. Growth was constrained either by savings or by foreign exchange availability, and the model demonstrated the high potential productivity of foreign aid (in providing foreign exchange), enabling otherwise redundant domestic savings to be used in capital formation. The model, reflecting the views of the day, had little role for the price mechanism.[26]

---

[23] See Chenery and Paul Clark (1959) for an exposition. Economists in India probably carried planning models the furthest into practice. The Indian Second Five-Year Plan was explicitly based on the P. C. Mahalanobis (1955) model, and contained estimates of output levels for the subsequent five years which were used as a basis for granting investment licenses. No licenses were issued once the increased capacity already had been allocated. See Bhagwati and Padma Desai (1970) for an account.

[24] There was a huge literature on this subject. See Bhagwati (1971) for a synthesis of many of the papers.

[25] See Christopher Bliss (1989, p. 1194) for a modern statement of the proposition that if demand and supply are sufficiently inelastic, prices do not matter.

[26] See Ronald I. McKinnon (1966), who provided the first demonstration of this important proposition at the time.

An example of an analytical effort to clarify circumstances under which one of the stylized facts could be realized was Bhagwati's (1958) and Harry G. Johnson's (1967) demonstration of the possibility of "immiserizing growth," under which a country might increase its output, only to find the price of exports falling so much that the country was worse off. As Bhagwati showed, the conditions under which that might happen were fairly extreme.

An important development was the theory of shadow pricing, which was an offshoot of programming and planning models. It was initially used to demonstrate how reliance on market prices might yield an inappropriate resource allocation. Quickly, however, analysts pointed to the distortions between domestic prices of import-competing and exportable goods because of the trade regime. There is little doubt that cost-benefit techniques improved project selection and enabled improved governmental decision-making with, inter alia, the insistence on use of border prices. The publication of the I. M. D. Little and James A. Mirrlees (1969) volume marked a milestone, after which there was almost no question about the appropriateness of using border prices in project evaluation.

In a related and important development, the theory of effective protection was developed by Johnson (1965a), W. M. Corden (1966), Bela Balassa (1965), and others, providing a framework for analyzing the protection accorded to industries engaged in light processing and much higher value-added activities on a comparable basis. The notion of domestic resource costs (Bruno, 1965; Krueger, 1966), showing the uneven allocation of resources to earning and saving a unit of foreign exchange across activities, was developed to meet the argument that market prices failed to reflect opportunity cost. This research provided a tool with which economists could measure the wide disparities in protection accorded to different import-competing industries.

Recognizing that these estimates were based in part on partial equilibrium analysis,[27] a number of researchers began work on developing techniques for computing general equilibrium results. Based on newly developed solution algorithms, techniques were developed for models which endogenized prices, and thus moved away from the linear models earlier used for analysis.[28]

---

[27] They did not, in principle, have to be partial equilibrium estimates if shadow prices were known and used in calculations. In practice, however, that was seldom feasible.

[28] For an exposition of the development of these models into the 1970's, see Kemal Dervis *et al.* (1982).

By the late 1960's and 1970's, there were significant contributions which undermined some of the premises on which import-substitution strategies were based. At an analytical level, one line of research focussed on whether the stylized facts of "market failure" in fact warranted the imposition of trade restrictions, Bhagwati and V. K. Ramaswami (1963), Johnson (1965b), Bhagwati (1969), and others demonstrated that a trade instrument (tariff or quota) was usually not a first-best, nor often even second-best, instrument for achieving the objectives in the name of which protection had been granted. The equivalence of tariffs and quotas, an old result in international economics, was revised and refined, as quotas became more frequently used.[29]

Research also began analyzing other aspects of the ways in which protection actually worked. Here, attention focussed on rent-seeking (Krueger, 1974) as a by-product of protection (and, indeed, as a user of resources as lobbyists sought protection — see Bhagwati and T. N. Srinivasan, 1980), as resources were used to obtain valuable import licenses, thereby incurring deadweight costs. This, in turn, showed that protection was more costly than earlier, area-under-the-triangle, estimates had indicated. It further enabled insights as to the buildup of vested interests that is likely to arise once any policy is undertaken. When policy reforms were attempted, it was clear that those administering earlier policies were in the forefront of those opposing change, alongside the beneficiaries of protection (or other policies).

Related to work on rent-seeking and the tendency for vested interests to spring up around the policies that were adopted, others worked on the theory of overinvoicing and underinvoicing (see Bhagwati, 1974) and smuggling (see Munir A. Sheikh, 1974; Mark Pitt, 1981), again focussing on some of the flaws of the system of protection as practiced in most developing countries.

As trade regimes became more chaotic, empirical work began to document these problems, bolstered by the development of the measurement tools embodied in the concepts of effective rates of protection and domestic resource costs. Researchers focussing on Pakistan discovered that there was actually negative value added in some circumstances, suggesting that it would have been cheaper to pay workers to stay home and import the final product.[30]

The Organization for Economic Cooperation and Development (OECD) sponsored a series of country studies on industrialization led by Little *et al.*

---

[29] See the survey in Bhagwati (1969).
[30] See Corden (1971 p. 51) for a summary of that literature.

The three synthesized (1970) the results and provided estimates of effective rates of protection in a number of developing countries. These showed how high and indiscriminate protection levels were and demonstrated the extent to which import substitution had failed to achieve many of the objectives set for it. A later series of country studies undertaken under the auspices of the National Bureau of Economic Research, synthesized in works by Bhagwati (1978) and Krueger (1978), provided further systematic empirical evidence of the economic wastefulness and irrationality of the inner-oriented trade regimes.

F. East Asian Experience

At the same time as evidence of the high costs of import-substitution regimes was accumulating, another important development occurred. Starting first in Taiwan, several East Asian economies began growing rapidly under policies diametrically opposite those prevalent under import substitution. Interestingly, the Taiwanese government seems to have listened carefully to the views of S. C. Tsiang,[31] a professor at Cornell University specializing in international economics. Following the precepts of comparative advantage, Tsiang advocated growth through industrialization, but with industrialization taking place through increased capacity for exports, as well as for the domestic market. Taiwan's transformation from a high-inflation, inner-oriented, aid-dependent economy to a major exporting economy is well known.

Korea, whose initial conditions appeared, if anything, even less conducive to growth than those of Taiwan, followed the same pattern. In the late 1950's, Korea's exports had averaged only 3 percent of gross domestic product (GDP) and were growing slowly, if at all, while imports represented 13 percent of GDP. The current account deficit was financed largely by foreign aid, and the domestic savings rate was virtually zero. Major policy reforms look place in Korea in the early 1960's, which greatly increased the return to exporters. There were fairly uniform incentives to all exporters and assurances that the real exchange rate would not appreciate to their detriment. Reforms also reduced the protection to import-competing producers and permitted exporters duty-free importation of needed intermediate goods and raw materials.

The Korean economic performance was transformed, as growth rates entered the double-digit range and living standards improved rapidly. Hong

---

[31] For an account of Taiwan's turnaround, see Tsiang (1985).

Kong and Singapore also became part of the East Asian "miracle" through policies designed to encourage exporting. Growth rates exceeded those previously thought to represent an upper bound on attainable performance.[32]

It was not until the 1980's, however, that the importance of the differences became unarguable. After the second oil price increase of 1979, the worldwide recession of 1980–1982, and the accompanying "debt crisis," the East Asian newly industrializing countries rapidly resumed growth, whereas other heavily indebted countries were unable to service their debts and were hard hit by events in the international economy. Research undertaken in attempting to understand the impact of the debt crisis on the developing countries made it abundantly evident that the debt-GDP ratios were not significantly different between the two groups of countries. What was significantly different was the debt-export ratios, as the East Asian countries were able to maintain debt servicing and resume growth because of the greater flexibility of their economies.[33] It also emerged that, even prior to the debt crisis, the rates of growth of inner-oriented developing countries had not increased despite substantial increases in their savings rates.[34]

This is not the place to enter into the debate as to the factors contributing to the success of the East Asian "tigers." For, while there is debate about whether government intervention in "picking the winners" was a key component of the growth strategy,[35] all recognize that the reversal from an import-substitution strategy, the opening up of the economy, and the relative uniformity of incentives across the board were necessary, if not sufficient, for success. Indeed, there is an irony in the fact that the East Asian experience has stimulated some to attempt to identify the "dynamic" factors in exporting

---

[32] Chenery and Strout (1966) actually had a third constraint, "absorption," which restrained growth to 8 percent of GDP or less, on the grounds that more rapid growth would not be feasible.

[33] See Jeffrey Sachs (1985) for an early development of the argument.

[34] The World Bank (1983) documented that this phenomenon of a greatly increased average savings rate with no increase in the growth rate and, therefore, a presumed relatively sharp increase in the incremental capital output ratio, affected most developing countries.

[35] It can be argued that this is a difference between those who see the East Asian trade policies as "free trade" and those who see them as intervention, but of a different type, from that under import substitution. The critical difference is probably between those who would stress uniformity of incentives for earning or saving foreign exchange (and, therefore, would argue that the East Asian NICs were arbitrarily close to a free trade regime), and those who believe the "dynamic externalities" earlier associated with infant industry protection really call for the "right kind" of intervention and argue that the trade strategy was really one of "export substitution."

that are absent from production for the domestic market. Thus, we have a complete turnaround: in the 1950's and 1960's, the neoclassical argument for an open trade regime was rejected on the grounds that it was "static" and ignored "dynamic considerations"; in the 1990's, there appears to be widespread agreement that the benefits of an open trade regime are largely "dynamic" in nature, and go well beyond the gains from trade under "static" models of an open economy. Just as was the case with the infant industry argument, however, there is a question as to how to identify and measure these "dynamic" gains.

II. HOW DID ECONOMISTS AND RESEARCHERS GO WRONG?

The "Washington consensus" is very different from the policy consensus that led to the adoption of import-substitution policies in the 1950's and 1960's. While there will no doubt be refinements in that consensus with further experience and research, it is highly unlikely that the ideas of the 1950's and 1960's will be revived.

One can raise three questions about the change in viewpoints. First, how could it be that the economics profession, whose consensus on the principle of comparative advantage was at least as great as that on any other policy issue, endorsed a highly protectionist policy stance?[36] Second, what factors contributed to changing the entrenched views of the 1950's and 1960's? Finally, what types of research were most (and least) productive in bringing about better understanding of the role of trade and trade policy in development? I address these questions in turn.

The first is the issue of how the principle of comparative advantage could have been so blithely abandoned. With hindsight, it is almost incredible that such a high fraction of economists could have deviated so far from the basic principles of international trade. What led them to do so? Can any lessons be drawn to avoid (or shorten the duration of) similar mistakes in other applied fields when new policy problems arise?

But, recall the stylized facts that were widely accepted. People were thought not to respond to incentives; exports earnings were thought to be predetermined and slowly growing at best; industrialization was necessary for

---

[36] It can also be asked why it took so long for policy makers in countries such as India to recognize that import substitution (and other policies) as a strategy for development was not delivering the hoped-for results and that a preferable path existed. That is an important question that is well beyond the scope of this paper.

development; supply response was lacking; and so on. These stylized facts, which were at best simplistic and in most instances simply wrong, permitted economists to conclude that developing economies were "different."

However, it took theory to support these conclusions. Here, one can distinguish several failures. First, there was misapplication of good theory. Second, there was what I shall call the "theory of negative results," which essentially could be used to provide a rationale for virtually any trade intervention. Third, there was good theory harnessed to erroneous stylized facts.

A. Misapplication of Good Theory

Misapplication of good theory was significant.[37] The identification of comparative advantage with the two-factor, two-good model, and the assumption that free trade would imply that developing countries would forever specialize in primary commodities, was an important misapplication. One of the puzzling aspects of the evolution of thinking about policy is the degree to which proponents of open trade regimes failed to refute the allegation that free trade would forever leave developing countries specialized in production of agricultural commodities.[38]

It was not until the 1970's (see Ronald W. Jones, 1971b; Krueger, 1977) that models — motivated in part by the East Asian experience — were developed in which three factors of production (land, labor, and capital) were allocated among sectors, each of which could produce many commodities. As the three-factor models demonstrated, comparative advantage lies within manufacturing and within agriculture, and not between them. Thus, poor unskilled, labor-abundant countries have a comparative advantage in labor-intensive agricultural *and* unskilled labor-intensive manufactured commodities, while countries with a much higher land-labor ratio have a comparative advantage in more land-using agricultural commodities and their comparative advantage in manufacturing lies more in goods with higher capital-unskilled labor ratios. In these models, the overall trade balance in manufactures is a

---

[37] Another example of misapplication of good theory was the early defense, such as that of Hagen (1958), of protection because of a domestic distortion. But it took the development of the theory of domestic distortions to correct that, as is discussed below.

[38] Some of Johnson's (1958) research on trade and growth went some way toward refuting this proposition, but still in a 2 × 2 framework. Moreover, Johnson's work implied that labor-abundant countries would, while accumulating capital, undergo "ultra anti-trade biassed" growth, which seemed to support import substitution.

function of the size of the manufacturing sector, itself a function of past capital accumulation and the land-man ratio.

A second serious misapplication of good theory arose because of the nonoperational nature of the theory itself, and the failure to identify circumstances under which policy implementation might be incentive compatible *and* potentially increase welfare. A key culprit in this case was the interpretation of the infant industry argument. As I already discussed, it was widely touted as a basis for import substitution, and generally recognized as a "legitimate" case for a departure from free trade.

One can hardly argue with the proposition that the presence of a positive externality gives rise to a basis for intervention; if the externality is dynamic and temporary, then temporary intervention, such as infant industry protection, can be called for.

The problem with the argument, as a basis for policy, is that it fails to provide any guidance as to how to distinguish between an infant that will grow up and a would-be producer seeking protection because it is privately profitable. It is not even clear how one could begin, empirically, to identify the domain of the externality. Moreover, even if there were a producer or producers whose increased production would generate dynamic externalities, it does not follow that any level of protection is warranted. And there is nothing in the infant industry argument to provide guidance for quantifying or estimating the likely magnitude of the externality.

Indiscriminate protection in developing countries was defended on infant industry grounds with arguments of capital market failure, labor market failure (as the costs of training, presumably, would be borne by first entrants into industries and then not recouped as others hired workers away), costs of investments in technology, and uncertainty all used. It was not until Baldwin's (1969) seminal article that it was demonstrated that, even when the presumed imperfection existed, it was unlikely that infant industry protection would help correct it. As Baldwin cogently argued, later entrants to an industry might speed up their investments if protection made domestic production more profitable, and the first entrant might even be worse off! It was only after critical examination of these circumstances that the defenders of the infant industry case for import substitution became less vehement.

The infant industry argument also is an excellent example of a theory that is nonoperational because criteria for bureaucrats to identify cases have not been put forward. Quite aside from the unpredictability and immeasurability of the future time path of costs in new factories and the moral hazard associated with asking individual entrepreneurs to indicate how much protection they need, there is nothing to my knowledge in the literature specifying how the policy maker might instruct a bureaucrat to identify (much less measure) a dynamic externality if it were present, how an incentive-compatible mechanism might be devised for improving welfare, how the bureaucrat might measure the height of warranted protection, nor how policy makers might credibly commit to temporary protection. Even *ex post*, it is not entirely clear how one might identify an industry as a successful infant: simply because a firm became profitable and exported does not prove that there was either an externality or a dynamic process at work![39]

B. Negative Results

Much of the theorizing that took place was concerned with what I call "negative results." That is, analysts sought to find reasons why, for example, an exception to free trade should be made. Once the principle of comparative advantage was laid down as a basis for policy, there was little left for theorists to prove supporting an open trading system, so the challenge to theorists was to find conditions under which the free trade precept did not hold. As theory, these findings were significant, but for policy they were unhelpful, and probably served to perpetuate inappropriate policies.

In most real-world circumstances, one strongly suspects that protection exists where theoretical exceptions do not justify it, and that moves to first-best policies would on average lower, and not raise, protection. Judged by that metric, research output relevant for policy would consist more of attempts to measure the costs of these excess levels of protection. In practice, it would be interesting to review the literature and ascertain how many articles, or pages, or other measures of research output were devoted to finding exceptions to the proposition that comparative advantage should form the basis for trade policy, contrasted with those focussing on circumstances where protection was too high! In undergraduate international economics courses, sections on trade policy spend considerable time addressing national defense exceptions, the optimum tariff argument, the infant industry argument, second-best arguments, and other arguments for protection. While attention is paid to the reasons why these arguments may not be correct, focus nonetheless centers on

---

[39] The same is true of the optimum tariff argument. In the presence of many goods with varying degrees of monopoly power, the formula becomes hopelessly complex. It is certainly true that many tariff structures would lead to lower, rather than higher, welfare in the presence of monopoly power in trade. Yet, in practice, many policy makers have been misled into thinking that they could defend very high tariffs (sometimes even on goods that their countries import in small quantities) on optimum tariff grounds.

the exceptions to the case for free trade, rather than on the reasons for it. While this may be inevitable as a way of reasoning, the temptation to draw inappropriate inferences seems high.

An example will illuminate the argument. Whereas theory suggests criteria for departures from laissez-faire free trade which normally would result in different levels of protection for different industries, a widely used prescription for policy makers is that, if there is to be protection, a uniform tariff is usually preferable to any alternative structure. This proposition rests on several considerations. First, only a uniform tariff can generate a uniform rate of effective protection in the import-competing sectors and, if different goods are subject to different rates of tariff, the resulting differences in effective rates of protection will lead to resource misallocation even within the import-competing industries and have no relation to underlying "dynamic" or market-failure considerations. Second, a uniform tariff simplifies customs administration, making evasion and/or bribery of customs officials more difficult than a varying rate structure. Third, a uniform tariff greatly reduces the opportunities for resource losses in rent-seeking and lobbying. Fourth, given international prices, international value added is more likely to be maximized under a uniform tariff structure than under a variable one.

None of these arguments is sufficient to prove that a uniform tariff is optimal. And, indeed, it is straightforward to develop models in which a uniform tariff is nonoptimal, especially in the presence of income-distribution considerations. In theory, the costs of protection can be minimized by imposing higher tariffs or taxes on goods whose supply and demand is relatively more price inelastic.

Those arguments, as put forward, are all couched in terms of demonstrating the "falsity" of the proposition that a uniform tariff is preferable to variable tariff rates and that there is a departure from uniformity that can potentially improve welfare. But the difficulty with that formulation is that it does not provide a criterion for which departures from uniformity might improve welfare, because a model considering, for example, income-distribution considerations, cannot simultaneously address issues of corruption and administration. And, the fact that income-distribution considerations can warrant a nonuniform tariff structure does not prove that any nonuniform tariff structure is preferable to a uniform one! As such, a negative result gives little or no guide for policy. Nonetheless, it arms lobbyists and others with ammunition to discredit technocrats' efforts to maintain a less irrational structure of protection.

Some good theoretical papers would have done less damage, or at least given less aid and comfort to policy positions that were clearly not those intended in the analyses, if the authors had taken greater pains to note the limitations to their analyses, and the other factors that would have to be taken into account, before their results were applied to policy.

In that regard, it is often overlooked that most policy implementation is carried out by government officials who cannot be expected to have advanced degrees, and sometimes even undergraduate degrees, in economics. In many instances (including formulae for optimal tariff differentiation), the degree of sophistication needed to interpret research results is well beyond that which most bureaucrats will have. As pointed out by Johnson (1970 p. 101):

> ...The fundamental problem is that, as with all second-best arguments, deter-mination of the conditions under which a second-best policy actually leads to an improvement in social welfare requires detailed theoretical and empir-ical investigation by a first-best economist ... it is therefore very unlikely that a second-best welfare optimum will result based on second-best arguments.

C. Good Theory Assuming Counterfactual Situations

The final abuse of theory was primarily a fault of inappropriate stylized facts. Nonetheless, in many instances, analysts *assumed* signs of variables that were certainly questionable, modelled the situation neatly, and then drew policy conclusions that could hold only if the posited signs were valid. Yet their claims often went beyond the assertion that "if these facts ... then" variety.

As an example to illustrate the point, I have deliberately chosen a good, widely cited paper, because the paper represents good theory, but interprets it, for policy purposes, with dubious "stylized facts." Sudhir Anand and Vijay Joshi (1979) considered a world, such as that envisaged by Hagen (1958), in which workers in the advanced sector receive a higher wage than in the rest of the economy due to unions or other (presumably unalterable) circum-stances. They then asked whether maximizing international value added for given employment of domestic resources is an appropriate criterion when income-distribution considerations cannot be separated from productive-efficiency considerations.

In their setup, the clear answer is no, because tradeables are produced by the advanced (presumably unionized) sector, and hence maximizing interna-tional value will pull more resources into that sector at the cost of a deteriorating income distribution. Interestingly, they do not address the ques-tion of whether the advanced sector is labor or capital intensive. If, as is true for outer-oriented developing countries, the exportables are labor intensive relative to import-competing activity, removing protection to induce a move of more workers to the "advanced" high-wage sector would presumably increase wages of those workers and also those in the rest of the economy: a more equal income distribution would be obtained at the expense of lower real wages for all. Without regard to factor intensity, however, Anand and Joshi (1979 p. 350) conclude that:

> The motivation behind the theory of distortions has been to criticise and to guide trade and industrialisation policies ... Our analysis emphasises the need for caution ... Departures from technical efficiency may be called for as part of the rational response by governments to the limitations they face in carrying out desirable income distribution policies ...[40]

Anand and Joshi (1979) *assumed* that moving toward economic efficiency in tradeables requires paying higher wages because of a distortion. Yet, in fact, the evidence suggests that it has been the highly protected, import-competing industries which have been able to pay above-average wages; removing protection has led to rapid expansion of employment in labor-intensive industries. If the latter stylized fact is correct, and if income-distribution considerations are important, it would suggest that the policy implications of the Anand-Joshi analysis are the opposite of what they suggest — namely, that policy makers should encourage, even beyond the optimum, a shift of resources out of protected industries (presumably by removing protection) and into exportable industries.[41]

III. WHAT RESEARCH CONTRIBUTED TO IMPROVED POLICIES

Policies that were not consistent with policy makers' growth objectives were cloaked in respectability in the 1950's and 1960's by theory and stylized facts

---

[40] Another example of the "negative results" research arises from early findings (see Bhagwati and Srinivasan, 1973; Jones, 1971a) that the resource pulls associated with raising an effective rate of protection did not necessarily accord with those associated with increasing a nominal rate of protection. These findings did not significantly affect research efforts in part because the authors made clear the relatively extreme conditions necessary to generate the "perverse" resource pull, and partly because other researchers were able to demonstrate that there seemed to be few, if any, empirical counterparts to the perverse pull cases.
[41] See Pranab Bardhan (1996), tracing how the presumed "efficiency-equity" trade-off has been shown to be false in considerable measure.

of the type I have already described. I have so far discussed properties of some theories that made them susceptible to misapplication or misuse.

A second question is equally important, however. That is, how did the change in economists' policy prescriptions come about? What led to the reversal to recognition of the importance of an open economy after the conversion to advocacy of import substitution in the 1950's and 1960's? I can address this question more rapidly because much of the answer was implicit in the description of the evolution of developing countries' trade policies.

Three sets of research efforts can be singled out as having been particularly useful in informing changes in policy, although others, no doubt, also contributed.[42] First, there was research analyzing how import-substitution policies were actually working. Second, and not unrelated to the first, there was the refinement and more appropriate interpretation of theory. Third, there was research demonstrating the feasibility of the alternative.

A. Challenging the Stylized Facts and Understanding How Import-Substitution Regimes Worked

Analyses of the evidence regarding the key stylized facts were in hindsight important steps in undermining the intellectual consensus. Demonstration that there were significant responses to incentives undermined the policy case for ignoring prices. Proof that the terms of trade had deteriorated very little, if at all, began to undermine export pessimism.

Empirical work on the ways in which import-substitution regimes functioned was crucial. Comparative analyses such as those of Little *et al.* (1970), Bhagwati (1978), Krueger (1978, 1983), and Michael Michaely *et al.* (1991) clearly contributed significantly to awareness that the effects of import-substitution policies were not idiosyncratic to individual countries. The comparative studies provided a great deal of evidence as to the shortcomings of reliance on import substitution. Evidence that protection was not temporary, that protection levels were high and idiosyncratic, that there was very great discrimination against exports, and that "foreign exchange shortage" was a function of policies and not an exogenously given datum, were all

---

[42] The ideas and events influencing policy makers in one country may not have been precisely the same as those in the next one. And, of course, no precise measurement of the relative influence of research results and of experience is possible. There is also the question of the role of research, relative to the role of experience itself. However, in fact, the ways in which people in other developing countries learned about the East Asian experience was largely the consequence of research efforts.

important in challenging the protectionist trade policies still prevailing in most developing countries in the 1980's.

If one considered the evidence regarding the workings of trade policies in any one country taken alone, there were ample grounds for criticism of inner-oriented trade policies, with the monopoly positions they conferred on domestic producers, the high costs of doing business, rent-seeking low quality of products, and so on. It was possible, however, to recognize that and nonetheless conclude that policy makers in that particular country had been inept, or had simply failed to implement policies appropriately. As evidence mounted across countries, the similarity in the evolution of regimes and their consequences was striking. It was increasingly difficult to dismiss the evidence from a particular country as being sui generis or the failing only of the particulars of policy execution in that country.

But, underpinning the analyses of individual country situations, either in the comparative studies or individually, were agreed-upon measurement tools. The empirical studies could not have had their impact without the development and use of measurement tools. As cost-benefit techniques were used, it became increasingly difficult to justify some highly uneconomic projects. And, as measurement of effective rates of protection was undertaken in country after country, the high and erratic nature of protection became evident. Techniques for cost-benefit analysis and measurement of effective rates of protection were important, first of all, in providing analysts with tools with which to demonstrate the chaotic nature of import-substitution policies. In addition, even before the policy consensus changed, there is little doubt that some of the earlier extreme irrationalities of policy were curbed through use of these tools. It became extremely difficult to defend the high average of, and wide variance in, effective rates of protection.

At an empirical level, it seems clear that early demonstrations of the great range of variation in rates of effective protection were useful both in demonstrating some of the problems with trade regimes and also in preventing at least a few of the worst excesses that might otherwise have occurred. More generally, recognition and reintroduction of the proposition that there is a response to incentives that cannot be overlooked in policy formulation, combined with the evidence on the erratic and arbitrary nature of incentives provided by trade regimes, forced a reexamination of the premises on which import-substitution policies were based.

Yet another contribution of empirical research was to focus upon the actual workings of policy implementation. In early policy prescriptions, there had been something of a naive tendency to assume that enunciating a desired outcome was itself sufficient to achieve it. This naivete was dispelled, as the theories regarding bureaucratic behavior, rent-seeking, smuggling, and over-invoicing and under-invoicing all enabled observers to examine more critically the ways in which alternative policy prescriptions might have side effects that had earlier been unanticipated.

B. Refinement and More Appropriate Interpretation of Theory

As already seen, some of the intellectual underpinning of import-substitution policies was provided by inappropriate interpretation of theory, or the failure of theory to take into account key institutional or behavioral variables. Analytical developments focussing on conditions under which these interpretations were valid, or examining the ways in which results had to be modified to take into account these institutional and behaviorial aspects, were clearly important in improving understanding.

The entire literature on optimal interventions in the presence of domestic distortions is one important example of a demonstration that earlier interpretations of theory had failed to examine the relevant alternatives. It was invaluable in demonstrating clearly that in most circumstances, the presence of a distortion warranted a first-best policy intervention other than a tariff.[43] For example, in the case of Hagen's (1958) employment-generating case for protection, the optimal intervention literature demonstrated clearly that a first-best intervention would be in the labor market, and that a tariff or quota could not achieve a first-best outcome.

Similarly, developments showing that the comparative advantage results were not the simple "specialize forever in primary products" precept proved significant in enabling policy makers to contemplate alteration in trade strategy. Baldwin's (1969) critical examination of the infant industry argument provides yet another example of an analytical contribution that was important in making those concerned with policy consider carefully the effectiveness of the policies they had adopted in achieving their desired goals.

Finally, there was theory that was developed in response to the functioning of import-substitution regimes. Here again, the theory of rent-seeking, as it pointed to the ways in which bureaucrats and others made protection very costly, was important. Further, when it was recognized that bureaucrats, businessmen, and others attempted to capture or thwart policy initiatives not in their self-interest and that they acquired an interest in maintaining the system, once established, and that resources were expended in

---

[43] However, those advocating import substitution seized upon the infeasibility of first-best policy as a defense for following the policies they wished in any event to follow.

operating the system, it had to be recognized that changing the system would be politically difficult.

Development of a better understanding of the incentives for underinvoicing and overinvoicing of exports and imports and for smuggling under exchange-control regimes worked in the same direction: not only could these activities prove costly to the exchequer and in terms of resource drains, but the very recognition of their presence served to remind policy makers of the limitations of their instruments.

Finally, good analyses demonstrating how individual import controls actually worked contributed to understanding and made empirical work more effective. The further refinement of theory showing tariff-quota equivalence has already been mentioned. Rent-seeking again comes to mind. But, in addition, individual mechanisms for encouraging import substitution each had their own, often idiosyncratic, incentive effects. A good example is Gene Grossman's (1981) classic analysis of domestic content regulations and their effects.

C. Demonstration of the Viability of Alternative Trade Policies

Research on the contrast between East Asian and other developing countries and reasons for it obviously turned out to be a major contributing factor in influencing thinking about policy. In a way, research on East Asian experience provided a final blow to the earlier uncritical acceptance of the stylized facts. For, the East Asian experiences demonstrated, as nothing else could have, the feasibility and viability of alternative trade policies: it was no longer possible to associate comparative advantage with reliance on primary commodity exports, and the East Asian experience certainly put an end to the belief that developing countries could not develop rapidly when relying on integration with the international economy.[44]

The experience of the East Asian exporters did several things. Most important, it provided concrete evidence that a developing country could achieve industrialization without relying on domestic markets to absorb

---

[44] To be sure, there are still doubters. Some claim that South Korea and Taiwan were major recipients of foreign aid, which is said to account for much of their rapid growth (although the announcement that foreign aid would diminish was what triggered policy reform in Korea). The status of Hong Kong and Singapore as city-states is alleged by some to render their experience of little relevance. Even today, those resisting policy changes assert that conditions in the 1950's and 1960's were conducive to export expansion in ways in which the world market of the 1990's is not — despite the rapid expansion of exports from China and Southeast Asian countries.

almost all additional output. That demonstrated the fallacy of the earlier view that industrialization could take place only through import substitution.[45] Also, the East Asian trade regimes offered significant opportunities for empirical research, and the evidence mounted that properties formerly thought to be those of all developing countries were, in fact, properties resulting from inner-oriented trade and payments regimes.

It cannot be said that either research results or the contrast in economic performance alone led to the change in policies in other developing countries.[46] Both research (especially that which brought the sharply contrasting experiences of the East Asian exporters and the import-substituting countries into focus) and experience contributed.

Whether one should regard the East Asian experience as entirely separate from economic theory, however, is an interesting question. As already mentioned, Tsiang (1985) was himself an international economist, and it was in significant part his efforts that led the Taiwanese authorities to abandon inner-oriented policies and attempt to develop through exports. The theory of comparative advantage was, at least in that instance, a pillar on which policy was built. And, while a variety of factors no doubt contributed to the Korean adoption of outer-oriented trade policies after 1960, the favorable experience of Taiwan undoubtedly facilitated the willingness of decision makers to try the new approach.

The East Asian exporters put to rest the mistaken belief that developing countries relying on the international market would forever be specialized in the production of primary commodities. They also showed that rates of growth well above those realized even in the most rapidly growing import-substitution countries such as Brazil and Turkey could be realized.

IV. WHAT LESSONS CAN BE LEARNED FOR RESEARCH IN NEW APPLIED FIELDS?

It is difficult to draw generalizations based on the evolution of analysis, empirical research, and policy in one applied field. Nonetheless, in the hope

---

[45] Some have argued that the East Asian outer-oriented trade strategy might not have succeeded without an earlier stage of import substitution. In that view, East Asia moved away from import substitution at the "right time," whereas other countries stayed with the strategy too long. See Gustav Ranis (1984) for one such argument.

[46] For that matter, trade policy reform is still resisted in many countries, notably most of Sub-Saharan Africa.

that insights from other applied areas may reinforce or amend the list, the effort seems worthwhile.

Perhaps the most obvious generalization from the various factors that have been discussed is that empirical research which tests for the presence and order of magnitude of stylized facts which are used in modelling and policy formulation can be invaluable. If the right stylized facts can be used as a basis for theory, and theorists have good indications of the relative quantitative importance of various phenomena, it is clearly far more likely that the theory itself can make a useful contribution.

In the case of trade policy and development, the demonstrations that there were responses to incentives and that developing countries could expand export earnings and did have comparative advantage in other than primary commodities, were clearly crucial to improved understanding of the relationship of trade to development.

For that reason, high marks must go to the analytical research that pointed to measurement techniques such as effective protection and cost benefit, which enabled policy makers and their analysts to obtain empirical quantification, however rough, of the relevant magnitudes.[47]

In like manner, the empirical demonstration of the similarity of policy responses across developing countries, and of the wide and largely irrational variation in incentives for import-competing industries, increased understanding of what was wrong with existing policies.

Overturning, or more accurately interpreting, the accepted stylized facts, therefore, was a first prerequisite for developing a better theory of trade policy for development. But theory was important in many ways, in addition to pointing to appropriate measurement tools. First of all, good policy-relevant theory provided blueprints for those windows of opportunity in which governments genuinely sought to improve economic performance, as was the case in Taiwan and Korea in the early 1960's, and in Chile, Mexico, and India in later decades, to name just a few.[48] Having the "blue-prints" on hand from good theory is obviously a major contribution. As already noted, however, that theory is often relatively dull — such as comparative advantage — rather than the more exciting and refined results of complex models.

---

[47] There is another example from a related field. As is well known, multilateral negotiations with regard to agricultural protection were completely stalled until the 1980's. In the 1980's, economists at the OECD proposed the use of a "producer subsidy equivalent" to measure the degree of government intervention in various agricultural commodities across countries. That tool permitted negotiations to begin restricting and dismantling agricultural protection.

[48] See Arnold C. Harberger (1993) for a discussion of the roles played by economists in some key policy reform episodes.

Second, theory was invaluable when it showed why simple interpretations of received doctrine were in fact wrong, This was the case with the theory of first-best intervention in the case of domestic distortions, and in the case with comparative advantage as interpreted to mean developing countries would specialize in the production of primary commodities, and with the infant industry argument.

These considerations suggest that research results, in order to be most likely to be amenable to policy relevance, should be interpretable into phenomena that are observable, hopefully quantifiable, and recognizable by the policy maker. A negative result, such as that theory does not *always* tell us, can be counterproductive precisely because the policy maker is informed only that a certain generalization (such as comparative advantage and the value of free trade) is not without exception; the generalization can then be ignored.

A more general statement of the problems inherent in theorems which show that major propositions are "not generally true" would encompass all of that theory which is cast in terms of "anything can happen." While it is certainly true that there are conditions under which a wide range of outcomes (Pareto-inferior, a bad equilibrium, Pareto-superior, etc.) are possible from the same policy instrument, it would have challenged the skills of even the most superb theorist to attempt to develop a case for the sorts of chaotic policies prevalent in Turkey in 1957, in Ghana in 1983, and in Argentina in the late 1980's. It is far too easy for analysts to ignore the fact that "an exception" does not rationalize all possible policy alternatives to free trade.

There is a criterion for efficient resource allocation, equating domestic and international marginal rates of transformation. Even if there are "dynamic" factors which contravene part of the static efficiency criterion, they too are measurable. Yet the "anything can happen" theories do not provide guides as to how the phenomena under examination may be quantified, and thus provide rationalizations (admittedly for those who want them) for policies that cannot by any realistic test pass muster.

Perhaps the lesson is that there is a significant danger that economic theory will be misinterpreted in the policy arena, and researchers could productively take more pains to distance themselves from policy conclusions that are not warranted by their analysis. Theoretical papers which end with "it has been shown that, under conditions x and y, policy z may no longer represent an optimum ... Therefore policy should ..." are obviously overstepping their bounds when the empirical relevance of x and y are not yet established, and even more so when conditions other than x and v also may be important (as, for example, with rent-seeking).

But many good theory papers are written where the authors assume that their audience will consist entirely of other theorists. In such instances, good theory may be misused, and it certainly will be in the self-interest of some to harness it to their own ends. It behooves applied economists, as well as the theorists, to be careful to interpret the policy relevance of results in ways which minimize the scope for misinterpretation. This is as true for those seeking to find "dynamic" aspects of exporting, or endogenous aspects of a "big push," as it should have been for those developing the infant industry or optimum tariff arguments. Complex results, such as those noted by Johnson (1970), are particularly suspect in that they can be interpreted in whatever ways suit the decision maker or lobbyist.

Finally, there is theory which provides no guidance as to when or how to observe the phenomenon. In such instances, it is difficult to find policy implications that will not be captured. One possible challenge for theorists might well be to ask for at least one plausible incentive-compatible mechanism under which the inefficiencies they identify might be improved upon by policy makers and bureaucrats. The existence of infant industries, of cases in which there are rents that *might* be captured by appropriate strategic trade policy, and of informational asymmetries and other market imperfections cannot be doubted. But until the magnitude of these phenomena can somehow be measured, or incentive-compatible mechanisms for correcting them can be devised, theorists asserting their presence are simply providing a carte blanche for policy makers and bureaucrats to intervene in whatever ways they like, and this will simultaneously be seized upon by special interests to bolster their causes.

No matter how careful economists are, special interests always will seize their research results in supporting their own objectives. And, no matter how sophisticated and careful research findings are, there always will be politicians formulating, and non-economists administering, policies. Recognition of these propositions could do much to increase the degree to which economists' research results can contribute (positively) to policy formulation.

REFERENCES

Anand, S and V Joshi (1979). Domestic Distortions, Income Distribution and the Theory of Optimum Subsidy. *Economic Journal*, 89(354), 336–352.

Balassa, B (1965). Tariff Protection in Industrial Countries: An Evaluation. *Journal of Political Economy*, 73(66), 573–594.

Baldwin, RE (1969). The Case Against Infant-Industry Protection. *Journal of Political Economy*, 77(3), 295–305.

Bardhan, P (1996). Efficiency, Equity and Poverty Alleviation: Policy Issues in Less Developed Countries. *Economic Journal*, 706(438), 1344–1356.

Bhagwati, JN (1958). International Trade and Economic Expansion. *American Economic Review*, 48(5), 941–953.

——— (1969). On the Equivalence of Tariffs and Quotas. In *Trade, Tariffs and Growth*, Bhagwati J (ed.), pp. 248–265. Cambridge, MA: MIT Press.

——— (1971). The Generalized Theory of Distortions and Welfare. In *Trade, Balance of Payments and Growth*, Bhagwati, J, R Jones, R Mundell, and J Vanek (eds.), pp. 69–90. Amsterdam: North-Holland.

——— (1974). On the Underinvoicing of Imports. In *Illegal Transactions in International Trade*, Bhagwati, J (ed.), pp. 138–147. Amsterdam: North-Holland.

——— (1978). *Foreign Trade Regimes and Economic Development: Anatomy and Consequences of Exchange Control Regimes*. Cambridge, MA: Ballinger Press.

Bhagwati, JN and D Padma (1970). *India: Planning for Industrialization and Trade Policies Since 1951*. London: Oxford University Press.

Bhagwati, JN and VK Ramaswami (1963). Domestic Distortions, Tariffs, and the Theory of the Optimum Subsidy. *Journal of Political Economy*, 71(1), 44–50.

Bhagwati, JN and TN Srinivasan (1973). A General Equilibrium Theory of Effective Protection and Resource Allocation. *Journal of International Economics*, 3(3), 259–281.

——— (1980). Revenue Seeking: A Generalization of the Theory of Tariffs. *Journal of Political Economy*, 88(6), 1069–1087.

Bliss, C (1989). Trade and Development. In *Handbook of Development Economics*, Volume 2, Chenery, HB and TN Srinivasan (eds.), pp. 1187–1240. Amsterdam: North-Holland.

Bruno, M (1965). The Optimal Selection of Export-Promoting and Import-Substituting Projects. In *Planning the External Sector: Techniques, Problems and Policies*. New York: United Nations.

Chenery, HB (1958). The Role of Industrialization in Development Programmes. In *The Economics of Underdevelopment*, Agarwala, AN and SP Singh (eds.), pp. 450–471. Bombay: Oxford University Press.

——— (1975). The Structuralist Approach to Development Policy. *American Economic Review (Papers and Proceedings)*, 65(2), 310–316.

Chenery, HB and M Bruno (1962). Development Alternatives in an Open Economy: The Case of Israel. *Economic Journal*, 72(285), 79–103.

Chenery, HB and P Clark (1959). *Interindustry Economics*. New York: Wiley.

Chenery, HB and A Strout (1966). Foreign Assistance and Economic Development. *American Economic Review*, 56(4), 679–733.

Cline, WR and S Weintraub (eds.) (1981). *Economic Stabilization in Developing Countries*. Washington, DC: Brookings Institution.

Corden, WM (1966). The Structure of a Tariff System and the Effective Tariff Rate. *Journal of Political Economy*, 74(3), 221–237.

——— (1971). *The Theory of Protection*. Oxford: Clarendon Press.

Dam, K (1970). *The GATT: Law and the International Economic Organization*. Chicago: University of Chicago Press.

Dervis, K, J de Melo and S Robinson (1982). *General Equilibrium Models for Development Policy*. Cambridge: Cambridge University Press.

Diaz-Alejandro, C (1976). *Foreign Trade Regimes and Economic Development: Colombia*. New York: Columbia University Press.

Grossman, G (1981). The Theory of Domestic Content Protection and Preference. *Quarterly Journal of Economics*, 96(4), 583–603.

Hagen, EE (1958). An Economic Justification of Protectionism. *Quarterly Journal of Economics*, 72(4), 496–514.

Harberger, AC (1993). Secrets of Success: A Handful of Heroes. *American Economic Review (Papers and Proceedings)*, 83(2), 343–350.

Hirschman, A (1982). The Rise and Decline of Development Economics. In *The Theory and Experience of Economic Development*, Gersowitz, M and WA Lewis (eds.), pp. 372–390. London: Allen and Unwin.

Johnson, HG (1958). *International Trade and Economic Growth*. Cambridge, MA: Harvard University Press.

——— (1965a). The Theory of Tariff Structure, with Special Reference to World Trade and Development. In *Trade and Development*, Johnson, HG and PB Kenen (eds.), pp. 9–29. Geneva: LibrarieDroz.

——— (1965b). Optimal Trade Intervention in the Presence of Domestic Distortions. In *Trade, Growth and the Balance of Payments — Essays in Honor of Gottfried Haberler*, Baldwin, RE (ed.), pp. 3–34. Chicago: Rand McNally.

——— (1967). The Possibility of Income Losses from Increased Efficiency or Factor Accumulation in the Presence of Tariffs. *Economic Journal*, 74(305), 151–154; reprinted in Johnson, HG (ed.), *Aspects of the Theory of Tariffs*, Cambridge, MA: Harvard University Press, 1972, 177–180.

——— (1970). The Efficiency and Welfare Implications of the International Corporation. In *Studies in International Economics*, McDougall, LA and RH Snape (eds.), pp. 83–103. Amsterdam: North-Holland.

Jones, RW (1971a). Effective Protection and Substitution. *Journal of International Economics*, 1(1), 59–82.

——— (1971b). The Three-Factor Model in Theory, Trade, and History. In *Trade, Balance of Payments, and Growth* Bhagwati, J, R Jones, R Mundell and J Vanek (eds.), pp. 3–21. Amsterdam: North-Holland.

Krueger, AO (1966). Some Economic Costs of Exchange Control: The Turkish Case. *Journal of Political Economy*, 74(5), 466–480.

———— (1974). The Political Economy of the Rent-Seeking Society. *American Economic Review*, 64(3), 291–323.

———— (1977). *Growth, Factor Market Distortions, and Patterns of Trade Among Many Countries*, Princeton Studies in International Finance, No. 40. Princeton, NJ: Princeton University Press.

———— (1978). *Foreign Trade Regimes and Economic Development: Liberalization Attempts and Consequences*. Lexington, MA: Ballinger Press.

———— (1983). *Trade and Employment in Developing Countries*. Chicago: University of Chicago Press.

———— (1990). Trends in Trade Policies of Developing Countries. In *The Direction of Trade Policy*, Pearson, CS and J Riedel (eds.), pp. 87–107. Cambridge, MA: Blackwell.

Lewis, WA (1954). Economic Development with Unlimited Supplies of Labour. *Manchester School*, 22(2), 139–191.

Little, IMD and JA Mirrlees (1969). *Manual of Industrial Project Analysis in Developing Countries*. Paris: Organization for Economic Cooperation and Development.

Little, IMD, T Scitovsky and M Scott (1970). *Industry and Trade in Some Developing Countries*. London: Oxford University Press.

Mahalanobis, PC (1955). The Approach of Operational Research to Planning in India. *Sankhya*, 16, 3–62.

McKinnon, RI (1966). Foreign-Exchange Constraints in Economic Development and Efficient Aid Allocation. *Economic Journal*, 76(301), 170–171.

Michaely, M, D Papageorgiou and A Choksi (1991). *Liberalizing Foreign Trade: Lessons of Experience in the Developing World*. Cambridge, MA: Blackwell.

Murphy, KM, A Shleifer and RW Vishny (1989). Industrialization and the Big Push. *Journal of Political Economy*, 97(5), 1003–1026.

Nurkse, R (1958). *Problems of Capital Formation in Underdeveloped Countries*. Oxford: Blackwell.

Pitt, M (1981). Smuggling and Price Disparity. *Journal of International Economics*, 11(4), 447–58.

Prebisch, R (1984). Five Stages in My Thinking on Development. In *Pioneers in Development*, Meier, GM and D Seers (eds.), pp. 175–191. New York: Oxford University Press.

Ranis, G (1984). Typology in Development Theory: Retrospective and Prospects. In *Economic Structure and Performance*, Syrquin, M, L Taylor and LE Westphal, (eds.), pp. 23–44. Orlando, FL: Academic Press.

Rosenstein-Rodan, P (1943). Problems of Industrialization in Eastern and South-Eastern Europe. *Economic Journal*, 55(210/211), 202–211.

Sachs, J (1985). External Debt and Macroeconomic Performance in Latin America and East Asia. *Brookings Papers on Economic Activity*, (2), 523–564.

Schultz, TW (1964). *Transforming Traditional Agriculture*. New Haven, CT: Yale University Press.

Sheikh, MA (1974). Smuggling, Protection and Welfare. *Journal of International Economics*, 4(4), 355–364.

Spraos, J (1980). The Statistical Debate on the Net Barter Terms of Trade Between Primary Commodities and Manufactures. *Economic Journal*, 90(357), 107–128.

Tsiang, SC (1985). Foreign Trade and Investment as Boosters for Take-Off: The Experience of Taiwan. In *Export-oriented Development Strategies*, Corbo, V, AO Krueger and F Ossa (eds.), pp. 27–56. Boulder, CO: Westview Press.

Williamson, J (1994). In Search of a Manual for Technopols. In *The Political Economy of Policy Reform*, Williamson, J (ed.), pp. 9–28. Washington, DC: Institute for International Economics.

World Bank (1983). *World Development Report*. New York: Oxford University Press.

Chapter 4

INCREASED UNDERSTANDING OF SUPPLY SIDE ECONOMICS[1]

It is perhaps fortuitous that the 50th anniversary of the Reserve Bank of Australia provides an opportunity to reflect on how far understanding of economics has come over the Bank's fifty years. For, while retrospectives are always instructive, they are especially so at present, when most analysts and commentators seem to believe that economics and economic knowledge has been static and unchanging throughout the postwar period, and that the Great Recession of 2007–09 indicates a failure of economies. I shall argue in this paper that much has been learned, often through experience and the challenges arising because of changes in economies, and that improved understanding has resulted in better policy making. However, there will always be new phenomena to understand and problems to resolve as economic growth leads to changes in the structure and responses of our economies.

This paper is divided into four parts. The introduction deals with some preliminaries, including the definition of supply-side economics. In the second, there is a necessarily somewhat stylized sketch of the general mindset of analysts and policy makers around a half century ago. Focus is on those major themes which drove decision makers and academics in their thinking about policy. For reasons to be discussed, some differentiation needs to be made between thinking regarding industrial countries' policies and that centering on policy for developing (or as they were then called, "underdeveloped") countries in that period.

The third section deals with those important changes in policy, and the thinking underlying them, that inform current thought and actions. As far as

---

[1] This is a slightly edited version of a paper presented at the Reserve Bank of Australia's conference held on February 9, 2010 celebrating its sixty years of existence. See Kent and Robson (2010).

possible, aspects of monetary and financial policy are dealt with briefly, as they are the subject of other papers to be delivered at this conference. A final section then turns to current changes in the international economy that constitute challenges for understanding and policy going forward.

I. INTRODUCTORY CONSIDERATIONS

A first task is to define supply side economics. Google gives many definitions, some of which associate supply side economics with the proposition that lowering tax rates will raise tax revenue, or with the proposition that lowering tax rates will induce more rapid economic growth. For present purposes, however, these definitions are too narrow. Broader definitions focus on the determinants of aggregate supply. In this light, "production or supply is the key to economic prosperity".[2] I shall define supply side economics to be the concerns with the determinants of potential output, or productive capacity, and changes in it over time.

Given that definition, it is quite possible to recognize that output is the outcome of the interaction of aggregate supply and aggregate demand and to recognize that there can be interactions between aggregate demand and supply. That is because shortfalls in aggregate demand can lead not only to current output at a level below potential, but also to reduced investment and thus lower future potential output. Nonetheless, for present purposes, I shall focus on understanding of determinants of the supply side and changes in thinking about the relative importance of supply and demand factors in determining output and growth. Supply side analysis then focuses on the determinants of increases in the supply of factors of production and total factor productivity.

A second preliminary observation has to do with the proposition that, as a broad first approximation, the past half century has witnessed the greatest economic success in human history for any comparable period in bringing living standards and the quality of life to levels heretofore not dreamt of. Whether we speak in terms of real per capita income growth or other measures of economic performance, or whether instead focus is upon life expectancies, infant mortality rates, educational attainments, and other indicators of the quality of life, there can be no question but that the world of 2010 is a different, and in economic terms, better place, than it was a half century ago.

---

[2] "Supply-side economics — Definition" at http://www.wordiq.com/definition/Supply-side_ economics.

Table l: Per Capita Incomes, by Region, 1950–2000 (1990 Geary Khamis dollars)

	Western Europe	Western Offshoots	Asia	Africa	World
1950	4,579	9,268	712	894	2,111
1960	6,896	10,961	1,029	1,066	2,777
1970	10,195	14,560	1,530	1,357	3,736
1980	13,197	18,066	2,034	1,536	4,520
1990	15,966	22,345	2,771	1,444	5,157
2000	19,002	27,065	3,817	1,464	6,012
Ratio: Income 2000 to 1950					
	4.15	2.92	5.36	1.63	2.85

Source: Madisson, A (2003). *The World Economy Historical Statistics,* OECD Development Centre Studies, OECD, Paris, p. 234.

Table 1 gives data on per capita incomes for various parts of the world, in purchasing power parity 1990 dollars, for decades from 1950 to 2000. As can be seen, for the world as a whole, real per capita income rose an estimated 2.85 times while world population was 2.41 times as large in 2,000 as it was in 1950. World real GDP rose approximately 6.9 times. Productive capacity had to increase enormously to underpin those achievements and that it was almost entirely supply side factors that enabled the rapid global rate of growth.

Increases in per capita income were accompanied by increases in other measures of quality of life and well-being. Life expectancy, for example, rose by about ten years for industrial countries and more than twenty years for the then-developing countries, while literacy rates have more than doubled.

The successes of the past half century have, of course, brought with them problems and challenges, which will be addressed in the final section. But it should not be overlooked that there have been major improvements in the quality of life in industrial countries, although changes in developing countries have been even more dramatic. Life expectancies in the developing countries have risen rapidly, literacy is almost universal among the young in most developing countries, some very poor countries (mostly in East Asia) have achieved living standards similar to those of industrial countries, and poverty has been greatly reduced in most middle-income countries and emerging markets. The sad exception, to which I shall return, is the group of countries referred to as "least developed", which includes most of sub-Saharan Africa and south central Asia. But the successes owe much to what has been learned about supply side issues, and the failures are attributable, in part, to a lack of acceptance of that learning. Indeed, many of the challenges facing the international economy today are the result of the successes of the past fifty years. These will be addressed in the final section.

II. THINKING ABOUT ECONOMIC POLICY IN THE 1950s

Prior to the end of the Second World War, little thought had been given to the economic conditions in developing countries: most had been or still were colonies[3] and it was generally taken for granted that their economies were "different". The leadership in almost all developing countries set economic development and rising living standards as a preeminent policy goal. When governments in developing countries embarked upon policy formulation to foster economic growth, they based their policies at least partly on a different understanding of supply side economics than that in developed, or as they were often called, industrial countries.

For ease of exposition, it is simplest to start with developed countries. It will be recalled that memories of the Great Depression were very strong, with many economists believing that there was a tendency for "secular stagnation" which would reassert itself once the initial postwar recovery was completed.

The intellectual contribution to policy making of the 1930s had been Keynesian: it was thought that private markets would work fairly well in allocating resources at full employment (with the exceptions to be noted below), but the major challenge to policy-makers was to maintain full employment. It was generally accepted that there was little or no automatic tendency for markets to achieve that outcome. Moreover, there was a widely-held view that there was a trade-off between price stability and the level of employment: by the 1960s this had been formalized as the Philips curve, which was deemed to show that higher rates of inflation would be consistent with higher levels of employment.

On macroeconomics, therefore, focus was largely on aggregate demand and determinants of the level of employment. It seems to have been more or less implicitly assumed that, if full employment were achieved and maintained, economic growth would be the automatic result and that few, if any, growth-oriented policies would be needed. To a significant extent, "supply side" issues were downplayed or ignored because of the belief that the major challenge for policy makers was to sustain aggregate demand along Keynesian

---

[3] There were, of course, a number of countries (such as those in Latin America, Turkey and Thailand) that had never been colonized. The general views on economic policy in those countries were much the same as in former colonies, as the "modernizing elites" and leadership believed that the developed countries had been sufficiently economically dominant so as to render them "virtual" colonies.

lines. Automatic stabilizers (in the forms of unemployment compensation, progressive income tax rates, and other schemes) were advocated and developed, and discretionary policies were advocated to stimulate the economy in times of underemployment and moderate economic activity in times of overly rapid expansion.

A major consequence of this focus was the neglect, or even the disbelief, in the role of incentives, and to some degree even of prices, in affecting the workings of the economy.[4] Marginal tax rates greater than 80 percent were not uncommon; replacement rates for the lost wages of the unemployed were often near 100 percent; and some industries were brought under government ownership. There was even a sizeable academic literature on whether devaluation of a currency might result in an improvement or a deterioration of the trade and current account balance (and little distinction was made between the nominal and the real exchange rate).

The belief in government regulation and/or ownership of economic activities stemmed from three sources: the Pigouvian argument that governments should compensate for externalities through taxes or direct interventions; concerns about market failures, especially in the labor market; and widespread belief that the great depression had shown that markets "didn't work". Many regulatory regimes, such as the Securities and Exchange Commission, the National Labor Relations Board, and the Glass-Steagall Act in the United States, had been established or tightened during the 1930s.Then, and in the first two decades after the War, there was little or no discussion of whether governments could regulate or run various economic activities; academic focus was on appropriate criteria for doing so, while policy makers simply acted.

A significant contributing factor to the acceptance of government ownership was the widely-held belief that the USSR had successfully been transformed into an industrial country through central planning, and in some industrial countries, government ownership increased in the early postwar years. This view even more strongly influenced economic policy makers in many developing countries and often resulted in policies that were detrimental to growth.[5]

---

[4] At a conference in the 1970s at which I presented a paper, my discussant began and ended his discussion with words to the effect that "this paper is based on the assumption that prices matter. They do not, and this paper is therefore irrelevant".

[5] India, for example, adopted a "socialist pattern of society", delineating industries into three groups: the "commanding heights" industries which could only be owned and operated by the government; the "mixed" industries in which both private and public sector firms could coexist, and industries (generally deemed "small-scale") that would be reserved for the private sector. Even those that were reserved were heavily regulated, and would lose their tax exemptions and other privileges if they grew "too large".

Even with respect to international trade, views were schizophrenic. If one examines the proposed charter of the International Trade Organization, the first half espoused the general principles that most free traders would adhere to: there should be open multilateral trade without discrimination among countries, and trade barriers should only be in the form of tariffs, and then the lower the better. There were, however, exceptions noted for developing countries to which I return below. But that first half became the articles of the General Agreement on Tariffs and Trade (now the World Trade Organization, or WTO). The second half of the proposed charter focused on what countries might do whenever they were confronted with less than the level of employment they deemed desirable: they were empowered to take trade protective measures in those circumstances. It was argued at the time, and in my judgment correctly, that the second half of the proposed ITO charter gave countries license to erect whatever trade barriers they liked in the name of achieving full employment.

Fortunately, the ITO never came into being, largely because the American Congress refused to ratify it, with objections based largely on the license the exceptions gave to countries to adopt whatever levels of protection they chose. Indeed, the conflict between the two halves of the proposed ITO charter has often been noted as puzzling to present-day observers. It seems safe to say that had the ITO charter been ratified, the unprecedented reciprocal lowering of trade barriers among the industrial countries that took place over the next several decades would have been quantitatively much smaller, if indeed reciprocal trade liberalization would have happened at all.

That the "free trade" GATT articles were adopted (by Presidential decree in the United States in order to begin the process of multilateral tariff negotiations while the American President still had "fast track" authority) was largely the result of American pressure. The multilateral tariff negotiations that took place under the auspices of the GATT were certainly a significant contributor to the rapid postwar economic recovery and sustained rapid growth among the industrial countries that took place in the 1948–73 period.[6] The more integrated global trading system and its results

---

[6] By most estimates, the average height of tariffs on manufactures prior to the first GATT round (in 1947) was between 40 and 50 percent in Europe, Japan, and North America. The European and Japanese tariffs understate the extent of protection because bilateral trading arrangements and exchange control were used to constraint imports in light of the "dollar shortage". The removal of quantitative restrictions on imports and adoption of Article VIII (full convertibility for current account transactions) in the 1950s was important for the speed of reconstruction and the rapid growth of trade in that era.

were certainly one of the key factors accounting for the greater weight placed on supply side factors in later years.[7]

In developing countries, Keynesian ideas on macroeconomic policies were similar to those in industrial countries. But the policy framework was even more inimical to private markets. The apparent success of the Soviet Union and the disaster of the Great Depression were viewed as having shown the fatal flaws in the capitalist system. But, in addition, there were two other factors. On one hand, the colonial legacy led many to believe that the west had developed through "exploitation" of its colonies, and that government support for economic activity thus lent to domestic industry had accelerated growth among the developed countries and thwarted it in the colonies.[8] On the other hand, there was a strong belief that high living standards resulted from having a large manufacturing/industrial base. The modernizing elites of most developing countries adhered strongly to the view that their countries must industrialize,[9] and that the head start of the developed countries made it necessary for governments to take the lead in establishing these industries, either in the public sector or through protection of the new infants from imports. The infant industry argument, long noted in economics textbooks as a key exception to the case for free trade, was invoked as justification.

In practice, most developing countries' governments adopted fixed exchange rates but undertook expansionary fiscal and monetary policies in the belief that these would spur investment and therefore accelerate growth.[10] The incremental capital-output ratio was seen as a given, virtually unaffected by economic policies, so that the investment rate (limited by savings and the current account balance) would determine the growth rate.

Policies resulting from these views led to inflation rates that were generally significantly higher than in the United States, at a time when dollar prices

---

[7] Transport and communications costs also fell significantly. However, by the middle of the century, they constituted about 20 percent of the fob prices of exports, and were thus less of a barrier than were tariffs and quotas.

[8] It was widely accepted that the terms of trade had worsened for primary commodities, and would continue to do so. That belief was also used as a rationale for "import substitution".

[9] As a stylized fact, industrial countries exported manufactures and imported primary commodities, while developing countries had large sectors producing and exporting primary commodities and imported most of the manufactured goods domestically consumed. This buttressed the belief that growth of industry was the key to rising living standards and economic development.

[10] It will be recalled that there was a "structuralist" school of thought in Latin America which held that "rigidities" were strong and that relatively high rates of inflation would be desirable to enable the breaking of the resulting bottlenecks.

generally were global prices. Since most countries pegged their currencies to the dollar, there was a strong tendency for real appreciation of developing countries' exchange rates. Real exchange rate appreciation served to discourage exports and of course also to lead to greater demand for importable goods.[11]

Development of "import-substitution" industries in the developing countries proved to be import-intensive, and excess demand for imports at the prevailing exchange rates generally led to greater and greater distortions over time. "Stop-go" cycles were the general rule, with each stop taking place when inability to finance even imports deemed essential resulted in a "stabilization" program in which fiscal deficits were reduced and monetary policy tightened, while devaluation adjusted the exchange rate. "Go" started after export earnings (and foreign exchange received as part of the stabilization as well as decumulation of speculative holdings of imports and exports) enabled an increase in imports. But each stop cycle was generally longer and more severe than the previous one, while each "go" was shorter and with a lower average rate of economic growth.

Policies toward international trade were central to this line of thinking. Underlying them was the view that prices had little or no effect on key variables. And once small, primarily agricultural economies were insulated from world markets because of high tariffs, quantitative restrictions on imports, and import prohibitions, governments also could and did intervene extensively in domestic economic activities. There was generally a strong bias against agriculture because of overvalued exchange rates used for valuation of exports, the high prices paid by farmers for nonagricultural items, and the suppression of domestic food prices through Agricultural Marketing Boards and other mechanisms.[12] But since it was believed that peasants were not responsive in any event to incentives, these policies were seen as supportive of industrialization and growth. Public sector enterprises were established, not

---

[11] An extreme example is provided by Ghana. In that country, the black market rate rose to 200 times the official rate before policies began being altered in the early 1980s. By that time, farmers had not only stopped replanting cocoa trees, but had even failed to harvest those that were still yielding. But most developing countries used import licensing, and import prohibitions for goods that could be domestically produced, in an attempt to restrict imports to the available foreign exchange.

[12] Agricultural Marketing Boards typically were the only legal buyers of farm commodities and were often the only legal source of farm inputs. They were used, however, as a means of collection of revenue for governments and as a source of patronage for politicians. As their costs rose, the return to farmers fell. It is estimated that in the late 1970s, there were many countries in which peasants earned less than a third of what they would have had they been able to sell their products and obtain their inputs and consumer goods at international prices.

only in utilities, transportation, and heavy industries, but even in activities such as tourist hotels, textiles and apparel, and food processing.

For activities not in the public sector, in most developing countries (and, in the early postwar years, many developed countries) governments placed low ceilings on interest rates that might be charged by banks, with many instances of negative real interest rates. With credit rationing, governments could and usually did direct credit to lines of economic activity (mostly in the "modern" sector) they wanted to encourage. Price controls, through loss-making public sector enterprises and on private economic activity, were extensively used in efforts to suppress inflation.

All of these policies were effected in industrial countries as well, but the degree to which government regulation, control, and ownership dominated economic activity was generally much, much greater. To the extent that the foreign trade regimes in developing countries were much more highly restrictive than in developed countries, the apparent room for government intervention was considerably greater, while the insulation of the economies from the rest of the world prevented feedback that might have signaled the extent to which these policies were detrimental to the very goals at which they were said to be aimed.

One result was that, until 1973, the average rate of economic growth of developing countries was below that of industrial countries despite the much greater potential for growth due to the catch-up possibilities. Although developing countries benefited from the rapid expansion of global trade, their share of world trade fell markedly, and for many purposes it was possible to view the world as split into the industrial countries, the developing countries, and, of course, the centrally planned economies, of which only the first group seemed significant for analysis of many global issues.

III. SUPPLY SIDE ECONOMICS TODAY

The contrast between the economic analysis underlying economic policy formulation then and now is almost stark: while many would accept that there may be a role for macroeconomic stabilization in the short run, most would hold that economic policies, macro[13] but especially micro, are key determinants of

---

[13] If one includes exchange rate regimes and controlled interest rates and repressed financial systems among macroeconomic policies, they would be regarded as equally important as microeconomic policies. In addition, as inflation has been tamed and fiscal balances brought under control in many countries, there is increasing acceptance that inflation, fiscal deficits, and high public debt/GDP ratios are more detrimental to economic growth than had earlier been supposed.

output and the longer run rate of economic growth, and that sufficiently ill-advised policies can result in economic stagnation, if not decline. Moreover, many of the policies that were regarded as output and growth-enhancing or neutral would now generally be viewed as detrimental to growth. In addition, the relative emphasis on the short-term and the longer-term aspects of economic policy has changed dramatically.

Here, I attempt to pinpoint some of the key changes in thinking, and the factors that led to those changes. Examination of what and why ideas changed is helpful in considering the challenges of the coming decades and the ways in which economic analysis and policy formulation may be influenced.

A key issue underlying many, if not most, of the changes, is how much incentives matter. An answer in the 1950s might have been "not much", as reflected in the tolerance, if not the advocacy, of high marginal tax rates, in the discrimination against agriculture in many countries, in the belief that the capital-output ratio was a given and not very much affected by policies, in price controls and credit rationing, and so on.

The change was starkest in developing countries, perhaps because the initial policies had become so extremely detrimental. There is now in general much wider recognition of the importance of incentives and the responses likely to occur when market outcomes are suppressed. This appreciation resulted from a number of factors, which can be mentioned only briefly here. In developing countries, failure of agricultural output to grow as expected was one phenomenon that helped. Peasant responses to incentives came to be recognized as not only existing, but relatively strong. This was pinpointed in the pioneering work of TW Schultz and his colleagues not only with respect to agriculture, but with respect to human capital formation more generally. They showed that human capital formation was an important source of economic growth,[14] and that rates of return to education mattered greatly in determining individuals' choices as to type and duration of education. Once it is recognized that investment in humans is an important determinant of factor productivity and growth, and that those investments are responsive to the costs and returns associated with them, it is no longer possible to regard the growth rate as a mechanical function of physical capital investment only. But the human capital paradigm was important in developed countries as well as in developing countries.

---

[14] In the early postwar years, it was often assumed that developing countries were poor because and only because they lacked physical capital. The incremental capital-output ratio was taken as a technological given, and policy prescriptions centered on raising the rate of capital formation. The human capital literature showed both that incentives mattered and that investment in human capital was an important source of economic growth.

As import-substitution progressed in developing countries, its evident costs became higher and the benefits lower. One might regard the first-round import-substitution industries as having been relatively close to low-income countries' comparative advantages. But as domestic demand for these unskilled labor-intensive products (footwear, apparel, matches, simple assembly industries, and so on) was satisfied (given the relatively high prices of the domestically-produced goods behind high walls of protection), further import-substitution investments necessarily entailed starting industries using physical and human capital more intensively, many of which had fairly large minimum efficient sizes of plant, while catering to small domestic markets. Few of the highly protected "infant industries" developed into export industries both because they were high-cost relative to international standards and because it was generally more profitable to develop a new domestic monopolistic position by producing an imported item and thus removing it from the list of eligible imports. Foreign exchange "shortages" persisted and worsened even with periodic stabilization programs, and infant industries became "senescent" without ever growing up. When, after twenty and thirty years, activities were still high-cost and insisted upon the need for continuing high levels of pro-tection, if not import prohibitions, some began questioning the efficacy of the import substitution strategy. While the primary lesson was in developing countries, difficulties with state owned enterprises and weak incentives came to be recognized in developed countries as well.

In both developed and developing countries, peoples' evasions of gov-ernment regulations also came to be recognized as a likely response to significant disparities between official prices and market-clearing prices. This was significant with rent seeking, corruption, smuggling, and unanticipated behavior within public sector enterprises. Sometimes, the behavior was legal, although uneconomic. It was demonstrated that "rate of return regulation" for public utilities led to overinvestment in many circumstances, for example. Cost-plus pricing was seen to be wasteful in many government contracts. When regulations (including high marginal tax rates, bureaucratic delays in obtaining necessary permissions, and price controls) surrounding the conduct of private sector enterprises became sufficiently onerous, "informal sector" economic activity developed. Small-scale enterprises sprang up beneath the radar screen of government officials. In India and other countries where reg-ulations were put in place to cover activities larger than a specified minimum, a large number of enterprises below that minimum, owned by relatives in the same family, would spring up in the same building, with each unit in a sepa-rate room or rooms. With high marginal tax rates, taxes were avoided, labor market regulations ineffective, and the small firms escaped oversight by the authorities. The costs, however, were generally significant as productivity in these informal sector firms was estimated to be one quarter or less that of larger firms in the formal sector. Meanwhile, even if the activities were unskilled-intensive, exporting was not feasible, as that would have required paperwork and official permissions only attainable by firms with large staffs.

But illegal activity also flourished and was more widespread the more restrictive the regulations, as there was greater scope for profit. Smuggling, black markets, tax evasion, over- and under-invoicing of imports and exports, bribery of officials, misallocation of government procurement from low-cost sources to those bribing the most, and a host of other activities reduced tax revenues, raised procurement costs, and thwarted the stated intent of government regulations.

The scale of these activities increased over time and was, in many instances, breath-taking. While some of this occurred as well in developed countries, it was usually on a smaller scale, both because the disparity between regulations and individual incentives was generally smaller and because institiutional mechanisms for enforcement of government edicts were further developed.

These developments, the stop-go cycles already mentioned, and failure of growth rates to accelerate would undoubtedly over time have led to some degree of rethinking in developing countries as to the degree to which the policies undertaken were supportive of the stated objectives. But at the same time as growth rates were failing to accelerate, if not decelerate, a small group of countries were rejecting the entire set of policies that had been adopted, and turning to policies much more closely identified with those economists would have said were conducive to economic growth. The pioneers were in East Asia: Hong Kong, Singapore, South Korea, and Taiwan. Because Hong Kong and Singapore were city-states, their experience was largely ignored and rejected by development economists and policy makers.

But South Korea and Taiwan were not so easy to ignore. Initially, they had very low per capita incomes in the 1950s and the ills generally associated with developing countries: heavy dependence on primary commodity exports, reliance on imports to supply most manufactured goods, an abundance of unskilled labor, relatively high rates of inflation and chaotic public finances. They had also relied heavily on import licensing and exchange controls to encourage domestic import substitution.

But starting in the mid-1950s in Taiwan and around 1960 in Korea, economic policies were reformed dramatically. Trade policy was shifted from a focus on restraining imports and encouraging domestic production of substitutes to an outer-oriented trade strategy. This entailed moving to relatively balanced incentives for sale on the home market and abroad: quantitative restrictions and import licensing were eliminated within a decade, and tariff levels were greatly reduced. The exchange rate was brought to more realistic levels.[15]

Although changes in the trade regime were perhaps the most visible and dramatic, reforms in these economies were more far-reaching. Price controls were abandoned, the tax structures reformed and fiscal deficits greatly reduced, nominal interest rates were permitted to rise to levels that made real interest rates positive (with unanticipatedly large effects on the domestic savings rate — which had been negative in Korea in 1960) although credit rationing did not entirely cease, to name just some of the major reforms. At the same time, government activities focused on the provision of infrastructure (a real challenge when real growth rates reached double digit figures as they did for well over a decade), education, and the creation of business-friendly environments, and public sector enterprises' shares of new investment and economic activity fell, with much greater reliance on the private sector.

The spectacular results in each of the Asian "tigers" were well beyond expectations. In Korea, for example, real wages and per capita incomes increased 7-fold between 1960 and 1995, while the unemployment rate fell from 25 percent to less than 5 percent. Exports grew at an average annual rate of 40 percent for the first decade of the new policies, and rose from 3 percent of GDP (in 1960) to 38 percent by the mid-1980s. Living standards and economic structure were transformed from those of poor developing countries to those of industrial countries.[16]

Foreign observers could not help but note the transformation of the East Asian economies. It changed thinking as to feasible growth rates[17] and altered the economic geography of the world as East Asians became major

---

[15] In Korea's case, uniform export "incentives" were provided per dollar of export earnings, with incentives initially in the form of preferential access to (subsidized credit), tax breaks, and import privileges, but these were largely offsets to the remaining protection accorded to import-competing production. By 1973, these "incentives" had been eliminated and tariffs reduced, as the exchange rate became the main mechanism for inducing exportable production.

[16] By one estimate, South Korea's per capita income was about the same as that of Ghana in the late 1950s, and 22 times Ghana's by the turn of the century. Indeed, South Korean incomes were estimated to be lower than those of many subSaharan African countries in the late 1950s.

[17] As late as the mid-1960s, most development economists regarded average annual growth of 5 or 6 percent as the maximum sustainable rate. Hollis Chenery, the chief economist of the World Bank, used that number to model development prospects.

international traders, and could no longer be viewed as "similar" to low-income developing countries. Southeast Asian countries also altered their economic policies starting in the late 1960s and the 1970s, with accompanying acceleration of growth rates. By 1980, China also began pursuing an outer-oriented trade strategy, with accompanying domestic reforms. Those results were as dramatic over the next two decades as Korea's and Taiwan's had been earlier, and rapid growth has proceeded, and even accelerated, more recently. India, which had a highly restrictive trade regime and heavy government involvement in economic life in the entire postwar period, began major policy reforms in the early 1990s,[18] and again experienced sharp acceleration in economic growth. Many other developing countries began dismantling their trade barriers and reducing the role of the public sector in directing economic activity by the 1990s,[19] although the reforms in the trade regimes and domestic economic policies were frequently far less reaching than they had been in the East Asian tigers and later the other rapidly growing economies.[20]

Although the shift in thinking was more dramatic in developing countries than in the industrial world, significant changes took place there was well. Disillusionment with public sector enterprises led to privatization; financial markets were considerably deregulated; tax structures were reformed so that marginal tax rates (on both corporate and personal incomes) did not greatly damage incentives, monetary and fiscal policies were altered so that inflation rates dropped sharply. There was also considerable deregulation of domestic

---

[18] The slowdown in growth rates in many developing countries also led many to reject their countries' earlier strategies for economic development. In India, for example, it was the foreign exchange crisis of 1991, combined with the contrast between India's continuing difficulties contrasted with Chinese and East Asian success, that induced the policy changes. The fall of the Soviet Union reduced the credibility of those still advocating a heavy role for the state in directing all economic activity.

[19] The aftermath of the oil price increases of the 1970s and the debt crisis of the early 1980s served to reinforce the lessons from East Asia. In particular, the "Asian tigers" were able to adjust economic policies and sustain economic growth in both decades, while many other developing countries were experiencing sharp slowdowns in economic activity and growth.

[20] Among countries undertaking major reforms, Chile should be noted. Starting in the mid-1980s, protection was dismantled and other reforms were undertaken that made the Chilean economic experience much more satisfactory than that of other Latin American countries. Focus is on the Asian countries largely because of their much greater size and economic importance to the global economy today.

economic activity.[21] In almost all industrial countries, trade had been liberalized and tariff barriers (in manufactures) reduced to low single digits. Those among the industrial countries where reforms began earliest and were most far-reaching (New Zealand, Australia, and the United Kingdom among them) were the earliest to experience improved economic performance.

Much has been learned. The costs of inflation are considerably higher than was generally thought 50 years ago, while the benefits are much lower. Fiscal policy is evaluated in terms of sustainability,[22] and few would question the negative consequences of high personal and corporate marginal tax rates.[23] Replacement rates for unemployment compensation, publicly-funded disability payments, and other facets of the social safety net are scrutinized and evaluated in terms of their incentives for labor force participation in a way that would have been unthinkable a half century ago. Rigidities in the labor market itself are subject to scrutiny, with issues such as portability of pension rights (to enable mobility) coming to the fore.

In general, the appreciation of the degree to which markets and individuals respond to incentives, including those arising out of uncertainty, is greatly increased. Part of this enhanced appreciation may result from the fact that the world is increasingly globalized. With that comes the recognition that capital and skilled labor can move across borders, that ill-advised regulation, be it of phytosanitary standards, financial sector activities, labor markets, or other, can be costly to the economy of the country imposing it. To name but a few of the highly visible examples, the interest equalization tax is regarded as having shifted the financial capital of the world from New York to London; Sarbanes-Oxley is thought to be responsible for the shifting of a significant number of corporate headquarters away from the U.S.; and the U.S. imposition of anti-dumping duties on drams led to the wholesale shift of computer assembly operations offshore.

---

[21] Deregulation of the airline industry in the United States was a watershed in the movement toward deregulation. Despite forecasts of loss of service for small cities and other major problems, the costs of air travel fell sharply and service in fact improved to small towns as small aircraft came to be used.

[22] The evaluation of fiscal policy in terms of sustainability has certainly been learned in the policy community. However, most industrial countries and all but a few emerging markets and low-income countries were running fiscal deficits in the boom years of the mid-noughties. During 2008, it became evident that the room for fiscal maneuver was much greater in those countries that had relatively low levels of public debt and had incurred surpluses or relatively small deficits.

[23] Especially in the case of the corporate income tax, the increasing importance of international private capital flows, and their responsiveness to tax and interest rate differentials, was a major factor in the rejection of high marginal rates.

IV. CHALLENGES FOR THE FUTURE

While unprecedented rates of economic growth for the world economy and associated successes have certainly led to greater understanding and appreciation of the importance of supply side determinants of output and growth, the world economy itself has changed markedly and, as a result, new problems have arisen. Some of these are the outcome of success itself; some result from the failure of the accepted policies to deliver the anticipated results; and yet others result from reactions to the greater constraints that this understanding has imposed on some aspects of traditional economic policy formulation. To a considerable degree, the challenges are interrelated, and can only briefly be addressed here.

Among the challenges posed by success must be counted the rapidly increased importance of large new emerging markets (which would not be such a challenge by definition if these countries were growing only at the rates they achieved in the 1950s and 1960s), which in turn means that the international decision-making processes for the world economy must appropriately reflect the voices of the emerging markets.

Challenges arising because of inability fully to solve past problems concern mainly the very low income countries. The low-income countries have not succeeded in generating rising living standards and improved well-being. Many have living standards below those of a half century ago.

Turning first to the fruits of success, the emergence of China and India, especially, but also of number of other countries,[24] has led to the need for their greater contributions to, and participation in, international economic policy formulation and execution. Fifty years ago, a few countries accounted for a sufficiently large share of world economic activity that they could consult each other informally or lead in international organizations and in effect reach decisions for the global economy.[25] Today, emerging markets' weight in the world economy is large enough so that they must participate in the process. Moreover, interdependence was considerably less than it is today, further challenging international governance.

---

[24] Brazil and Russia are often lumped with China and India as the BRICs, but there are a number of other countries, some such as Indonesia fairly large, and others much smaller but which collectively are increasing their share of world output and trade.

[25] The U.S. and the U.K. together held 52 percent of the votes in the IMF and the World Bank at the inception of those institutions. The "quad" of the U.S., Japan, Europe, and Canada constituted a "core" group in the GATT. The "G-3", then "G-5", and then "G-7" of industrial countries was often the forum in which problems requiring international coordination were addressed.

Although the IMF was generally consulted throughout the fifty years about exchange rate changes, most of its authority came from its ability to lend funds to countries in severe economic difficulties, and these were mostly developing countries. Efforts to coordinate international macroeconomic policy were generally left to the large industrial countries, as for example in the Plaza and Louvre accords. An effort in the mid-noughties to induce the major countries, the U.S., China, the EU, Japan, Britain and Saudi Arabia, to agree to simultaneous policy measures that could address global imbalances ended with agreement that action should be taken but without agreement on who should take it. Large countries were not willing to adjust their macro-economic policies because of international ramifications. Current account surplus and deficit countries each believed that adjustments should be taken by the other side. While willingness to adjust in coordination with other countries may be somewhat increased by the experience of 2007–09 (and was agreed by the G-20 with a process of peer review intended to achieve that result), there is still a gaping hole in international economic policy formulation when each large country believes the others should adjust.[26] Without agreement on a credible process to enforce needed adjustments, it will be of interest to see whether peer pressure can achieve the desired outcome.

But the issue is not only one of macroeconomic coordination. At the GATT/WTO, until the Doha Round developed countries engaged in multilateral tariff negotiations and reductions, with the developing countries claiming "special and differential" treatment and essentially being free riders, benefiting from the tariff cuts of industrial countries but offering few of their own. Even in the past two decades when there have been large reductions in protectionist measures in emerging markets, those reductions have generally been undertaken unilaterally.

International trade was certainly an engine of growth. Whereas world real GDP grew by a factor of almost 7, international trade in goods and services grew by a factor of 22 from 1950 to 2000. Some of that increase was attributable to the fall in costs of transport and communications; some was attributable to growth in the international economy; but much was the result of trade liberalization through the GATT/WTO, and surely growth of trade stimulated growth of real GDP as well as vice versa.

---

[26] Appreciation of the importance of coordination was enhanced by a number of events during the financial crisis, including issues regarding the supervision of banks, deposit insurance guarantees, bailouts for industrial firms, and "buy local" provisions in stimulus packages, to name just a few.

However, the increased importance of the emerging markets in the international economy implies that increased participation of those countries will be needed to enable the system to foster further integration of the global economy. Yet, to date, the emerging markets are still largely claiming their earlier place as developing countries without acknowledging their interest in rapid and healthy growth of international trade in goods and services.[27] Achieving increased participation by the emerging markets and their support for multilateral decision making processes has begun, but the challenge remains, and will even increase, as emerging markets sustain their rapid growth.

The open multilateral trading system is challenged in a number of other ways. The WTO's procedures, with a requirement of "consensus" (the full membership make most decisions) is cumbersome, and has become more so as membership has enlarged. And, while the GATT/WTO has been successful in the removal of quantitative restrictions and reductions in tariffs on trade in manufactured goods, there has been little success to date in achieving comparable disciplines over agriculture, trade in services, and capital flows. For the international economy as a whole, bringing agriculture, services and capital flows under GATT/WTO disciplines would do much to enable achievement of growth rates at or above those achieved in the past half century.

The final major challenge for the international trading system relates to the proliferation of preferential trading arrangements (PTAs). Those arrangements have, on some occasions, resulted in freer, welfare-improving trade for member countries. But they have also permitted the rise of protectionist pressures and reduced the support for multilateral trade. Finding ways to make PTAs more consistent with an open multilateral system is urgently needed.

The functioning of the WTO is important. But however that issue is resolved, there will be the challenge associated with the increasing share of rapidly growing countries in world markets. The entry of newcomers always engenders protectionist pressures, as was seen vis-à-vis Japan in the 1980s. With the rapid ascent of India and even more of China, the temptation to protectionist measures in the "old" countries must be recognized. A well-functioning and legitimate WTO is the best bulwark against such pressure, but achieving it (or otherwise thwarting those pressures) will be difficult. Of course, completion of the Doha Round would be a major step forward,

---

[27] There is also a major lacuna in the international system when it comes to international capital flows. At present, there is no international agreement to prevent discriminatory treatment of these flows, and indeed some preferential trading agreements have contained clauses that could result in discrimination against third countries.

while failure to do so weakens the WTO at a time when its value to the international economy could be extremely high.[28]

Success has also resulted in bringing environmental issues to the fore. Obviously, the rapid growth of the world economy, and the emergence of the BRICs has resulted in greater urgency than would have occurred had growth been slower. But no one can defend the view that emerging markets' growth should be severely restrained because of environmental concerns. Finding a multilateral regime in which the "public good" of the environment can be protected with an agreed-upon mechanism for allocating the burdens of reducing negative externalities, while simultaneously enabling the sustained growth of emerging markets and enabling other poor countries to develop more rapidly, is challenging, as witnessed by the Copenhagen outcome. There is also a danger that environmental concerns can motivate calls for protectionist measures if producers believe that they must compete with imports not subject to the same costs imposed by environmental protection in particular countries.

The other major challenge arises because a number of countries have as yet failed to adopt policy reforms that achieved rapid growth. By and large, these considerations are centered on the low-income countries. At the extreme, there are the failed states which either have not undertaken reform or where the state itself is so weak that reforms cannot be implemented even if decision-makers attempt to adopt them. The challenge of failed states is huge: they have failed in part because the existing economic framework has led to stagnant or deteriorating standards of living, as can be seen in Table 1. There has been civil war in some cases, but whether civil war resulted in deteriorating living standards or vice versa is an open question. The inability of key groups within those countries to agree has led to political conflict that has prevented meaningful changes in the framework.

But, in an important sense, the problems of failed states are the problems of low-income countries (and to a lesser extent other countries) writ large. The absence of strong institutions, such as the judiciary, discredits the law at the

---

[28] Much of the discussion of the challenge of emerging markets has been framed in terms of "voting rights" at the international institutions. The chief issue, of course, is that those members whose relative weight has diminished are reluctant, if not entirely unwilling, to surrender any of their shares. Although there has been some reallocation of shares toward emerging markets, allocation of shares at present fails to reflect economic realities. There is also confusion about the "representation" of NGOs in international organizations. Presumably, NGO members have their voices within individual countries and are already represented. The demand for a "voice at the table" has confused a number of discussions.

same time as it reduces the efficiency of the economy. Without an enforceable
and meaningful commercial code, the scope for efficient organization of production and exchange is greatly reduced. When the state cannot enforce the
law because civil servants use their posts for immediate personal profit, the
burden on the economic system can prevent any significant increase in output
and even result in decline. Per capita incomes in many sub Saharan African
countries fell in the twenty years after independence. In some of them, civil
war was the triggering factor, but in others, ill-advised economic policies and
rapacious politicians and civil servants were among the chief culprits.

Addressing the issues surrounding low-income countries and bringing
them into the international community of more successful countries is clearly
desirable on humanitarian grounds. In addition, the fact that the failed states
among them are believed to be major locations for terrorist activity makes the
task urgent. To date, however, there have been few successes in reversing the
declines. Research attempting to diagnose the problems has led to a focus on
what is called the "institutional framework" within which economic actions
(both policies and response to incentives) are undertaken. The challenges of
failed states, as well as those of countries where reform outcomes have fallen
far short of desired (and believed to be realistic) outcomes are a major issue
that must be addressed.

A final challenge lies in the political economy of economic policy formulation. Resistance to reforms and political pressures in support of special
interests (agriculture, protection, etc.) are facts of life in all economies, and
especially in failed states. Indeed, there is some evidence that a crisis, bringing about the "suspension of politics as usual", may be the best hope for
achieving major policy reforms. One of the great improvements in understanding of economic policy formulation in the past half century has been the
increased understanding and awareness of political economy issues. It was
earlier assumed that ignorance of good economics, such as the superiority of
free trade and the efficiency of competitive markets, was the problem and
could be addressed by better education. The role of interest groups, and their
influence on policy-making, is an issue of concern, especially with respect to
trade policy, but also in addressing almost all economic and financial issues.

More generally, one of the big improvements in understanding of economic policies over the past 50 years has been to recognize and analyze the
political pressures that arise and surround economic policy formulation,
including economic policy reform. In many instances, potential winners from
reforms are unaware that they might benefit, while many individuals believe
that they are at risk of losing when in fact a relatively small fraction of them
will. But efforts to compensate potential losers fully have sufficiently negative

incentive effects that it is difficult to formulate policies to reduce resistance to reforms. In addition, pressures for policy reforms typically arise when economic conditions are close to, or at, the crisis stage. At that point, the crisis generally mandates reductions in fiscal deficits, so that compensation is in any event infeasible.

In many poor countries, those most threatened by possible reforms are often not the very poor, but those in urban areas, and especially the capital, where demonstrations can put great pressure on politicians even if those participating represent a small fraction of the entire populace. Some observers have claimed that strong teachers' unions in some developing countries are one of the biggest obstacles to progress. Achieving a consensus as to the appropriate role for interest groups relative to other influences on public policy is a major challenge for the years ahead.

Fifty years ago, it was thought that per capita incomes in "underdeveloped countries", as they were then called, could "never" catch up with those in advanced countries. But some have. That South Korea could be transformed from the third poorest country in Asia to an industrial country in the space of 35 years would have been regarded as wildly unrealistic. Had anyone been told that tariffs on manufactured goods would fall from an average level of 40–50 percent in industrial countries to 3–4 percent, while quantitative restrictions would disappear, they would have reacted with total skepticism. Indeed, in the early postwar years, it was assumed that the key economic challenge was to prevent the world from sinking back to another great depression.

Major steps have been taken in resolving, or at least severely reducing the magnitude of, the problems of poverty reduction, and liberalization of trade. If past ability to address the problems of the day is a predictor of present capacities, one can expect that the conference celebrating the 100th anniversary of the Reserve Bank of Australia will look back on the progress in, or total resolution of, the problems of today, and enumerate a new set of issues that would then dominate the policy agenda going forward.

REFERENCES

Kent, C and M Robson (eds.) (2010). *Reserve Bank of Australia: 50th Anniversary Symposium*, Reserve Bank of Australia, Sydney, Australia.

Part II

ECONOMIC POLICY REFORM

Chapter 5

DETOQUEVILLE'S 'DANGEROUS MOMENT': THE IMPORTANCE OF GETTING REFORMS RIGHT[1]

With much discussion of the need for economic policy reform, it is important to recognize that reforms are normally difficult for policy makers to plan and implement. There will almost always be opposition, and it is important to achieve successful reforms whenever possible on the first try. A failed reform, for which much has been promised, makes successful reform at a later date more difficult.

My focus is on the difficulties that all governments inevitably encounter in judging what reforms to introduce; when; and how fast. Opportunities for reform are infrequent and if critical efforts go wrong, reforms get discredited. Once that happens it can be difficult to get another chance to introduce reform.

I will start with what we have learned about the way economic policy reform can most successfully be implemented. A first task is to define what we mean by economic policy reform: I would argue that a successful economic reform is much more wide-ranging than we realized until relatively recently. I will then suggest some ways, based on past experience, in which governments and policy makers can best cope with the problems of uncertainty that invariably accompany the reform process.

Past policy failures provide the motive for reform. In the postwar era that saw the creation of the multilateral economic framework — including the IMF — many of what we now call the emerging market countries pursued dirigiste policies. Import substitution was actively encouraged. State owned and managed enterprises were given a central role in economic activity.

---

[1] This chapter is a slightly edited version of the World Economy Lecture given at the University of Nottingham on September 19, 2004.

Government spending was high, and high levels of taxation and regulation discouraged entrepreneurial activity. Some of these policies were pursued in many industrial countries too.

The fundamental weaknesses of these policies gradually became apparent. Economic growth slowed or stagnated; or a crisis erupted. Living standards rose only slowly, if at all. Poverty increased. Private sector enterprises had little or no incentive to compete in overseas markets and sheltered domestic industries — often monopolies — could remain high-cost and turn out low-quality products. Economies that pursued such policies experienced slow economic growth or stagnation over a long period, often punctuated by balance of payments crises and "foreign exchange shortages". This often provided the political impetus for reform.

In some cases, policy failures were so acute that they precipitated major economic or financial crises. This was the case in India in 1966 and 1991; in Turkey in 1980; in Mexico in 1982. In these and other cases, the old policy stance was not consistent with continuing economic growth.

I. DEFINING REFORM

As the need for change became widely accepted, reform became part of every politician's vocabulary. No political program seems complete without a plan for economic reform. Economic success has long been recognized as making a crucial contribution to the political success of democratic governments. The well-being of ordinary citizens, measured by rising real wages, full employment and price stability, is seen as an important factor in determining electoral winners and losers. The number of democratic states has increased markedly in the past twenty or thirty years, of course. And even in those states with authoritarian governments, there seems to be a greater desire for economic growth, and the rising living standards and falling poverty that such growth brings.

So the need for reform has become almost a mantra for many politicians and policymakers. To be successful, or to remain so, economies need to be constantly adapting. Economic policy needs to enable economies to become flexible so as to adapt to change in consumer tastes and demand as incomes rise; in technology; and in the external environment.

But what do we — or more precisely, those policymakers — mean by reform? Not every small change can deliver the sort of welfare improvements that policymakers say they want. Not every change in the direction of economic policy will have a beneficial impact on economic performance. I would define reform as a measure, or set of measures, that are expected to result in a significantly improved framework for economic activity because of the way these measures alter behavioral incentives and thus improve the alignment between private behavior and economic welfare. These changes can be direct — tariff reductions or the elimination of quantitative restrictions on imports. They can be institutional; such as the introduction of a proper commercial code, or the establishment of an effective financial regulatory framework. Good, well-planned reforms will involve both types of change.

Reforms deliver the best results when they are complementary. A series of changes is likely to bring far greater returns than a one-off shift in policy direction. Trade liberalization and a move to a floating exchange rate regime will together have more impact than either one carried out in isolation. The two can bring greater benefits when accompanied by reforms that increase labor market flexibility. The whole really is greater than the sum of its parts.

But reforms haven't always brought the improvements anticipated — sometimes quite the reverse. In the past two decades or so, we have seen a number of countries pursue wholesale economic policy reforms that have ultimately proved disappointing — because of weaknesses in design or implementation; or because of political opposition that led to their reversal before benefits could be realized. The consequence was often slow or non-existent growth, high and often rising inflation, debt burdens that soared out of control — often cumulating in a major financial crisis, and yet another reform effort.

Some reforms are, at best, misguided. When duties on intermediate goods are removed or lowered, but those on finished goods left untouched, effective protection increases and makes later reform more difficult.

Consider another example: When duties are removed but the exchange rate is left unchanged, the demand for imports will rise but there will be no offsetting pressure to increase exports. Hence, economic activity in import-competing sectors will fall, but that in exportables would remain largely unchanged, thus raising unemployment in most cases.

II. CONTEXT AND CREDIBILITY

Crises force significant policy reforms on a government, Hence my reference to a dangerous moment. In a crisis, there is little enough time to act, let alone think. The exact nature of the crisis will determine what reforms are needed and in what order. In the Asian crisis countries in 1997, a key factor in the crisis was chronic weaknesses in the banking sectors of many countries,

Reform of the financial sector subsequently became a high priority in those countries, although some made more progress than others.

But the immediate need was to halt the drain on foreign exchange reserves that resulted from huge capital outflows in a fixed rate regime. Korean reserves had been virtually exhausted in 1997, for example. The IMF-supported programs in the Asian countries were intended to stabilize the situation as quickly as possible. Only then could the governments involved start to implement the longer-term reforms needed to prevent a repetition of the crises.

Other types of crisis require similarly rapid responses. Foreign exchange crises, usually under a fixed rate regime, force governments to take unpalatable decisions rapidly. Britain in 1967 and 1992, Mexico's tequila crisis in 1994, Argentina in 2001 — all involved significant devaluations. But devaluation by itself does not usually end the crisis. Confidence will only be restored by tackling the underlying economic problems that led to the crisis; and tackling them in a credible way, The debt crisis in Mexico in 1982, when the government announced it could no longer service its debt obligations, was also a symptom of economic weaknesses that went well beyond the problem of the sovereign debts to commercial banks that it could not repay.

Loss of confidence in a government's ability to deliver economic growth and prosperity can precipitate a different sort of crisis situation. This is arguably what happened in 1984 in New Zealand when the Labor government came to power aiming to reverse decades of relative economic decline or when Margaret Thatcher won the 1979 election in the U.K.; or in France when "cohabitation" was forced on President Mitterrand in 1986 after the first years of his socialist government in France.

Governments acting in a crisis situation appear to have a better chance of implementing reforms: that was certainly true of the Callaghan government in the UK when it introduced reforms as part of a Fund-supported program in 1976. The sense of crisis made it more difficult for the opponents of the reform program to marshal support. Similarly, the Indian reforms implemented in response to the crisis in 1991; those introduced in Mexico in 1994; and in Asia in 1997–98. It is easier for governments to marshal support for reforms in a crisis, in part because there are fewer obvious alternatives.

In fact, crisis seems sometimes to lead to a suspension of "politics as usual" and provides a government with considerable freedom — more than is usual in politics — to undertake reforms.

New governments may enjoy something of an advantage, especially those in democracies that enter office with a mandate for change.

But reforms are painful (or they would have been undertaken already!) and the deeper the reforms, the greater the opposition they are likely to arouse. So politicians have to weigh the magnitude of reform (the size of tariffs cuts, the magnitude of devaluation, the cut in government expenditures) and its projected benefits against the likely opposition they will encounter.

Building credibility for a reform program is essential. The economic actors, whose behavior the reforms are intended to influence, will respond to the altered incentive structure more rapidly if they are persuaded by the speed with which a program of reforms is introduced, by the comprehensiveness of the program, and if they are convinced that the reforms will be adhered to. International credibility is important too. Access to the international capital markets will be easier. And support from institutions like the IMF always depends on a government being able to demonstrate credible commitment to a reform plan.

But the more opposition there is and hence the greater likelihood that reforms will be reversed, the more slowly will economic actors respond to changed incentives.

The global economic environment in which reforms are introduced will have a crucial impact on their success. Unfortunately, in many cases crises erupt when economic vulnerabilities become apparent in a global downturn. In such cases, governments are not only pressed for time: they also have little room for maneuver.

III. UNCERTAINTY

Crisis by definition is a dangerous moment and requires a response. But when profound changes in the structure of an economy are desperately needed if long-term prospects are to improve — as has been true in most emerging market economies as the shortcomings of earlier policies were recognized — then considerable uncertainty surrounds the outcome.

The authorities do not know how much opposition there will be to reforms. They do not know how much change it will take to convince economic agents that the new policies are firmly in place and that there is no point on betting against their reversal. Nor do the authorities know how quickly speculative pressures will subside, how some economic actors will respond to the realigned incentive structure and how quickly.

There is equal uncertainty for economic decision-makers. They do not know how likely it is that reforms will stick. They cannot judge, in many instances, how reforms will affect them, their competitors, and the economic environment in which they operate. Economic actors often decide to fight against reforms rather than adjusting to the new incentive structure. They often delay their response until their likely impact becomes clearer.

We can make judgments about the likely economic response when we do certain things, based on what we know about how economies work, and on past experience. But though we can often predict the direction of change, when we alter incentives in an economy we cannot predict the timing or degree of the response with any great certainty.

In 1966, in the midst of a foreign exchange crisis, India devalued the rupee by a little over 35 percent but exports did not appear to respond. This was largely because the removal of export subsidies at the same time as the devaluation had, in effect, acted as a disguised appreciation of approximately the same magnitude as the devaluation, so the rupee price of exports had not increased significantly, and in some cases had fallen. To make matters worse, a bad harvest in a then predominantly agricultural economy led to a drop in real GDP. The outcome was a political backlash which gave reform a bad name and resulted in a fifteen year period before reforms could be tried again.

It is clear when we start trying to put some numbers on these variables — the magnitude of a devaluation, the scale and speed of tariff reduction, the time-line for reducing the fiscal deficit be reduced — that the challenge of getting reforms right becomes truly formidable. There are no guarantees, but there are ways in which the risks inherent in the reform process can be reduced, though not eliminated.

But there are things we do know, Without reforms things will get worse and, while we may not know exactly how a program of trade liberalization will affect a particular economy, there is plenty of evidence across countries and over time to support the view that opening up economies to trade is beneficial. The competition it brings is a powerful force for increased economic efficiency because it helps ensure that resources are allocated in the best possible way; it helps eliminate domestic monopolies; it drives down prices both for domestic consumers — as well as producers in import-consuming industries — and in the international marketplace.

Trade liberalization generally leads to higher growth rates than would otherwise have been the case. Warcziarg and Welch (2008) have shown that of 133 countries they surveyed between 1950 and 1988 those that liberalized their trade regimes enjoyed annual growth rates of about one half of one percentage points higher after liberalization. And opening up to international trade seems to have become increasingly important: the same study showed that removal of trade barriers during the 1990s raised growth rates by an estimated 2.5 percentage points a year.

Studies of trade reforms in individual countries also confirm the magnitude of gains that can be had. Korea's sustained focus on trade liberalization as part of the reforms introduced from the late 1950s onwards played a major role in that country's spectacular growth performance. Over a long period Chile also reduced its tariffs and opened up its economy. In 1974, tariffs often exceeded 100 percent; the World Trade Organization estimates the simple average tariff for 2003 to have been 5.9 percent. The Chilean economy has experienced sustained growth over a long period.

Similarly with labor market reform. Rigid labor market regulation stifles employment growth in the formal sector while increasing the size of the informal sector. We know that the less rigid and more flexible labor markets are, the better economies perform and the higher growth rates will be.

We may not be able to predict how the labor market in any one economy will respond to changes in labor laws — how rapidly unemployment will fall; how employment will rise and/or shift to the formal sector; and the impact of the changes on overall economic performance. But we have plenty of evidence to support the argument that such changes will result from greater flexibility.

There is always a fortuitous element in reform programs. This is partly because of the domestic context in which they take place: a good or bad harvest can make a big difference to the extent of opposition to difficult reforms. It will be easier to tighten fiscal policy in more buoyant domestic conditions.

The global economic environment is also important. It is much easier to introduce large-scale reform when the global outlook is more benign. Trade liberalization is likely to bring economic benefits more rapidly at a time of global economic expansion, when trade is growing. As a general rule, governments are wise to seize the opportunity to press ahead with reforms in the context of growth — one reason why we at the IMF have been urging emerging market economies to reduce their public debt burdens now, during the current upturn. But there the sense of urgency that provides the main impetus for reform is likely to be lacking when the global outlook is brighter and politicians will be understandably — but mistakenly — tempted to postpone uncomfortable decisions.

When reforms are introduced, specific measures might work more quickly or more slowly than anticipated; and that could in turn affect the ability of policymakers to sustain support for further reforms.

For politicians there is a trade-off — between implementing tough reforms that will bring considerable benefits down the road and confronting opposition to unpopular measures. There will always be a temptation to do the minimum necessary. But that inevitably increases the risk that the reforms will not deliver the hoped-for results, and in some cases will fail, only to be followed by another crisis and another reform package — and that in turn will meet yet greater opposition.

The stronger a reform program — in terms of its scope and the speed with which it is implemented — the greater will be its chances of success. And the more signs of success there are, the more the government will have to build on and the better it will be able to cope with opposition to change.

IV. WINNERS AND LOSERS

Building support for change is an important element in ensuring a reform program can be implemented successfully. Ideally, one would be able to identify the winners and losers of any reform process; make sure the winners realized who they were; and then seek ways of countering the opposition.

But it is usually difficult to identify winners and losers with any great certainty. Some short-term losers might recognize that they are vulnerable — protected domestic industries facing the prospect of greater foreign competition might have good reason to worry. But not always, One of my favorite stories concerns Mexican refrigerators. A major refrigerator manufacturer in Mexico was strongly opposed to NAFTA because he reckoned that opening up trade would enable American manufacturers to make significant inroads into the Mexican market.

This turned out to be a misjudgment. A big weakness with Mexican-made fridges was the poor quality of compressors previously available to the fridge-makers. NAFTA made it possible to import and use higher quality US-made compressors in Mexican fridges and so enabled the manufacturer in question to become a leading player in the American refrigerator market for smaller models.

In the short-term, though, predicting such outcomes is difficult and beneficiaries do not recognize their prospective gains. It takes time for the full effect of reform measures to work through the economy. Removing subsidies and moving to a flexible exchange rate regime will help export-oriented firms increase their overseas markets, for example: but it is unlikely to do so overnight.

And in the meantime, people are uncertain and afraid. You cannot know that you will be hired by an expanding exporting firm: but you can guess that your job — or your profits — are threatened by greater import competition.

Better understanding of the reform process can dampen some opposition. The removal of agricultural export subsidies is often opposed without recognition that exchange rate change can confer bigger benefits.

Winners will become evident as a reform program progresses; and then they can be enlisted to support further reforms. In the short-term, though, it is not possible to identify the firms and workers who will start up or expand businesses as reforms take hold. Ending protection and freeing up trade makes it easier for new firms to compete successfully — but the identity of those firms and those workers who get the jobs they create will only become apparent later.

Losers are similarly difficult to identify in advance, but their identity might become apparent more quickly as firms lay off workers, or go out of business, in response to more competitive pressures.

It is clearly important that reforms that are introduced do not create vested interests that might then oppose future reforms. Establishing preferential trade agreements that create trade diversion can make further trade liberalization more difficult. A misguided regulatory framework could also make it difficult to deepen financial markets at a later stage.

V. COMPREHENSIVENESS

The main focus here has been on trade and labor market reforms — in deference to the audience here this evening. But similar considerations apply in many other areas. A successful reform program means tackling problems on a wide front.

Major areas of reform include governance issues and the establishment of secure property rights and predictable legal systems; better government expenditure management; the move to less distortionary tax systems; pension system reform; and the privatization of state owned enterprises, among others.

VI. COMMITMENT AND FOLLOW-THROUGH

I have talked about the difficulty of framing a reform program because of the huge uncertainties involved; and I have mentioned some of the ways in which those uncertainties about the outcome can be reduced.

The importance of commitment and perseverance cannot be overstated. Too many reform programs have lost momentum because policymakers lost their appetite for change, or were overwhelmed by opposition, or because uncertainty on the part of economic actors led to a slow response that helped engender political opposition. The lack of follow-through can have a significant economic cost, and it can also be politically painful for governments whose enthusiasm for reform faded at the wrong moment. The cost of failed or partially implemented reforms can be high.

Look at Argentina, an economy still recovering from the impact of the crisis in 2001. Yet in the 1990s, Argentina's reform program was, initially, seen as a model.

After the experience of the 1980s, when the Argentine economy had contracted by about half a percent a year, while inflation had soared — to a peak in the late 1980s of 3,000 percent — the 1991 Convertibility Plan was seen as the centerpiece of reform. The aim was to deliver high growth and low inflation, based on disciplined macroeconomic policies and market-oriented structural reform. The Argentine government wanted to escape from past inflationary failures: and at the start the government showed every sign of a readiness to take the difficult steps needed to deliver macroeconomic stability.

Central to the convertibility plan was its guarantee of peso convertibility with the dollar at parity. Having a fixed exchange rate system was seen as crucial for building up the anti-inflationary credibility that the government needed. A quasi-currency board was established in order to underpin the system and so reinforce the government's commitment. The early results were promising. For such a plan to work in the longer term, however, fiscal restraint is required.

In the first two years of the plan, Argentina experienced real annual GDP growth of over 10 percent, and more than 5 percent in 1993–94. Inflation was down to single digits by 1993. There was a huge surge in capital inflows. The loss of confidence in emerging markets that followed Mexico's so-called Tequila crisis of 1995 seemed to do little more than interrupt performance improvements temporarily. Argentine growth rebounded in 1996–97.

But this apparently impressive performance masked structural weaknesses that weren't confronted. The convertibility plan was only sustainable if there was fiscal discipline and sufficient flexibility in the economy to adjust to shocks. However, fiscal control was undermined by off-budget expenditures; and it was too weak to prevent growing reliance on private capital flows to finance government borrowing. The estimated structural fiscal position went from rough balance in 1992–93 to a deficit of about 2.75 percent of GDP in 1998. In addition, there was persistent off-budget spending, mainly as a result of court-ordered compensation payments after the social security reforms of the 1990s, and arrears to suppliers. This raised the government's average new borrowing requirements to more than 3 percent of GDP a year over this period. In 1996, for example, when off-budget spending is included, the total deficit was 4 percent of GDP.

The problem was made worse by overoptimistic assessments of the economy's growth potential. There were more temporary factors at play than was realized at the time. This, of course, meant that the authorities had less room for maneuver on the fiscal front than they believed. The decentralized system of government in Argentina made fiscal control particularly difficult. The provinces, for example, had little incentive to improve revenue performance or constrain expenditure growth: and this important weakness in the fiscal structure was not tackled.

Exports grew, but nowhere nearly as rapidly as imports. By the late 1990s, there was an uncomfortably high debt to export ratio: it was 455 percent in 1998, and jumped, unexpectedly, to 530 percent in 1999.

Added to all this was the fact that the pace of structural reforms lost momentum in the mid 90s; indeed, some reforms were reversed. Perhaps the biggest weakness here was the labor market which was heavily regulated in Argentina. Individual workers have long enjoyed considerable protection, with high barriers to dismissal and the guarantee of generous fringe benefits. Yet a fixed exchange rate regime required labor market flexibility to enable the economy to respond to shocks.

Some labor market reforms were introduced in the 1990s. In 1991, for example, there was some modest improvement in flexibility. In 1995 came equally modest steps that made it easier to hire temporary workers and introduced more flexible working hours. But these improvements did not go far, and reform in this area quickly lost momentum. To make matters worse, Congress diluted a further government attempt to increase labor market flexibility — so much so, in fact, that the final outcome promoted further centralization of collective bargaining. The result of all these lukewarm changes was predictable: unemployment rose, to 12 percent in 1994; and productivity growth fell to zero in the second half of the 1990s.

These structural rigidities were all the more problematic in the light of the fixed exchange rate regime. It became increasingly clear during the 1990s that successful operation of the quasi-currency board required much better fiscal control than the government was able to deliver. Since the collapse, of course, there has been much debate about whether the pegged exchange rate regime was ever appropriate as a long-term policy instrument.

The arguments over the exchange rate regime have ensured a plethora of different explanations of the eventual crisis in 2001. Both the then government and the IMF have been criticized, most recently by the Fund's own Independent Evaluation Office, in a report published last month. But it is clear that the impact of the crisis would at least have been mitigated if the original reform program had been more ambitious — specifically if it had included serious reform of the labor market and if it had tackled the problem of fiscal relations between central and provincial governments; and if this more ambitious program had been fulfilled.

Effective implementation of fiscal, labor market and structural reforms could have meant that the economy was robust and flexible enough to cope with unanticipated shocks and thus could have avoided the economic collapse that resulted from the abandonment of the convertibility plan.

Instead of Argentina I could equally well have pointed to Turkey in the 1980s, when an ambitious, and initially very successful, reform program petered out. Some reforms were enduring. Quantitative restrictions on imports were removed, the exchange rate became more realistic, and the structure of the economy was transformed — exports went from 5–6 percent of GDP to about 20 percent.

But by the late 1980s, the then Turkish government displayed a reluctance to confront the re-emerging problem of persistent high inflation and to impose fiscal discipline. In Turkey's case, of course, that meant the reform program was left unfinished and that the potential benefits were, therefore, not fully realized. This ultimately led to a series of financial crises.

The current Turkish government has shown itself to be committed to a tough reform program that should bring Turkey's debt down to sustainable levels and deliver rapid economic growth over the medium and long term. But the cost of adjustment this time is higher than it would have been if the 1980s reforms had been adhered to and if those reforms had encompassed the financial sector which was the proximate cause of the most recent crisis in 2000.

There are many examples of countries where experience illustrates what benefits commitment can bring. Korea was a poor, rural peasant economy in the 1950s. There was a widespread view that it was not a viable economy without significant injections of foreign aid. The realization that financial aid from America was going to decline was part of the motivation for embarking on a wide-ranging series of reforms starting in the late 1950s.

These reforms had the objective of turning Korea into a fully-fledged market economy. They systematically addressed fundamental problems. There was a determination to tackle structural problems in the economy, and to stick with a reform program. Sound macroeconomic policies were put in place.

In 1960, there was a large but necessary devaluation, and export incentives were adjusted to relative constancy in the real returns to exporters over time. Over the next few years, almost all quantitative restrictions on imports were converted to tariffs. In 1964, a major fiscal reform was introduced, which greatly reduced the government's budget deficit; at the same time interest rate cellings were relaxed and the exchange rate regime was changed to a crawling peg.

Tax policy was reformed and tax collection improved. Public spending was brought under control and high tariffs reduced. The huge budget deficits of earlier years were virtually eliminated in just a few years. At an early stage, the importance of infrastructure investment as an aid to exporters and import-competing firms was recognized-and appropriate measures taken.

Later in the reform process, greater emphasis was put on further liberalization of trade and the financial sector. And the reform process has continued as Korean policymakers adapt to deal with the problems that come with further growth. But the main thrust of economic policy has remained largely constant-an outward orientation with strong incentives for exporters, and a commitment to growth through trade. This has meant that the country has been well-placed to cope with the fresh challenges that economic success brings.

The rewards Korea reaped from these ambitious reforms are well-known. Economic growth was spectacular, especially in the 1960s and early 1970s. GDP per capita rose seven fold in the three decades to 1995. The third poorest country in Asia in 1960 became one of the region's richest by the mid-1990s. It is a performance of which any country would, and should, be proud.

Korea's successful performance was reinforced by policymakers' ability and willingness to try to anticipate bottlenecks and potential crisis points. They were arguably successful in this until the 1990s when they failed to anticipate the problems that weaknesses in the financial sector could bring for the wider economy.

Roger Douglas, New Zealand's finance minister in the 1980s when that country's far-reaching reforms were undertaken, is clear that ambitious reforms bring great rewards. He has described how in the decade before 1984, New Zealand's economic growth rate was half the OECD average, with unemployment rising apparently inexorably and, with it, government spending and government debt and debt servicing costs. In the quarter of a century up to 1984, New Zealand's standard of living had fallen from being third-highest in the world, to a ranking somewhere in the mid-twenties.

The economy Roger Douglas found when he became finance minister in 1984 was highly regulated, with quantitative import restrictions and subsidies for exporters; high tariffs, distorted price controls, expensive social policies and low workforce skill levels.

The reform program introduced by the Labor Government of which Roger Douglas was a member was sweeping. The exchange rate was floated, industrial subsidies were removed, the tax system was reformed, financial markets were deregulated as were prices and incomes, quantitative import restrictions were scrapped, the labor market was reformed. A long list of changes, in fact, and all introduced at a breathless pace.

Douglas (1994) says it is impossible to go too fast, that speed is essential, in part because many structural reforms will anyway take several years to implement and have their full impact.

> "When an economy has been driven down a blind alley and ends up facing a brick wall, what matters is to back it out as soon as possible and get it back onto the high road to a better future".

VII. WHAT, WHEN AND HOW

So what have we learned about the best way to implement reforms, and when? Of course, the specific reform measures will depend on the circumstances of individual countries, and so too will the most appropriate timing. But it is clear that some general principles appear to hold good.

Roger Douglas is emphatic that reforms should be pursued on a broad front: that clearly brought results in New Zealand and in Korea; I think Chile's experience supports that thesis too.

But it is also clear that trade and exchange rate reforms should be.an early priority. The more rapidly an economy is opened up to the rest of the world, the better. This is partly because opening brings considerable economic benefits, as I mentioned earlier; and partly because the more open the economy the more difficult it will be to reverse the reforms.

Fiscal discipline has to be a key component of any sound economic reform program. Its absence helped undercut the Turkish reforms of the 1980s and was clearly a major factor in Argentina's more recent crisis.

Fiscal rectitude is difficult in countries that have pressing social needs and serious shortcomings in infrastructure that can impede growth. But better targeted spending — to those most in need — can help. So can more efficient tax collection which will boost tax revenues, and a widening of the tax base.

Beyond identifying winners and losers and building support for change, it seems clear that political leaders need to be ready to confront their opponents. How this is done can be critical. In Britain, Margaret Thatcher successfully took on the miners in 1984: but the Heath government failed when it confronted the same group in 1973–74. Confronting opponents is partly a matter of picking fights that are winnable — and luck plays an important part here — and it is partly a matter of having the courage to see the battle through to the end.

Effective reform also requires good communication, so that citizens know what the aims are and what the potential ramifications are. Transparency is also important because it is an important means of building support.

VIII. THE IMF'S ROLE

The IMF has an important role in all this. The Fund's principal objective, as it always has been, is the maintenance of international financial stability. That gives the Fund an important role in crisis prevention and resolution. Reform is, in a very broad sense, the Fund's business. Article IV surveillance on our member countries provides an annual assessment of economic policies, along with recommendations for reform, as appropriate. This applies equally to the largest industrial economies, emerging market countries and the poorest countries. This evening I have referred mainly to the reform process in emerging market countries. But the Fund also regularly recommends reform in our richest members; we recently made recommendations relating to the fiscal situation in the United States.

The Fund's role in the reform process under surveillance is an advisory one. This is partly in order to respect the sovereignty of member governments. But it also reflects the recognition that national policymakers are those who have to adopt reforms and try to ensure their success. It is they who have to secure the support of civil society and the various economic actors involved and whose response will contribute to the success or otherwise of the reforms.

But for countries receiving financial assistance from the Fund as they try to resolve crises, such assistance is provided on a conditional basis, with payments provided in installments against agreed benchmarks. The terms of such assistance are agreed with member countries, the government must "own" the reform programs that are undertaken. The Fund's role is to be assured that the program has a reasonable prospect of success.

There is a third way in which the Fund assists countries implementing reforms; technical assistance. This can be more important than is often realized. On a wide range of policy issues, from tax administration to budget accounting, from financial sector regulation to the development of commercial codes, the Fund has amassed considerable expertise and experience that can benefit governments seeking advice on formulating and implement such measures. It is clear from the wide range of governments that seek technical assistance from the Fund that this expertise has become a valuable and valued resource.

Currently, for example, the Fund is actively supporting banking reform in Turkey, providing technical advice for budgetary reforms in China and encouraging trade reform in Africa. The Fund has actively supported countries adopting floating exchange rate regimes and pension reforms.

CONCLUSION

Let me briefly conclude by reiterating that reform is obviously important — and often urgently needed. Many countries need to implement change if they are to continue to grow. Or are to achieve sustained growth. But well-judged and effectively implemented reform is also important — and difficult. Misguided or overly timid reforms can undermine the reform process and make it difficult to muster support for future reform programs.

Perseverance is crucial. Reforms have to be followed through. There is no scope for talk of 'reform fatigue'. Reforms bring the flexibility that is essential for economies to adapt successfully to changes in the global economy.

Finally, there is one ingredient alien to economists' luck. We do not like admitting that there are things that we do not know and, more importantly, can not know. But the reform process is, inevitably, something of a mystery. We cannot predict the exact outcome. But by proper and effective implementation we can increase the prospects of success.

REFERENCES

Douglas, R and L Callan (1987). *Toward Prosperity*. Auckland: David Bateman Ltd.
Wacziarg, R and KH Welch (2008). Trade Liberalization and Growth: New Evidence. *World Bank Economic Review*, 22(2), 81–124.

Chapter 6

THE CRUCIAL ROLE OF FINANCIAL INTERMEDIATION FOR RAPID GROWTH[1]

Everyone understands that money is essential for any economy. Students of economics learn about the use of shells and stones as money in very primitive societies, and about cigarettes becoming a medium of exchange in prisoner-of-war camps. It makes sense that there must be money: everyone knows it and uses it. But the crucial role of the financial system is not so obvious, in part because many financial transactions are not an everyday experience, and in part because the work that goes into a financial transaction and the bene-fits it brings are often invisible to most people.

Economists have always taught that the financial system enables an econ-omy to be more productive because it uses savings from those with few prospects of investing in high rate of return activities and enables those with investment opportunities but few resources to use those savings productively. In the absence of such a system, savers would obtain and hold low-return assets (such as gold and land) or simply store money (if there were a fairly sta-ble price level) while enterprises with profitable investment opportunities would be restricted in the rate they could expand by the amount of their available cash flow.

This conventional wisdom was always known and accepted by the devel-opment-growth community. But until the Asian crises of the late 1990s, most economists underestimated the positive value of a well-functioning and dynamic financial system that develops as the economy grows. Similarly they

---

[1] This is an abridged and slightly edited version of a paper "The Crucial Role of Financial Intermediation for Rapid Growth", presented at "International Derivatives and Financial Market Conference", Campos do Jordao, Brazil. A short section on the lessons from the financial crisis of 2007–08 has been added.

failed to comprehend the damage that was done to productivity and economic growth prospects when financial systems were repressed.

To be sure, some economists knew this. My colleague at Stanford, Professor Ronald McKinnon (1973), was in the forefront of those underlining the importance of a well-functioning financial system for growth. As early as 1973, he was writing extensively on the topic, terming poorly functioning financial systems "repressed". In his view, repressed financial systems were ones in which government regulation and controls — through state-owned banks, development banks that directed lending to priority projects and firms at below-market rates, and through directives to private banks as to the maximum interest rate they could charge and how they should allocate credit — led to low interest rates, credit rationing, and misallocation of resources. While the truth of his argument was recognized, liberalizing the financial system usually seemed to be a reform that was not "of top priority", and could be delayed until a later date or undertaken very slowly.

But with the financial crises of the 1990s, economists and policy makers sought to understand what had happened and why. It became evident to all that the financial sector played a crucial role in economic growth, and in many ways in addition to the savings-investment linkage. Moreover, it was seen that repressed financial sectors had been major contributors to the difficulties that the crisis countries experienced.

In this chapter, I first spell out in somewhat more detail the importance of a well-functioning financial sector's role in economic growth. I will then turn to the Korean experience, and sketch out what happened in Korea in the 1990s leading to the crisis of 1997–98. The analysis of that experience well illustrates the problems that can arise and cumulate with a repressed financial system. Finally, consideration is given to the ways in which the financial crisis of 2007–08 has affected our understanding.

I. THE ROLE OF THE FINANCIAL SECTOR IN GROWTH

A major economic function of the financial system is to enable savings of those with few productive opportunities to be used by those with highly productive opportunities. There are benefits to both savers and investors and to the rest of society: savers get a higher rate of return on their savings, while investors with worthwhile investments can do more and thus earn more income as well; that enables more capital accumulation in the economy, which results in more rapid overall economic growth with benefits for the whole society. The financial system has other functions as well (money as a store of value and medium of exchange, for example), of course, but I will not dwell on them here.

But to achieve an environment in which this apparently simple "loan" of resources from savers to investors can efficiently be achieved is not as straightforward as it might sound. Savers must be reasonably confident that they will receive a positive return on their investments. The riskier the investment, the higher the proffered or expected rate of return will have to be. Similarly, investors who make major efforts to bring a project to a profitable state must be confident of their rights to some of the returns. For both parties to have the appropriate assurances, society must have measures in place to insure that contract terms can be fulfilled. That, in turn, underscores the importance of an efficient and effective legal system, an effective commercial code, and a framework for the functioning of financial institutions that enables them to fulfill their role.

In the process of economic growth, new activities are undertaken, and old activities are undertaken in new ways. Almost all investments are made in the context of uncertainty: in general, investments with the highest prospective rates of return also have relatively high risks. And, since savers and investors are generally not the same (and since would-be investors may not be the best judges of their prospects) the financial sector's sorting of investment opportunities plays a much bigger role than the words "linking savers to investors" indicates.

To assess risk appropriately, those who would potentially extend resources to investors must have information about the investor and the likely prospects that the proposed investment will be profitable. This includes an assessment of many aspects of risk, including not only the likelihood that the costs and expected revenues of the proposed project are realistic (and risks evaluated), but also of the creditworthiness of the investor, his ability to carry out the proposed activities, and so on. If each potential creditor had to assess these attributes, the "transactions" and "information" costs would be huge, and many savers would simply not be able to form the necessary judgments. Information provided by credit bureaus and other external assessment sources is very important. But so, too, is the experience of bankers and others who specialize in particular lines of activity, understand businesses, and make the appropriate judgments. In modern large-scale industry, the financial sector plays a key role in monitoring the performance of managers of large public companies. It is also crucial in assessing the prospects of start-ups, supporting initial public offerings (IPOs), providing advice as to financing techniques and alternatives, and much more.

Financial intermediaries enable savers to receive higher returns than they otherwise would. And investors are able to attract resources for prospectively high-return investments. And since industry specialists can professionally assess activities, financial intermediaries add value for both the investor and the saver, and contribute importantly to the growth of the real economy.

Beyond that, however, financial intermediaries enable larger investments than would otherwise be possible; pooling the savings of many savers may be necessary to finance investments of economically efficient size; if investors had to raise the funds themselves, many investments would be uneconomically small. There is a wonderful quote from the eminent English analyst, Bagehot, that makes the point well[2]:

> "We have entirely lost the idea that any undertaking likely to pay...can perish for want of money: A citizen...in Queen Elizabeth's time...would have thought it was no use inventing railways...for you would not have been able to collect the capital with which to make them. At this moment [1873] in colonies and all rude countries, there is no large sum of transferable money; there is no fund from which you can borrow, and out of which you can make immense works."

In addition to appropriate allocation of new resources, there are many other aspects. A well-functioning financial system can provide: better corporate governance; a diversification of financial instruments that can enable investors and savers better to match their risks and time dimensions of returns (and thus reduce risks for savers who are risk averse and offer higher returns to those willing to take risks). And, it is often forgotten, economic growth requires the freeing of resources from inefficient uses; when financial intermediaries are effective, withholding of funds from inefficient enterprises, and offering higher rates of return for those enterprises to invest elsewhere, is an important contributor to growth.

Thus, appropriate risk-return assessments play a crucial role: a financial system that appropriately evaluates alternatives will generate a much higher rate of return on investment than a repressed financial system; and those higher rates of return themselves are part of higher rates of economic growth.

Consider the contrast between a primitive economic system in which families must finance their own enterprises. Families with activities yielding a high rate of return will be enabled to invest more than those with low rates of return, but the differential in those rates is a lost growth opportunity: if the

---

[2] Quoted in Levine (1997), p. 699.

financial system permitted the low-return resources to be invested in the high-return activity (with compensation, of course, to the low-return family), overall economic growth would be higher and both families could be better off. And, to the extent that the high-return activity entailed risks, the ability of the owners to diversify risk would be limited and would likely curtail even their investment.

Since the growth rate is the outcome of the investment rate and the rate of return on capital, as well as factor productivity growth and the growth in quantity and quality of the labor force, it will be lower than would be attained with a well-functioning financial systems. A great deal of evidence shows that total factor productivity growth is in large part a result of the increased shares of more efficient firms and the reduced shares of less efficient firms, both within particular industries, and between them.

This can be seen with some simple numbers. Suppose that the rate of investment is 20 percent of GDP while the average rate of return on capital is 5 percent. Then growth attributable to investment will be only 1 percent of GDP. If productivity growth is 1 percent, and the labor force grows one percent, the overall growth rate of real GDP will be 3 percent.

If, by contrast, a well functioning financial system raised the savings-investment rate to 30 percent and the average rate of return to 15 percent (and these numbers are very plausible), growth on that account alone would be 4.5 percent (compared to the 1 percent with 20 percent investment and a 5 percent return). If, in addition, productivity growth doubled to 2 percent — again a very reasonable number, overall growth would be 7.5 percent, instead of 3 percent. Of course, in per capita terms, the difference is even more pronounced. If the growth rate of population and the labor force were the same, the growth rate of per capita income would be 6.5 percent contrasted with 2 percent.

Judging by what has happened in some countries after economic policy reforms, these orders of magnitude of potential gains do not seem unreasonable. Of course, almost all countries, even the poorest, have some financial intermediation, and policy changes conducive to more rapid economic growth encompass more than simply the financial sector.

But, in fact, there are usually different degrees of risk associated with different investments. Most people, including savers, are risk averse, and are unlikely to be willing to invest in a more risky venture unless it offers a higher expected rate of return, to offset the additional perceived risk. Because of this, the role of the financial sector becomes even larger. Individual investors cannot have the time and knowledge sufficient to judge the likely risk-reward profiles of alternative investments. Even if they could allocate the time to learn about the prospects of potential investment streams, it would be inefficient and a waste of their time for individual investors each to undertake the research necessary to evaluate them.

Hence, a well-functioning financial system enables savers to choose investments with risk-adjusted rates of return appropriate to their situations. And, while risks may be high for individual investments, it will generally be the case that the higher risk investments on average yield a higher return. The financial system evaluates the risk-reward profiles of alternatives, and enables savers to choose the degree of risk with which they are comfortable. Savers themselves may choose a portfolio with some investments more risky than others, but the evaluation role of the financial system is essential.

Technical change and innovation themselves need financing, and well functioning financial systems generally provide it. Venture capital firms, angel investors, private equity firms, and other financial instruments enable start-ups to develop their products and services to the point where they are large enough to secure other forms of finance. The initial public offering (IPO) is a major milestone in the life and growth of most companies.

So a well functioning financial system contributes enormously to economic growth. Almost equally important, the demands on the financial system grow with economic growth itself. The economic history of the now-rich countries is a history of financial development alongside the development of the real economy. Even the development of simple banking started relatively recently; a shift to use of bank deposits as a medium of exchange required trust in the banking system, which came only gradually until regulatory systems were put into place. Even in the nineteenth century, economic growth was frequently interrupted by "banking crises"; in the United States, banks issued their own money, which often exchanged at a fraction of the face value.

Banking reforms and lessons from earlier crises — such as Bagehot's famous *dicta* regarding the role of a lender of last resort — gradually resulted in greater stability in the money supply over time. But even the Great Depression was as severe as it was in large part because of inappropriate monetary reactions on part of the central banks, as Friedman and Schwartz (1963) demonstrated so convincingly for the United States.

The Great Depression resulted in a number of reforms in the financial sector, including measures to provide greater security to depositors (with government-provided deposit insurance), greater information to investors (in the United States, through the Securities and Exchange Commission which required registration of public companies and specified information that was required to be reported quarterly and annually), and a separation of functions between various financial institutions — including commercial banks, investment banks, insurance companies, and equity markets. Some of these measures served very useful functions for years after they were enacted, but have needed to be revisited in light of the recent financial crises.

But of course, economic growth resumed, and as it did, the demands on the financial system increased still further. Most recently, financial markets have increasingly spun off risks in the forms of derivatives. Banks, which earlier assessed alternative investments and lent, became intermediaries themselves, selling the loans they made to other investors once they had extended them. Banking income in the United States and other financial centers now comes in significant part from the fees received for placing loans, rather than from interest on the loans themselves. Current discussions focus on the appropriate kind and degree of regulation in derivative markets. Appropriate resolution of the issues associated with derivatives will no doubt be crucial in determining the future growth of the major financial centers and other countries dependent for their financing upon them. However, it has been widely recognized that, in the Great Recession of 2007–09, it was not the hedge funds that experienced extreme difficulties: the shadow banking system was far more to blame.

Additionally, financial markets have become increasingly globalized, with further benefits but also issues, over the past two decades. Private capital flows to emerging markets have mushroomed. Banking branches and subsidiaries have been opened by most major banks. Issues arise as to how regulation should be accomplished so that the financial institutions in the countries with least regulation (as, for example, by having lower capital requirements) do not benefit, and how banks where ownership is spread across two or more countries should be dealt with. These are important questions, and are the subject of intense consideration in the policy community in the wake of the financial crisis.

As this thumbnail sketch of financial history indicates, financial development took place accompanying growth of the real side of the economy. Had financial markets failed to develop, growth of the industrial countries would certainly have been slower than it has in fact been.

For the now-emerging markets, there are lessons from this. After the Second World War, almost all developing countries had very repressed financial systems, along the lines described by McKinnon. Of course there were banks, but those banks were controlled by governments, if they were not government-owned. And in efforts to foster import-substitution and for other purposes, banks were directed to lend specified amounts or fractions of their loans to industries or sectors specified by the government. Moreover, these, and usually all, loans were often required to be extended at controlled low interest rates. "Credit rationing" was the result. With low interest rates and profitability seemingly assured by protection against imports, firms demanded considerably more credit than was available from the banks. In those circumstances, banks could lend without much concern for risk: they could choose the safest among potential borrowers; and even if a borrower encountered financial difficulties, chances were good that borrower could plead for greater protection, tax breaks, or other relief. And, at any event, most interest rates were below the rate of inflation so the likelihood of inability to pay was very low. A firm that would realize a zero real rate of return on investment could nonetheless profitably borrow, as long as the real rate of interest at which it borrowed was negative.

As growth proceeded, however, financial systems also developed. While government ownership of banks still persists in many countries, others have privatized some or all of their previously state-owned banks. And, in most countries, the problems arising from negative real rates of interest have generally led the authorities to raise permitted interest rates so that they are positive in real terms, if they have not abandoned credit rationing altogether. Regulation, meanwhile, has developed as well, relying more on incentives within a prudential framework and less on direct controls of banks' lending.

There is a growing body of empirical research substantiating all of this.[3] There is a strong relationship between economic growth and measures of how well the financial system functions. Measures of economic growth are straightforward; the functioning of the financial system is usually measured by several variables. These include the ratios of: liquid liabilities to GDP, claims on the non-financial private sector to domestic credit, gross claims on the private sector to GDP, and others. For rich countries, for example, private sector credit as a percent of GDP is 71, while in poor countries it is 47 and in very poor countries it is 37. Similarly, the ratio of gross claims on the private sector to GDP is 53 in very rich countries, 20 in poor countries, and 13 in very poor countries. The correlation between these measures and real per capita GDP is surprisingly high, given all the variables that affect real per capita incomes. There are a variety of other empirical studies, too many to review here. But almost all researchers report significant relationships between the aspect of the financial system's development studied by them and real per capita income and/or the rate of growth.

II. LESSONS FROM THE ASIAN CRISIS

It is thus clear that the financial system must develop at a pace sufficient to meet the needs of the real economy if growth is to be sustained. And, the

---

[3] See Levine (2005).

more efficiently the financial system allocates resources, taking into account both expected returns and risks, the more rapidly the economy will grow. But with growth, the real economy becomes increasingly complex: in early days when most economic activity is subsistence agriculture and there are few applicants seeking bank credit, a simple banking system may suffice, and credit rationing may not be severely inimical to growth prospects. But with economic growth, the demands for credit increase in type and variety, and hence the costs of misallocating bank credit (and thus investment) and not having a sufficient array or quantity of alternative financial instruments (such as bonds and equity) become higher. Although all of this was known prior to the Asian crisis, the quantitative impact of an underdeveloped financial system in affecting growth was probably underestimated by most policy makers and development economists.

The experience of South Korea vividly illustrates what goes wrong when the financial system fails to develop alongside the real economy. South Korea was one of the poorest countries in Asia in the 1950s. After the devastation of the Korean War (when the fighting went up and down the South Korean peninsula three times), recovery was anything but robust. The South Korean government adopted many of the measures then in vogue in developing countries: quantitative restrictions on imports and high tariff levels, encouragement of import substitution activities through prohibition on imports when domestic production was available, establishment of state-owned enterprises, credit rationing, and so on.

In this process, South Korea reached the highest recorded rate of inflation in the world in the 1950s (about a 25 percent annual average, although price controls probably resulted in an understatement of the true rate) and yet resisted and delayed altering the nominal exchange rate both in an effort to reduce inflation and for other reasons. One result was that exports were low even relative to the size of the economy, and grew very slowly: by 1960 exports (of which 88 percent were primary commodities) were only 3 percent of GDP. Worse yet, the domestic savings rate during the 1950s was very close to zero: investment was around 12–13 percent of GDP and foreign assistance was about 10 percent of GDP. And, of course, there was credit rationing, with an interest rate below the rate of inflation. South Korea's economic prospects appeared very poor.

But by the late 1950s, it was evident to the South Koreans that if they did not alter their policies, their economic prospects were dismal. Starting in 1958, therefore, the foreign exchange and trade regime began to be liberalized; by 1960, the exchange rate in real terms had been altered enough so that exporting became profitable for many. During the 1960s, there were fiscal reforms that enabled the reduction of inflation to single digits; tariffs were lowered; quantitative restrictions on most imports were removed; and the government shifted from direct controls to greater reliance on incentives. As part of its drive to accelerate growth through an outer-oriented trade strategy, the government provided uniform incentives to all exporters including the attractive real exchange rate, exemption from any taxes or controls for imports of goods used in producing exports, favorable tax treatments, and access to rationed credit. All exporters were entitled to equal treatment, proportionate to their export earnings. In addition, while credit rationing was not abandoned, the rate of interest charged to borrowers was raised above the rate of inflation (which fell substantially due to fiscal reforms).

For purposes of understanding the role of the financial sector, there are two important features of subsequent South Korean growth. First, as you know, it was a spectacular success. South Korean per capita incomes are estimated to have increased seven-fold between 1960 and the mid-1990s. South Korean export earnings in dollar terms grew more than 40 percent annually for the first ten years of growth at a time when world dollar prices were fairly constant. Real wages grew an average of about 8 percent annually. By the late 1980s, the investment and savings rates which were 12 percent and zero in the late 1950s, were each over 35 per cent. Exports, which had been just 3 percent of GDP, were over 30 percent, and imports had grown as well. The South Korean economy had been transformed from a very poor, agrarian one to a middle income country — at first called newly industrializing, and soon called newly industrialized. No one could doubt the fantastic success story.

During the period after the beginning of reforms, there was no year in which the South Korean economy did not grow, and the average growth rate was of course very high. By the 1990s, most observers believed that South Korean policy makers had responded to various threats to sustained growth in a timely fashion, and that sustained growth was assured.

But that leads to the second major feature. That is, the very high rate of South Korean economic growth in the early years took place in the context of financial repression. The authorities adopted a macroeconomic stance compatible with a much-reduced rate of inflation and finally single digit rates of price increase. That reduced the degree to which the real interest rate was negative. They also raised the ceiling on the interest rates that banks could charge so that real interest rates became positive. But they still enforced interest rate ceilings and did not liberalize the entire banking system. These measures led to some misallocation of resources, but in the early growth years, there were enough highly profitable opportunities so that the economic costs of financial repression were not too high. In an economy starting with exports equaling only 3 percent of GDP, it was probably economically efficient that a large fraction of new resources be allocated to exportable goods, as incentives to export had been increased.

But the situation then and later was complicated by the fact that the great success of the South Korean economy in the 1960s and 1970s had been accomplished in large measure through the *chaebol*, which were the large industrial conglomerates which dominated South Korean business. These *chaebol* expanded output rapidly and greatly increased their share of economic activity. They were successful exporters and demonstrated their ability to compete on world markets. But the *chaebol* were also required to maintain their employment, so that as productivity rose in existing lines of activity, they took on new ones to keep their labor forces employed. At the same time, many of the banks were affiliated with *chaebol*. Hence, when one or more businesses within a *chaebol* were performing poorly, the *chaebol* bank extended additional funds to them. Not only did the banks have no experience of evaluating risks and returns, but the connected lending that resulted was another impediment to any sound judgment of the situation. Over time, rates of return on investments fell.

The fact that interest rates were repressed made it more difficult for any efforts at diversification of the financial system. The development of bond and equity markets as means of financing *chaebol* (and other) activities was undoubtedly restrained by the fact that bank lending was at below-market rates and hence would-be borrowers did not seek to diversify their funding sources while the development of diverse financial institutions — equity, bonds, etc. — was undoubtedly slowed because of the relatively low cost to borrowers of bank credit.

Hence, the *chaebol* were financed largely by bank borrowing, and had relatively small equity bases. Over time, they became more and more heavily indebted, and continued borrowing to enable them to roll over existing debt and increase output.

By the 1990s, bank returns on assets and equity were falling sharply.[4] In the early 1990s, the government raised the interest rate ceiling, in an effort to help the banks' profitability. But by that time, the *chaebol* were heavily indebted, and many were servicing their debts only by additional borrowing, or evergreening of their loans, as it came to be called. *Chaebol* had debt-equity ratios as high as 700 and 800 percent. It was obviously a situation that could not be sustained. But before the collapse, banks started

---

[4] See Krueger and Yoo (2002), for a full analysis.

investing offshore, and especially in currencies where the interest rate they could receive was higher, in an effort to forestall their incipient difficulties. Some of the major currencies were in Southeast Asia, and when those currencies were devalued, bank losses mounted. By that time, both domestic residents and foreigners were selling won-denominated assets, and the Korean crisis was unstoppable.

Thus, financial repression became increasingly costly over time. By the late 1970s, returns on investments were falling although the negative effects were not perceived as the rate of investment was rising rapidly. By the 1990s, rates of return were, as already stated, turning negative.

When the authorities did finally address the root causes of the difficulties, they undertook major reforms in the financial sector, which enabled a resumption of growth within 18 months of the depths of the crisis. Korea's economic growth since that time has not been at the same rate as earlier occurred, but has still been well above that of most other emerging market countries.

Thus, South Korea could and did experience rapid growth for a considerable period of time, during which the degree of financial repression (although it was somewhat relaxed), while a negative, could not offset the factors contributing to strong growth. When policies were changed in the early 1960s, the degree of imbalance in the economy toward import-substituting activities was so great that it is probably true that anyone who had potential exports should have been supported. The high growth rate does not prove that there was no resource misallocation resulting from credit rationing in the early years of rapid growth, but there was surely not a lot.

As growth continued, however, the ability of the authorities to direct credit, or the ability of the banks to perform appropriate risk-reward calculations, was increasingly impaired. The real rate of return on investment — very high in the 1960s — naturally fell over time as the initial imbalances were gradually corrected. As that happened, however, selection of the right investments got harder. Banks couldn't do it, because they had been accustomed to lending in circumstances where there was little choice (and little risk) as to which borrowers to support. They had to evergreen loans when ailing businesses could not service their debts. But, over time, as rates of return fell and the number and proportion of loans that would have been nonperforming rose, had it not been for evergreening, the situation became unsustainable. But lending to enable service of existing loans does not have a high rate of return, and the growth rate plummeted.

The South Korean case presents an important lesson. Growth, and even rapid growth, may be achievable with a given set of economic policies at a particular stage of development, although growth will be less than attainable were resources allocated more efficiently. But the same set of policies and institutions will not support further sustained or rapid growth over the longer term. The art of good economic policy making is to identify those policies and institutions which are not likely to support the economy's move to the next stage. The same policies that may not detract too much from growth at one stage may be a key bottleneck that has to be corrected to continue economic growth. And, the more rapid is economic growth, the more quickly the authorities must adapt the policy framework to the needs of a growing economy.

Korean policy makers had been unusually astute at identifying growth bottlenecks and correcting them for over thirty years. But they failed to recognize the weaknesses of the financial sector, and the role those weaknesses would play in undermining growth, until the crisis was upon them. Had they proceeded more rapidly with liberalization of the financial system, it is likely that growth in the late 1980s and early 1990s would have been at a higher rate, and the crisis would probably have been avoided.

CONCLUSION

To conclude, a well functioning financial system itself contributes to acceleration in potential economic growth, and a repressed financial system acts as a brake on potential growth. Even with distortions in the real sector of the economy, countries with better-functioning financial systems grow faster than those with more repressed systems. As the importance of a well functioning financial sector has become increasingly understood, more and more countries have undertaken reforms, thus further disadvantaging those whose financial systems are repressed. Moreover, as growth proceeds, there is need for still further reform — at all stages of development — simply for the financial system to meet the new demands that a more advanced economy places on it.

The Great Recession of 2007–09 raised doubts in many peoples' minds about the financial system in all countries. While the lessons of the preceding several decades had pointed to the desirability of encouraging a competitive, diversified, and innovative financial system, the lessons being learned from recent difficulties point to the need for appropriate regulation and to the importance of reaching international agreement on it. Some factors underlying the Great Recession, including especially global imbalances and the consequent incentives for a "search for yield", will, if appropriately addressed, reduce the incentives for excesses in the financial system. But such measures will need to achieve balance between reducing systemic risk and enabling the financial system to fulfill its functions as the international economy grows. Multilateral agreements on many of these issues are clearly desirable, assuming they can be negotiated with appropriate balance between the competing demands of systemic risk reduction and a well-functioning financial system for supporting growth.

But three conclusions are nonetheless possible: reforms which improve the functioning of the financial system will surely improve growth prospects, especially in lower income countries where existing financial systems are rudimentary or repressed; improved efficiency of the financial system will yield a bigger payoff to reforms undertaken in other sectors; and, equally important, if reforms are not undertaken, there will come a time when further growth is significantly impeded.

REFERENCES

Friedman, M and AJ Schwartz (1963). Monetary History of the United States, 1867–1960. Princeton, NJ: Princeton University Press.

Krueger, AO and Y Jungho (2002). Falling Profitability, Higher Borrowing Costs, and Chaebol Finances During the Korean Crisis. In *Preventing Currency Crisis in Emerging Markets*, Sebastian, E and JA Frankel (eds.), pp. 601–649. University of Chicago Press.

Levine, R (2005). Finance and Growth: Theory and Evidence. In *Handbook of Economic Growth*, Philippe, A and S Durlauf (eds.). The Netherlands: Elsevier Science.

Levine, R (1997). Financial Development and Economic Growth: Views and Agenda. *Journal of Economic Literature*, XXXV(2), pp. 688–726.

McKinnon, RI (1973). *Money and Capital in Economic Development*. Brookings Institutions, Washington, D.C.

Chapter 7

LESSONS FROM THE ASIAN FINANCIAL EXPERIENCE*

Until the 1990s, East Asia's economic growth was the economic marvel of the world in the post-World War II period. Japan, a low-income country prior to the war, had emerged from war in dire economic straits, but postwar reconstruction was completed by the mid-1950s and economic growth accelerated sharply in the late l950s. By the mid-1960s, Japan's "economic miracle" had transformed it into an industrial country whose economy and productivity bore no resemblance to that of the late 1940s, as signified by its joining the OECD in l964.

In the immediate post-war period, the rest of East Asia was even poorer than Japan. Korea was partitioned in 1946. What became South Korea[1] endured the partition, and experienced hyperinflation in the late 1940s and war on its territory in the early 1950s. In the aftermath of the war, Korea had one of the lowest per capita incomes in Asia, the highest density of population on the land of any country in the world, and population characteristics (life expectancy, literacy, infant mortality) found only in very low-income countries.[2] Although reconstruction usually enables an above-average rate of

* This paper was presented at a conference, Asia and the Global Financial Crisis, sponsored by the Federal Reserve Bank of San Francisco, and published in Glick and Spiegel (2009). I am indebted to Takatoshi Ito, Il Sakong, and Andrew Sheng for helpful comments on the penultimate draft of this paper, and to Erin Berg for research assistance. None of these are responsible for the views expressed herein.
[1] Formally, the south became the Republic of Korea and the north the People's Republic of Korea. Since North Korea is not discussed at all in this paper, I shall refer to South Korea as Korea.
[2] Korea's per capita income is estimated to have been below that of many African countries at the time. Maddison (2003) estimates South Korean per capita income in 1960 to have been $1105 in 1990 international purchasing power parity dollars.

economic growth for at least a few years, Korea's postwar economic growth rate remained below 5 percent (with per capita income growth at less than 3 percent).

Taiwan experienced a large immigration in the aftermath of the Chinese civil war, and was also very poor, although significantly better off in terms of per capita incomes and other measures of well-being than Korea. The two city states, Hong Kong and Singapore, were likewise poor. Southeast Asian countries had higher per capita incomes than their East Asian neighbors, but were also "underdeveloped countries", the term used at the time, by any measure.

But starting in the mid-1950s in Taiwan, in the early 1960s in Korea and the city-states, and in the 1970s in Thailand, Malaysia and Indonesia, economic growth accelerated rapidly.[3] By the late 1980s, Japan's economic prowess as a high-income industrial country was recognized globally. The four "Asian tigers" (Hong Kong, Singapore, South Korea, Taiwan), as they came to be called, had sustained unheard of rapid growth rates even higher than Japan's and become industrial countries. The Southeast Asian countries were also growing rapidly, although not quite at the pace of Japan and the "tigers". Many observers believed that all these economies were immune to the difficulties faced by countries in the rest of the world, as they weathered almost without notice the 1973 oil price shock, the second oil shock, the "debt crisis" of the early 1980s, and other challenges that affected almost all other oil-importing economies negatively.[4]

But in the 1990s, when it was believed that the success of these economies was entrenched, things changed dramatically. In 1990, Japan entered into a period of stagnation more than a decade long, often referred to as the "Great Stagnation" (Hutchison, Ito and Westermann, 2006). In the late 1990s, Thailand, Malaysia, Indonesia, and South Korea all experienced severe crises, and a number of the other successful Asian economies were severely challenged. In many ways, the Japanese stagnation and the Asian financial crises were as surprising to the world in the 1990s as the financial crisis in the United States has been over the past two years.

It is the purpose of this paper to examine the factors contributing to the difficulties in these economies in the 1990s and to analyze the policies that

---

[3] Of course, rapid economic growth also started in the People's Republic of China in the early 1980s, although that experience is not covered here.

[4] Japan's rapid economic growth had slowed sharply after the first oil price increase in the early 1970s. However, the 'tigers" all continued rapid growth. Their success in so doing, relative to the difficulties faced by other developing countries, was a major factor in convincing the policy community of the wisdom of an outward orientation in trade.

were adopted in addressing them. Focus is on Japan and South Korea as their experiences largely capture the lessons to be learned. When experience from other countries is relevant, or significantly different from that of Japan and South Korea, that will be noted.

A first set of lessons focuses on the rapid growth leading up to crisis and the importance of a well-functioning financial system for growth. A second set of lessons is relevant mainly for developing countries and emerging markets, and is addressed next. The third set, primarily from Japan and Korea, concerns the financial sector. Finally, crisis and postcrisis management issues are addressed.

A significant difference that sets Japan, on the one hand, and the other crisis countries, on the other, apart has to do with their economies' exposure to foreign-exchange risk. In the Japanese case, Japan was incurring current account surpluses and held ample foreign exchange reserves; the difficulties were, in that sense, purely "domestic". For the other "crisis" countries, mismatches in the foreign-currency composition of assets and liabilities in the financial system were major immediate triggers of the crises, although they led to problems in the financial sector that were much the same as those of Japan.

LESSONS FOR EMERGING MARKETS AND DEVELOPING COUNTRIES

The Asian crisis countries other than Japan all faced problems in their banking systems, but to a considerable extent, the origins of the emerging markets' banking systems' problems differed. In many regards, as already mentioned, the Korean experience typifies the lessons from the East Asian emerging markets that went into crisis. Some, such as Taiwan, Singapore, and Hong Kong, were severely threatened, but managed to avoid a full-blown crisis either through the use of (a high initial level) reserves or through other interventions.[5] From these experiences in the 1990s, there is widespread consensus on several lessons, although most are relevant primarily for emerging markets and of limited relevance for the major industrial countries. However, they do apply to a significant degree to the economies of Eastern Europe.[6]

---

[5] They also had positive or at worst small negative current account surpluses, which was partly reflected in the high reserve levels.

[6] Most of those economies have maintained fairly fixed, if not rigid, exchange rates, relatively low levels of foreign exchange reserves, sizeable short-term capital inflows, and fragile banking systems. In many of them, households had taken out mortgages in foreign currency, rendering them highly vulnerable to any exchange rate change and increasing political resistance for necessary changes.

Lessons include: the wisdom of choosing an exchange rate regime consistent with the use of other policy instruments, which in most cases is a flexible rate regime;[7] the need to avoid mismatches between banking assets and liabilities that can result because banking assets are denominated in domestic currency while liabilities are denominated in foreign currency; and the desirability of a ratio at least above one between government holdings of foreign exchange reserves and short-term liabilities.

Turning first to the exchange rate issue, there is an almost-universal consensus that, in the absence of a willingness and ability to adjust domestic monetary and fiscal policies to the dictates of the balance of payments under a fixed exchange rate regime, a floating exchange rate regime serves as a preferred buffer for individual countries.[8]

Ito (2007) believes that the maintenance pre-crisis of fixed exchange rates was a crucial mistake: "For emerging market countries...the danger of a de facto dollar peg was again confirmed. The de facto dollar peg may result in an overvalued real exchange rate if the domestic inflation rate is higher...than the U.S. rate. The de facto dollar peg encouraged borrowers and lenders to engage in financial transactions that underestimated exchange rate risk." (p. 26)[9]

Prior to the 1997 crises, Thailand and Malaysia had supported almost entirely fixed exchange rates for several decades, while Indonesia and Korea had permitted only limited managed floating. In consequence, earlier adjustments which might have removed some of the pressure from those countries in 1997 were not made, and the swings in exchange rates which accompanied the onsets of the crisis (when countries could no longer defend their rates) were commensurately larger and resulted in much larger shocks to the domestic economy. The price of a dollar almost doubled in Korea, for example. But the biggest change was in Indonesia, where the pre-crisis exchange rate was Rs. 2380 per U.S. dollar at the end of 1996 and peaked during the crisis at over Rs. 17,000 per U.S. dollar, falling back to Rs. 9,000–10,000 by 2000–01.

---

[7] Hong Kong has operated a currency board throughout the past several decades. The regime was successfully defended during the Asian financial crisis.

[8] In the current crisis, countries such as Australia, India, South Korea and Chile that have let their exchange rates adjust appear to have fared better than those that have kept their exchange rates within narrow bounds. The obvious exception is China, although that country has a relatively closed capital account and its currency was widely believed to have been undervalued.

[9] The "again" reference is to the Mexican crisis of 1994. Ito's analysis pinpoints the maintenance of a quasi-fixed exchange rate as a major contributor to that crisis as well.

In analyzing the Asian financial crises, IMF researchers have concluded that when a flexible exchange rate facilitated the needed external adjustment in the 1990s, the response to policy changes was accompanied by larger output gains than under fixed exchange rates. (Ghosh *et al.* 2005, pp. 107ff).[10] But there are other reasons why a flexible exchange rate is probably preferable. When exchange rates are fixed (or heavily managed), expectations form that the exchange rate will stay within a relatively small range, and the temptation not to hedge foreign-currency borrowing is strong. Insofar as uncovered dollar liabilities in the banking system (or of banks' borrowers) are larger under fixed exchange rates, the shock to the system when the exchange rate is forced to change is larger.[11]

The danger of mismatches between currency denominations of assets and liabilities is clear. The difficulty, as perceived by many policy makers in emerging markets, has been that foreign loans have been available largely, if not exclusively, in foreign currency. The result has been that changes in the exchange rate have resulted in increased liabilities of the banking system (and the banks' borrowers) with little change in bank assets, since they are mostly denominated in local currency.[12]

A strong lesson from Asia in the late 1990s is the importance of insuring that banks' assets and liabilities are either in the same currency or appropriately hedged.[13] Another advantage of a floating exchange rate regime is that borrowers and lenders are more aware of the possibility of exchange rate fluctuations than they are under fixed exchange rate regimes.

The final macroeconomic lesson, important for emerging markets and low-income countries but less relevant for industrial countries, is the desirability of

---

[10] See also Edwards (2003).

[11] This advantage is somewhat diminished when the domestic banking system has become significantly dollarized.

[12] An extreme case was Argentina after the 2001 crisis. The authorities "pesified" the banks' liabilities (i.e. deposits, which had been denominated in pesos when the exchange rate to the U.S. dollar was one-to-one)) at the rate of 3 pesos per U.S. dollar, while the assets were left at the 1 peso = U.S. $1.

[13] Even with such hedging, the problem is not entirely solved. If banks' loan portfolios are heavily weighted towards firms whose costs have a large component of imports while their revenues are mostly from the home market, those firms can be negatively affected by exchange rate depreciation. Obtaining data on the sensitivity of individual firms' revenues to exchange rate fluctuations is extremely difficult.

Recently, in some Eastern European countries, the same problem has arisen with respect to mortgages. Households borrowed from foreign banks because of lower interest rates, and have encountered major increases in liabilities when exchange rates have depreciated.

maintaining sufficient foreign exchange reserves to be able to cover short-term foreign exchange liabilities.[14] Speculation against a currency is considerably less likely when speculators can observe that foreign exchange cover may be adequate to withstand an attack.[15]

LESSONS FROM GROWTH

Prior to considering the lessons of relevance to industrial countries from the Asian crises, it is useful to sketch some of the characteristics of the growth experience of those countries, especially as they relate to the financial sector. This is important because it is sometimes thought that financial crises prove that the financial sector does not contribute to economic growth. But nothing could be further from the truth. Financial development is an essential concomitant of economic growth. While the crises were painful, they took place when they did because of failures of the financial and real components of the growing economies to develop synchronously.

All but the most primitive economies must have a financial sector. Even at very early stages of development, when 70–80 percent of economic activity is still in agriculture and other subsistence activities, the absence of a well-functioning financial sector suppresses economic activity somewhat (as most non-farm activities are family-owned and family-financed) but is not a major deterrent to more rapid growth because activities of a size and a character to require finance are such a small part of the overall economy.

But with economic growth, the costs of financial "repression" (to use McKinnon's apt term) rise. Indeed, if a relatively efficient low-cost banking system does not develop, possibilities for growth are limited. But when there are only a few "nontraditional" nonagricultural activities — often textiles and clothing, footwear, and the like — a banking system of even relatively small size can enable a small nontraditional sector to function and grow, and it can

---

[14] Ito (2007, p. 34) also makes this point. Some of the transition economies seem not to have paid heed to this lesson.

[15] Having foreign exchange reserves greater than short-term liabilities is not a guarantee, however. Sharp changes in prospects, whether originating from global shocks or from shifts to highly expansionary fiscal and monetary policy, can induce speculators to attack. But the magnitude of the impact of the projected shock or fiscal expansion has to be considerably larger if foreign exchange reserves are adequate. Some have argued that the Asian countries have over-learned this lesson from the crisis. As seen from the warnings of those concerned about a decision by foreigners to sell U.S. treasuries in large amounts, even large dollar holdings will not necessarily ward off an attack.

be reasonably evident (as it was in Korea in the 1960s) which activities (unskilled labor-intensive exports in Korea's case) should be financed.

But to move beyond the constraints of family finance requires the ability of promising enterprises to finance investments in addition to those that can be undertaken with plowed-back profits (and mechanisms for assuring owners of low-return or loss-making enterprises that they can invest in businesses other than their own with reasonable confidence that they will be fairly dealt with).

The history of economic growth of the West is one in which new financial innovations came about to meet the increasingly complex financing needs of the growing modern sector.[16] Since new activities must be financed and inherently involve uncertainty, the financial sector plays a crucial role for economic growth in appropriately assessing risk-return trade-offs and channeling funds to those investments that are most promising. It is no coincidence that the World Bank has repeatedly found that countries with deeper and better functioning financial markets are countries with higher per capita incomes.[17] Interestingly, in rich countries credit to the private sector averages 71 percent of GDP, while in low income countries it averages 47 percent and in the very poorest 13 percent. Other measures of financial depth show similar patterns.

That lesson is highly relevant to understanding the Asian experience in the 1990s. The Korean experience illustrates. Korea had a very underdeveloped financial system in the 1950s. Although some policy reforms started in 1958, the commitment to an outer oriented strategy and wholesale reform really began in the early 1960s. Economic growth accelerated sharply, and growth momentum was sustained for the next three and a half decades, as many reforms in the fiscal system, in government regulations, in the trade regime, and elsewhere were undertaken.

However, there was little effort to develop the financial system. Instead, the government mandated credit allocation with credit rationing (directed credit). Exporters were entitled to a specified amount of credit at a subsidized interest rate per dollar of exports,[18] and other activities deemed socially

---

[16] See Rosenberg and Birdzell (1986) for an economic history focusing in significant measure on the interactions between technological advances in the real sector of the economy and financial innovation.

[17] See World Bank (2004), Chapter 6 and references therein.

[18] Exporters were also entitled, in the early days of the outer orientation of the Korean economy, to other privileges including the ability to import needed inputs duty-free (with minimum delays) and tax credits. These entitlements were extended equally to all who exported per dollar of exports (except for inputs for which duty-free treatment was based on an estimate of use of imports per unit of exports). They were thus export incentives, but the incentive was essentially uniform across all exporting activities. See Krueger (1979, pp. 87ff.) for a full description.

desirable were also eligible for subsidized credits. Other entities either managed on self-finance or went to the (thriving) curb market where interest rates were much higher.

While there were undoubtedly inefficiencies in credit allocation, two considerations suggest that these were limited. First, Korea had entered the 1960s with exports equal to approximately 3 percent of GDP and imports 13 percent. Foreign exchange was rationed and there was a significant black market premium despite high tariff levels and import licensing. To allocate most new resources to exportable industries undoubtedly made sense, and the fact that borrowers had to export successfully in return for their credit meant that there was something of a market test to sort out potential borrowers. Second, given Korea's very high growth rates in the 1960s, it is difficult to argue that improved credit allocation could have made the growth rate very much higher.

Partly because of credit rationing, and partly for other reasons, much of the initial growth in Korea was concentrated in the *chaebol* — the industrial houses that grew very rapidly in response to the incentives offered by the government. The *chaebol* naturally established or acquired their own merchant banks (and some small commercial banks), and lent to the various companies within their specific groups. The larger commercial banks also bought *chaebol* debt.

Over time, the hugely profitable opportunities for expansion for the *chaebol* diminished, but they were still large and visible and subject to special regulations. They had been prohibited from laying off any workers, and had thus expanded into new activities as productivity rose (or, in the case of some very labor-intensive industries, exports were no longer profitable). Over time, as each *chaebol* ventured into more and more new lines of activity, managerial challenges undoubtedly became increasingly difficult and the requirement that they retain all workers more onerous. At much the same time in the mid-1980s, the government was attempting to liberalize the financial system. The banks lent (or rolled over loans) to their less profitable businesses to keep them afloat as profitability fell. For the *chaebol*, mechanisms for increasing profitability such as reducing the workforce were unavailable to them.

One question might be why Korea ran into difficulties in 1997. But another, more fundamental, question is how the authorities managed macroeconomic and financial policies so well that there were more than 30 years of growth before the first crisis. The first oil price increase, in 1973–74, hit South Korea particularly hard because of the total dependence on imported oil.[19]

---

[19] A rough estimate would be that the 1973–74 oil price increase resulted in a deterioration in Korea's terms of trade equivalent to 15 percent of GDP (and there had been increases in food and other commodity prices in 1972 and 1973 which also constituted a negative shock).

But the authorities adjusted policies, passing on the oil price increases and raising taxes, so that growth quickly resumed.

During the early 1970s, the Government had also decided to embark on a heavy and chemicals industry (HCI) program, believing that Korea's rapid economic growth warranted that decision. In fact, the HCI drive resulted in sharp changes in the economy, tripling the compensation of engineers, leading to the first decline in exports (in an export-growth-led economy) since 1960, and generating inflationary pressure. But before the harm could extend too far (and before the second oil price increase, which would probably have been disastrous had policies not been altered), the mistake was recognized, and the HCI drive was greatly curtailed, if not abandoned. The second oil price increase and the worldwide recession that followed it also posed a challenge for Korean economic growth, but, as in earlier instances, the authorities were able to adjust so that Korean growth in fact accelerated.

Over the thirty years prior to the 1990s, many fundamental policy adjustments had been made. The rapid-growth era started with (uniform) export incentives for exporters, consisting of access to credit (which, as already seen, was provided at below-market interest rates), tax credits, and other privileges. Over the next ten years, these "incentives" were gradually phased out, while simultaneously import protection was reduced, as the exchange rate depreciated and replaced both incentives and tariffs. Likewise, fiscal reforms were undertaken, the nominal interest rate was raised (although it remained below market clearing levels) so that the real interest rate was at least not negative, and tariffs on imports were reduced and the trade regime liberalized.[20] The authorities successfully addressed these and many of the other bottlenecks that would otherwise have put downward pressure on the growth rate over time.

Korean policy makers had identified and corrected many potential bottlenecks and crisis points over the thirty year period of rapid growth some of the challenges came from the world economy; but many were needed to address the archaic policies that had done little damage to a stagnant economy but which were incompatible with Korea's increasingly complex modern economy. However, the domestic financial system was not sufficiently altered to keep pace with the changing economy. Suppression of bank interest rates in

---

[20] Exporters were from an early stage permitted to import goods they used in the production process. A first step on the import side was to move from a positive list (of permitted imports) to a negative list (of those prohibited). The exchange rate was also gradually unified as tariffs were reduced and export incentives reduced while the real exchange rate depreciated. Later, tariffs were further reduced and the exchange rate fully unified.

the early 1990s as growth seemed to be slowing, which in turn induced the banks to lend offshore at higher interest rates, and other measures, retarded the development of the financial system.

For present purposes, the important points are two. First, the financial system, and government policies toward it, must adapt and be able to handle the increasing demands put upon it as economic growth progresses.[21] The same (flawed) financial system which had been able to support rapid growth in the 1960s and early 1970s could no longer do so as the economy had modernized and become increasingly complex.

Second, even if a financial crisis is a cost of rapid economic growth, most observers would conclude that it was a cost worth paying, judging by the differences in growth rates between the rapidly growing countries and the others. If one thinks of the financial crises in the now-industrial countries in the 19th and early 20th centuries, it is more likely we should regard Korean policy choices during the decades of rapid growth (during which Korea grew more in a decade than Britain did in the entire 19th century) as having been appropriate. Failure to let the financial system develop more was the first major (and insufficiently addressed) policy issue that led to crisis. To be sure, lessons have been learned so that in future, policy makers in countries undergoing rapid growth will have learned and be enabled to reduce the severity, if not prevent, crises.

But proposals for altered and intensified regulation of the financial system must be evaluated not only in terms of the likelihood that they will prevent, or at least reduce, the incidence and/or severity of, financial crises but also in terms of the likely effects of those regulations on the financial system's capacity to support future economic growth.

The Japanese story is also one where successful growth preceded the stagnation of the 1990s but it differs in that a financial crisis was triggered by domestic events without any foreign currency mismatches or related foreign exchange crisis. In Japan's case, rapid economic growth had resulted in a bubble in the real estate market. The "main bank" system meant that banks lent to other companies within the same keiretsu (but to other companies outside the group as well), so connected lending was a problem. In addition, the banks held equity, real estate, and commercial loans. When the bubble burst,

---

[21] The same can be said of any number of other policy arenas: the foreign trade regimes that many countries (including Korea) adopted during their early years of growth would have, if unaltered, certainly retarded and perhaps even prevented a continuation of that growth. To be sure, in many countries, these regimes were sustained until it became evident that they were inconsistent with sustaining growth. Turkey (see Krueger and Turan, 1992) in the late 1970s is one example, but there are many more.

bank equity was greatly reduced, as real estate prices and equity prices fell. Simultaneously, many of their borrowers had borrowed to finance equity and real estate investments, and nonperforming loans began increasing rapidly. In Japan's case, however, there was a current account surplus and a relatively freely floating exchange rate. The result was a decade of stagnation, with an unresolved financial crisis throughout the decade despite repeated efforts to stimulate the economy. I return to the lessons from that below.

A fundamental lesson from the Asian experience in the decades after 1960 is the power of economic growth. Some countries set their economic policies for rapid economic growth, while others were far more cautious. Even if financial crises were an inevitable cost of economic growth,[22] the Asian experience suggests that rapid growth is worth it. Graph 1 charts Indian and

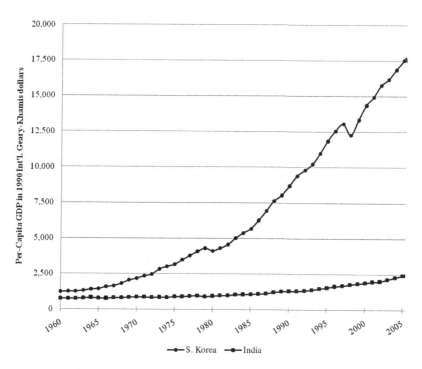

Graph 1:   Indian and Korean Per Capita Incomes 1960–2006

Source: Maddison (2009).

---

[22] Tornell, Ranciere and Westernmann (2003) have provided extensive evidence that over the period through the 1990s those countries that had financial crises in fact grew more rapidly than those that did not. Their explanation is that more rapid credit expansion is a concomitant of more rapid economic growth; more rapid credit expansion means that more risk, and more high-return activities, are financed. Hence, the overall growth rate is higher.

Korean per capita incomes after 1960, when their per capita incomes were fairly similar. The most dramatic feature of the chart is the much more rapid rate of growth of Korea than of India until the 1990s. But what is hardly noticeable is the crisis and the drop in South Korea's income in the 1990s. India, of course, had no financial crisis in 1997 (although there had been a balance-of-payments crisis in 1991).

EVENTS LEADING TO CRISIS IN KOREA

As already seen, despite their many reforms in other sectors of the economy, the Korean authorities did little to modernize the financial system once they had taken measures to assure a positive real interest rate. The lending to the chaebol, and the use of the banks' lending rate as an instrument of growth policy, continued. Failure to develop a more flexible financial system commensurate with the growing economy's needs was a major factor in contributing to the 1997-98 crisis.[23]

Despite that failure, Korea liberalized short-term capital transactions as one of the measures needed to join the OECD in the early 1990s. It is often asserted that it was premature external liberalization that caused the crisis. In fact, the falling ROA and ROEs of the banks suggest that the causes were deeper than capital account liberalization, although the presence of significant offshore deposits and buildup of short term foreign debt certainly contributed to the severity of the crisis (see Kim, 2006 for a full description). It is clear that the sequence of capital account liberalization was a mistake and exacerbated the 1997 crisis: long term capital flows should surely have been liberalized sooner.

As the *chaebol* expanded into ever more lines of activity, their profitability fell and loans were "evergreened".[24] The rate of return on bank assets and equity began falling in the early 1990s. No longer could an economy as developed as the Korean had then become grow with such a constrained financial system.[25] In an effort to sustain growth, the Korean government mandated a

---

[23] See Krueger and Yoo (2002).

[24] There is considerable evidence in both Japan and Korea that a major reason for the retardation of growth was the reduced credit available to support expansion of small and medium enterprises, as banks could not free their resources from the large but nonperforming borrowers.

[25] It might be argued that the converse was also true: high rates of growth had been sufficient so that the financial system had been able to survive the problems that showed up once growth had slowed down. For present purposes, it matters little whether slowing growth led to financial difficulties that were already there, or whether financial repression led to slowing growth.

sharp drop in interest rates, but nonetheless the return on assets continued falling and evergreening (lending so that borrowers could meet their debt service obligations) was increased. Indeed, by 1997 the return on bank assets had turned negative.[26]

To finance themselves, the banks (and others more generally) increased borrowing domestically and placing the proceeds offshore, especially in countries such as Thailand and Indonesia where they hoped to earn a higher return. This was easy because of the liberalization of short term capital flows, already noted.

After the early 1960s, the exchange rate had no longer been fixed, but there was a managed float. By the early 1990s, there was strong market pressure for exchange rate depreciation. However, the authorities resisted, permitting a series of relatively small depreciations, but preventing a market outcome. During that period the U.S. dollar was depreciating against the yen, and the depreciation of the won relative to the dollar was much smaller, so that the won appreciated relative to the yen. That reduced export profitability (both directly and because many Japanese and Korean exports were competitive and this gave the Japanese an advantage). It is generally agreed that the effort to manage the won's float intensified the Korean crisis (Kim, 2006, p. 7).

Without recounting all the gruesome details, the downward pressure on the growth rate was not reversed[27] and the authorities responded by encouraging credit expansion and foreign borrowing (mostly short term). To add to the problems, the government of President Kim Dae Jung had changed Finance Ministers and Ministers of Economy frequently, the fifth change in his five-year term coming in March 1997 (despite the fact that a new government was to be formed in 1998 after elections in December 1997). The lack of continuity contributed to unease in Korea. Foreign debt was increasing rapidly (rising from 13 percent of GDP in 1990 to 32 percent in 1996), and short term debt rose from 45 percent of the total to 64 percent of the total over the same period.[28]

---

[26] See Krueger and Yoo (2002) for a full analysis.

[27] The Korean growth rate was, however, more than respectable by contemporary standards, with a growth rate between 7 and 9 percent in the 3 years preceding the crisis, and inflation less than 5 percent. The current account deficit and foreign debt (especially short-term), however, were increasing. By 1996, the current account deficit was 4.4 percent of GDP. It fell in 1997 (presumably as financing was not available), and turned strongly positive in 1998. Foreign debt had risen from 20 percent of GDP in 1990 to 33 percent in 1997 and 47 percent of GDP in l998. See Hahm and Mishkin (1999), Tables 1 and 2.

[28] Yoo and Moon (1999), p. 266.

As already mentioned, the rate of return on bank assets turned negative, and failures of chaebol further contributed to a sense of panic. Hanbo Steel had been bankrupt on January 23, 1997, while Sammi Group went bankrupt in March. Spreads between Korean bonds and U.S. treasuries were rising, from 49 basis points in January to 67 basis points in March, to 87 basis points in July, to 220 basis points by the end of October (as Moody's downgraded the credit rating of the Industrial Bank of Korea), and 559 basis points on December 12, 1997 (having risen from 253 basis points on December 4th, the date on which an IMF US\$55 billion program was announced).

By the fall of 1997, many of the offshore accounts held by banks had lost value, if not become worthless, while foreigners and Koreans alike were trying to get their funds out of Korea and the crisis became full-blown.[29]

By the beginning of December, gross reserves were fast reaching zero, and the Korean authorities approached the IMF (after a period during which all three presidential candidates said they would never do so).[30] Korean *chaebol* had become significantly overleveraged, with many having debt to equity ratios well above five. That many banks had borrowed in foreign currency and lent in Korean won made matters worse.[31] When the won was finally allowed to depreciate, more borrowers were unable to service their debts and rescuing the banks became a major part of the reform package needed to stabilize the economy and improve growth prospects.

Once in crisis, however, the South Korean authorities acted forcefully. Accepting an IMF program, NPLs were rapidly transferred to asset management companies, and chaebol deleveraged. Interconnected lending was prohibited, and financial regulation reformed.

---

[29] The crisis could probably have been prevented as late as the summer of 1997 had appropriate policy actions been taken at that time. Kim Kiwhan believes that if Parliament had passed a financial legislative package that went before it on November 16, 1997, even then the full-blown crisis might have been averted (Kim, 2006, p. 21).

[30] The triggering event for acceptance of the IMF program in December 2007 immediately prior to the election was that reserves were literally exhausted. After months during which all 3 presidential candidates insisted that they would not accept support from the IMF, gross reserves fell to zero by December 3, and the Korean government would have been forced to default had not IMF support been forthcoming. It is often forgotten that the IMF team had virtually no time in which to devise a program, as they had not been able to meet with their Korean counterparts until very shortly before the crisis.

[31] The interest rates in some Southeast Asian countries were below those in Korea, so banks were borrowing in Thailand, Indonesia, and other countries to lend in Korean won at a higher interest rate. When the crises came in Southeast Asia, and currencies were devalued, the banks lost heavily.

In South Korea's case, real GDP fell by 6.7 percent for the full year 1998, but began recovering in the middle of the year. In 1999, real GDP growth was about 10 percent, so that economic activity had reattained its pre-crisis level. Growth continued in subsequent years. Hence, while the crisis was costly, the willingness of the government to address problems in the financial sector (and the chaebol) promptly enabled a sharp recovery and resumption of growth.[32]

LESSONS FOR THE FINANCIAL SECTOR FROM JAPAN (AND KOREA)

As already indicated, by the 1980s, Japan had long since joined the group of advanced industrial countries, after three decades of economic success and rapid growth.[33] During that decade, real estate and other asset prices had risen rapidly. At one point in the late 1980s, the market-based value of Japan's real estate was reported to be greater than that of all American real estate! Price-earnings ratios in the stock market had been rising almost continuously during the period of rapid growth. Capital account liberalization in the first half of the 1980s, which had been expected to lead to capital outflows, in fact was followed by capital inflows so that the yen appreciated, obscuring some of what might have been inflationary pressure on goods prices in addition to the bubble.

By the early 1990s, however, real estate and other asset prices started plummeting. Economic activity slowed, and bank assets, which included real estate and equity as well as other loans, fell. Throughout the 1990s, efforts to stimulate the economy were undertaken. Economic policy in Japan in the 1990s seems to have been predicated on the assumption that a resumption of economic growth would take place and that in itself would enable debtors to resume servicing their debts to the banks. Neither resumed economic growth nor a sufficient reduction in NPLs happened.[34]

There were repeated stimulus packages, and some stimulus was clearly necessary.[35] But in large part, the government's policy toward the banks

---

[32] In Ito's view, Korea's crisis was one of liquidity only, whereas other Asian crises were solvency crises. See Ito (2007), p. 38.

[33] As indicated above, Japan had joined the OECD in 1964.

[34] Much bank lending was connected within the same *keiretsu*. The extent of evergreening was almost surely underestimated. See Hoshi (2001).

[35] In 1997, economic activity was rising, and the government increased consumption taxes. That was quickly followed by another downturn in economic activity.

(where there was clearly inadequate equity) was one of forebearance, except in the cases of clearly insolvent institutions. Until 1997, this period was characterized primarily by stagnation and relative monetary ease, although 1996 saw growth of over 5 percent following a large fiscal stimulus package in 1994. But despite several (relatively small) programs to help the banks, nonperforming loans on the banks' books continued to increase.[36]

After November 1997, Japan entered into a crisis phase for the following sixteen months. Credit became tight. Recapitalization of the banks, with 8.7 trillion yen (about 1 percent of total bank assets at the time), was undertaken in 1998, but that seems to have been far below the amounts needed for adequate recapitalization. The banks were again recapitalized in March 1999 and credit flows resumed, but many of those flows were directed toward enterprises that were themselves in difficulty, often at the direction of the government.

Hoshi and Kashyap (2009, p. 29) estimate that between 1992 and 2005, the Japanese banks wrote off about 96 trillion yen of loans, or about 19 percent of GDP, and that efforts to fund the banks fell far short of needed magnitudes. While there was some recovery early in 2000, and the Japanese government's position was that the 1999 measures would jump-start the economy, stagnation once again set in and NPLs began increasing again, with capital erosion following. Hoshi and Kashyap (2009) show that whereas NPLs resulting from the 1980s bubble were mostly removed from the banks' books by 2000, difficulties in small and medium enterprises (SMEs) starting at that same time resulted in rising NPLs once again. In the boom of the late 1980s, lending to these SMEs had accelerated, and as deflation and stagnation continued, more and more SMEs were unable to service their debts, thus giving rise to a new spate of NPLs.

The Financial Services Agency (FSA) was established in 1998, and two large banks were resolved in that year. That was an important milestone in the restructuring of the banks. But it was not until 2003 that the new FSA seems to have been able to insist upon the banks' write-offs of NPLs and recapitalization. Thereafter, the NPL problem diminished, and by 2005 it is estimated that credit flows had resumed. The evergreening of loans by the banks kept

---

[36] Until 1998, public reporting of nonperforming loans was undertaken only by large banks, and the definitions of nonperforming loans were very loose, with only those loans to failed enterprises or on which there had been no payments for more than 6 months were recorded. There were also other changes that enabled banks to show more favorable balance sheets up to that time, including permitting banks to record assets at either cost or market value. After 1998, reporting became standard, and the criteria for NPLs were tightened. See Hoshi and Kashyap (2009) for an account.

loss-making companies alive, but simultaneously reduced the supply of credit for new firms (Caballero, Hoshi and Kashyap, 2008).

Hoshi and Kashyap (2009, p. 21) conclude that

"The main cost of allowing the banks to operate with a capital shortage was not a prolonged credit crunch. Rather the undercapitalization limited the banks' willingness to recognize losses and they took extraordinary steps to cover up their condition and in doing so retarded growth in Japan."

For present purposes of understanding lessons, probably the most important features of ultimately successful policies were the establishment of asset management corporations (which took toxic assets off the balance sheets of the banks), and the nationalization and restructuring of large failed banks.[37]

A major lesson from the contrast in the Korean and Japanese experiences comes from the speed and determination with which the authorities addressed issues in the financial sector. In the Korean case, a "bad bank", the Korean Asset Management Corporation, was created to assume the toxic assets in the banking system, *chaebol* were required to deleverage and separate their banking activities from their production activities. By contrast, in Japan, until 2003 the authorities' measures were largely of the "too little, too late" variety.[38]

Some observers have noted that a significant contrast between the rapid Korean action and the tardy Japanese response was the result of the perceived source of the difficulties. Whereas the Korean authorities were virtually forced by their foreign obligations to react speedily, the fact that the Japanese difficulties were seen as almost entirely domestic made a decisive and rapid response far more difficult.

Lessons from the Japanese experience are several. A first, and perhaps the most important, one is that an undercapitalized banking system can retard, if not entirely stifle, an incipient recovery even when fiscal policy is expansionary. Permitting evergreening of lending is a disastrous policy. Second, efforts by banks (and acquiescence by the government) to hide their difficulties not only delay recovery but create uncertainty about the financial system as a

---

[37] Among other problems, the banks had recorded "deferred tax assets" as part of their capital base. These "assets" were the tax deductions the banks might (if profitable) use in the future once they became profitable again, because they had recorded losses. These were sizeable and of course were not fungible, and were usable only against profits, which the banks did not have.

[38] It is unclear how much equity banks really had. Hoshi and Mishkin have shown that much of the reported capital should not have been treated as equity. Moreover, had banks recognized nonperforming loans and charged them against assets, reported equity would have been considerably smaller.

whole.[39] Third, unless measures to restore healthy banks are sufficiently large, they do not significantly contribute to the resolution of the problem. In the Japanese case, the NPLs written off by the banks are estimated to have equaled 19 percent of GDP, while the largest amount allocated to support the banks was about 3 percent of GDP. Fourth and finally, when banks continue to roll over NPLs, they are starving the potential new entrants (especially small and medium enterprises) of credit, and hence reducing growth.

The "lost decade" of the 1990s in Japan was marked by successive stimuli and financial interventions. But most of these were too little, too late.[40] Taken alone, the Japanese experience would not conclusively suggest a lesson. But across the other crisis Asian economies, strong actions taken initially were associated with a more rapid and stronger recovery, and almost certainly smaller losses.

The South Korean response was the strongest, and the trough was reached by mid-1998. The reduction in leverage, the removal of toxic assets, and other measures recounted above were sufficient so that recovery started within six months and was strong.

For each of the other Asian countries, the response was slower and weaker, and the upturn was later and less rapid. Indonesia, with the weakest and slowest response in large part because of political upheaval, took the longest time for recovery to resume.

There is a general lesson that immediate credible strong action (with regard to removal of toxic assets, recapitalization of banks and deleveraging of firms, and to fiscal stimulus) is economic, both in the sense that government expenditures and losses in the financial system would be smaller, and in that the length and the severity of the downturn is more limited, while the upturn not only comes sooner but is stronger.

The Korean experience reinforces the Japanese lessons. Although the crisis was triggered by difficulties within the banks that were intensified by the exchange rate regime, the crisis was financial once the exchange rate had been allowed to depreciate and float. It was already seen that the underlying problem had been a failure of the financial system to develop commensurately with the needs of an increasingly complex modern

---

[39] Hoshi and Kashyap (2009) report that in 2002, when the banks reported increased equity, six independent financial analysts all reported that the same banks had negative equity.

[40] Hoshi and Kashyap (2009) point out that, although Japanese politicians felt politically constrained as to the amounts they could spend to attempt to restore the banking system, the actual amounts voted in by Parliament amounted cumulatively to 3 percent of GDP. This compares with the 60 percent of GDP increase in Japanese government indebtedness that resulted from repeated fiscal stimulus efforts. It therefore seems reasonable to conclude that larger expenditures in the early years of the banking difficulties might have led to lower overall expenditures.

economy. This was connected to the problems of the chaebol. They had been heroes of Korea's hugely successful growth experience, but had accepted government restrictions and had their own banks each financing much of the needs of the individual groups.

The spillover from the exchange regime to the financial situation is evident from the evolution of the economy as detailed earlier. First, in the runup to the crisis, short-term foreign debt was about seven times Korean foreign exchange reserves. The authorities attempted to defend the currency initially (after the Thai crisis was under way) but simply were unable to continue doing so.

The exchange rate was depreciating rapidly, and the authorities tightened the money supply, including a sharp rise in the interest rate. While this stabilized the currency, it made the plight of the banks, already hit by a mismatch between their loans (denominated in won) and their liabilities (denominated in foreign exchange), still worse. The *chaebol* were highly leveraged, averaging about 400 percent debt relative to equity, so rising interest rates (when there had already been a buildup of nonperforming loans) made their situations worse and increased the banks' NPLs.[41]

During the runup to, and in, the crisis, a factor that apparently intensified difficulties in many of the Asian economies, and certainly in South Korea, is that market participants quickly learned that earlier information they had received had been inaccurate. (Cho, 2009, p. 19). Cho points out that, even in 2008 when the Koreans held high reserves, "The past record of credibility of the Korean government's statistics on the amount of total foreign debt and usable foreign reserve did not help in gaining full credibility for the government guarantee." (p. 19).

LESSONS FOR POST-CRISIS POLICY

Perhaps the most important conclusion that can be drawn from crises in many countries is that delays in recognizing and confronting the difficulties in the financial sector are costly. Denial by officials may be understandable, but when the measures taken are timid relative to the magnitude of the problem, or when they are undertaken after significant delays, the costs of the cleanup mount.[42]

---

[41] The authorities also instituted blanket deposit insurance for a period of 3 years. It was withdrawn at the end of 2000. This seems to have been essential to stop runs on banks after some merchant banks had been closed early in the crisis, leading depositors in other banks to wonder how long their banks would remain open.

[42] Korea's reforms were far-reaching and undertaken rapidly. Reforms included the reduction of trade barriers and promotion of FDI inflows; improved corporate governance measures especially in the *chaebol*; recapitalizing the financial system and removing NPLs; creation of a new financial regulatory framework; privatization of many state-owned enterprises; and removal of some labor market regulations. See OECD (2000, p. 29 ff).

The credibility of the authorities, the transparency of the situation, and the measures taken are all crucial. If it is widely believed that the authorities do not fully recognize the difficulties, or that they are taking only half-hearted measures to change the situation, policies are unlikely to succeed.[43]

Moreover, in almost all crisis situations, the crisis happens because of underlying weaknesses in the economic policy framework and economic structure. It is now generally recognized in Korea that the cleanup of the banking system, and the reduction in chaebol-linked bank lending, were essential.[44] But in the first weeks of December after the initial IMF program, capital outflows continued, as there were considerable doubts about the determination of the newly elected government to address the issues sufficiently. It is noteworthy that, despite considerable speculative pressure, the economies of Hong Kong, Taiwan, and Singapore survived without a crisis.[45] They all had stronger economic policies during the period, reflected in many ways including large foreign exchange reserves and relatively low short term debt and took strong measures as soon as pressures on their currencies and finances were evident.

It is also notable that growth can resume fairly quickly when strong measures are taken. Most forecasts of post-crisis growth in the Asian countries were unduly pessimistic (with the probable exception of Indonesia).[46] Once the situation was stabilized, growth rapidly resumed.

For emerging markets, further lessons derive from the necessity to maintain consistency between policies toward exchange rates and monetary and

---

[43] This seems to have been the case initially in Korea. Even after the IMF program was announced in early December, large capital outflows continued. It was not until the major private banks committed to rolling over their loans to Korean entities and pledged some new money that the downward pressure and massive outflows ceased. The magnitude of the new pledges was evidently sufficient to restore credibility, whereas the initial IMF package had been insufficient to do so in light of the magnitude of private debt.

[44] The Korean authorities went far beyond the measures discussed here, as they took measures to improve corporate governance, regulation of the banks, the transparency of accounts, and addressed a number of other issues. These measures may or may not have been essential (although they were almost certainly beneficial to the economy) but they certainly reinforced the credibility of the government's commitment to strengthen and restore the financial system.

[45] These economies were all threatened, however, and the responses of the authorities were clearly crucial in preventing crisis. How one should classify the Philippines is questionable. For a considerable period of time, it appeared that the Philippines would confront a crisis. But policies were adjusted with the support of the IMF, and an outright crisis was avoided.

[46] The same much-better-than-expected recovery has taken place in other countries where the far-reaching cleanups have been undertaken. Turkey after 2001 and Russia after the 1998 crisis are prominent examples.

fiscal policies. Maintenance of adequate foreign exchange reserve levels, and guarding against significant mismatches in the currency denomination of assets and liabilities (of the financial system and of large borrowers) are also vital.

But perhaps the strongest lesson from all of the crisis situations is the urgent necessity of restoring the financial system by recapitalizing the banks, removing the NPLs from bank portfolios, and enabling the resumption of the flow of credit. Fiscal stimulus may be necessary and can provide a temporary boost (as it did in Japan in 1996), but if the financial system remains crippled, recovery is not sustainable. Growth can resume before credit starts expanding, but sustaining that growth requires a healthy financial system.

REFERENCES

Caballero, RJ, T Hoshi and AK Kashyap (2008). Zombie Lending and Depressed Restructuring in Japan. *American Economic Review*, 98(5), pp. 1943–1977.

Cho, YJ (2009). The Role of State Intervention in the Financial Sector: Crisis Prevention, Containment, and Resolution. Paper presented at ADB Conference on Global Financial Crisis, Tokyo.

Edwards, S (2003). Exchange Rate Regimes. In *Economic and Financial Crises in Emerging Market Economies*, Feldstein, M (ed.), pp. 31–92. Chicago.University of Chicago Press.

Fukao, M (2003). Financial Sector Profitability and Double-Gearing. In *Structural Impediments to Growth in Japan*. Blomstrom, M, J Corbett, F Hayashi and AK Kashyap (eds.), pp. 9–35. Chicago: University of Chicago Press.

Ghosh, A, C Christofides, J Kim, L Papi, U Ramakrishnan, A Thomas and J Zalduendo (2005). *The Design of IMF-Supported Programs*, IMF Occasional Paper No. 241, International Monetary Fund, Washington, D. C.

Glick, R and MM Spiegel (2009). *Asia and the Global Financial Crisis*, Federal Reserve Bank of San Francisco, San Francisco.

Hahm, J-H and FS Mishkin (2009). Causes of the Korean Financial Crisis: Lessons for Policy. Korea Development Institute.

Hoshi, T (2001). What Happened to Japanese Banks? *Monetary and Economic Studies*, 19(1), pp. 1–29.

Hoshi, T and A Kashyap (2009). Will the U.S. Bank Recapitalization Succeed? Eight Lessons from Japan. NBER Working Paper No. 14401.

Hoshi, T and A Kashyap (2004). Japan's Financial Crisis and Economic Stagnation. *Journal of Economic Perspectives*, 18(1), pp. 3–26, includes a good growth-finance link statement, citing the paper by Caballero, Hoshi and Kashyap (2003). Zombie Lending and Depressed Restructuring in Japan, Working paper, University of Chicago, may be in AER December 2008.

Hoshi, T and A Kashyap (2009). Will the U.S. Bank Recapitalization Succeed? Eight Lessons from Japan. NBER Working Paper NO. 14401, Revised in August 2009.

Hutchison, MM, T Ito and F Westermann (2006). The Great Japanese Stagnation: Lessons for Industrial Countries. In *Japan's Great Stagnation*, Hutchison, M and F Westermann (eds.), pp. 1–32. Cambridge, Massachusetts: MIT Press.

Ito, T (1996). Asian Currency Crisis and the International Monetary Fund, 10 Years Later: Overview. *Asian Economic Policy Review* (2007), Vol. 2, pp. 16–49.

Kashyap, AK (2002). Sorting out Japan's Financial Crisis. *Economic Perspective*, Federal Reserve Bank of Chicago, 4th Quarter, pp. 42–55.

Kim, K (2006). The 1997–98 Korean Financial Crisis: Causes, Policy Response, and Lessons. Paper presented at The High-Level Seminar on Crisis Prevention in Emerging Markets, Singapore, July 10–11.

Krueger, AO (1979). *The Developmental Role of the Foreign Sector and Aid*. Studies in the Modernization of the Republic of Korea, 1945–1975.

Krueger, AO and I Turan (1993). The Politics and Economics of Turkish Policy Reforms in the 1980s. In *Political and Economic Interactions in Economic Policy Reform: Evidence from Eight Countries*, Krueger, AO and RH Bates (eds.), pp. 333–386. Basil Blackwell.

Krueger, AO and J Yoo (2002). Chaebol Capitalism and the Currency-Financial Crisis in Korea. In *Preventing Currency Crises in Emerging Markets*, Edwards, S and J Frenkel (eds.), pp. 601–649. University of Chicago Press.

McKinnon, RI (1973). *Money and Capital in Economic Development*. Brookings Institution, Washington, D.C.

Maddison, A (2003). *The World Economy Historical Statistics*. OECD Development Center Studies, Paris.

Organization for Economic Cooperation and Development (2000). *OECD Economic Surveys: Korea*. OECD: Paris.

Rosenberg, N and LE Birdzell, Jr., (1986). *How the West Grew Rich: The Economic Transformation of the Industrial World*. New York: Basic Books.

Tornell, A, R Ranciere and F Westermann (2003). *Crises and Growth: A Reevaluation*. National Bureau of Economic Research Working Paper 10073.

World Bank (2004). *World Development Report 2005*. Washington, D. C. and New York: World Bank and Oxford University Press.

Yoo, J-H and CW Moon (1999). Korean financial crisis during 1997–98: Causes and Challenges. *Journal of Asian Economics*, Vol. 10, pp. 263–277.

Chapter 8

ECONOMIC POLICY REFORMS IN BRAZIL AND TURKEY

At the turn of the century, Brazil and Turkey both had economies in very serious difficulties. Both had entered into IMF programs, Brazil late in 1999 and Turkey early in 2000. High rates of inflation and other difficulties had led to attacks on the currencies. Each country was unable to borrow sufficiently to finance government borrowing requirements for fiscal deficits and needed rollovers of debt at reasonable interest rates. In each country, pressures eased after the start of each program, but rapidly began mounting again. Both countries' governments had committed to reductions in their fiscal deficits and some tightening of the money supply as part of their programs, but in both cases the authorities were unable fully to carry out their commitments.

Brazil had adopted a "nominal anchor" exchange rate regime in the early 1990s in order to try to bring down the rate of inflation from triple digits. By 1999, the country was forced to float the real. The inflation rate had fallen markedly, but the currency had appreciated in real terms. Turkey had experienced inflation rates above 50 percent in all years in the early 1990s, and adopted a nominal anchor exchange rate as part of the 1999 IMF program. For Turkey, too, adjustments in the exchange rate were far below the realized inflation rates and hence the Turkish lira also had become increasingly overvalued.

By 2001 in the case of Turkey, and 2002 in the case of Brazil, the situation was again becoming critical. In Turkey, there was a full-blown crisis as banks became insolvent (for reasons discussed below) and the inflation rate increasingly outstripped the preannounced changes in the exchange rate. In Brazil, a crisis was building rapidly in the middle of 2002 as elections loomed late in the year. Observers expected Lula to win and thought him unlikely to adhere even to existing fiscal and monetary disciplines.[1] In each country, sovereign indebtedness rose sharply, and spreads on the public debt rose dramatically.

---

[1] See Lapper (2002).

In both countries, the programs adopted in 2001 and 2002 were more far-reaching than their predecessors, addressing some of the underlying problems that had led to such severe difficulties. In the Turkish case, the domestic banks were insolvent, as extension of credits (many mandated at low interest rates by the government) had mushroomed and bank equity was largely wiped out. In Brazil's case, the inflation rate was rising but, above all, there was concern for the likely course of monetary and fiscal policy after the elections and anticipated change of government at the end of that year.

In each program, cutbacks in fiscal deficits and tighter monetary policies were adopted. And in each case, there were many doubters questioning whether the programs were realistic and whether they could succeed. But there the similarity ended. In Brazil, the major challenge was convincing the markets that fiscal and monetary policies would be maintained in a new government so that Brazilian debt and debt service would be sustainable, while simultaneously bringing the rate of inflation down and enabling sustainable growth. In Turkey, a major challenge was to bring the banking system back to health, but that, too, entailed reduced fiscal deficits and tighter monetary policy to bring down inflation and to reduce the burden of the debt to a sustainable level. These changes were necessary to enable the resumption of growth.

From the start of their respective programs in 2001 and 2002, both the Brazilian and the Turkish economies performed well, as will be documented below. Even during the global recession of 2007–2009, the two economies were less adversely affected than they had earlier been in international recessions, and their recovery was appreciably quicker. Turkey, by 2010, had the highest rate of growth of any European economy, while Brazilian economic growth was strong and a main concern was overheating. Other key indicators were also greatly improved: debt ratios had fallen markedly, fiscal deficits were reduced, and inflation lower.

The Turkish economy has in many ways been transformed, as inflation reached single digits while growth accelerated. In Brazil's case, a looming crisis in 2002 was nipped in the bud: commentators and analysts discussing the evolution of the global economy after 2000 seldom even list Brazil as having had a crisis in the 21st century.

There are several key lessons. First, tighter fiscal and monetary policy may in fact be followed by more rapid economic growth.[2] Second, even when the situation is dire, appropriate economic policy reforms can fundamentally alter

---

[2] There are many other cases, including rich countries such as Canada and Australia, in which fiscal consolidation has been followed by accelerated growth.

the economic prospects of an economy. But, third, economic policy reforms are crucial to alter significantly the trajectory of an economy caught in a downward spiral of rising inflation, slowing growth, and a trajectory of increasing pressure on the exchange rate and of rising spreads on outstanding government debt.[3] These lessons are spelled out in more detail in the final section of this chapter.

In the next section, the evolution of the Turkish economy from the 1999 crisis to 2010 is analyzed, while section 3 covers the behavior of the Brazilian economy from 1999 to 2010. Section 4 summarizes the state of the two economies at the time of writing, focusing largely on their successes and the role of the IMF in these two situations.

TURKEY: CRISES AND RESOLUTION[4]

From the end of the Second World War until the 1990s, the Turkish economy had experienced an above average rate of economic growth, but with high macroeconomic volatility. The growth rate had also trended downward, with more frequent periods of macroeconomic slowdown and crisis, and shorter periods of resumption of (slower) growth. Periods of rapid growth had been followed by slowdown and usually crisis, with IMF programs to support stabilization in 1960, 1970, 1976, 1980, and 1994. Inflation in the CPI had averaged well over 50 percent annually during the 1980s and 1990s, and had dipped below 35 percent only in a few years after the macroeconomic crisis in 1979–80.[5] The inflation rate had not fallen below 50 percent after 1988. In 1994, inflation (producer prices) reached an annual rate of 119

---

[3] A fourth lesson that emerges from the study of crises more generally is that the costs of delay can be quite substantial. These include a longer period of slow growth or even decline in real GDP and higher interest rates on government debt (both because the authorities were incurring new debt and because higher spreads were necessary for debt rollovers). In many cases, fiscal deficits are also widening as policy makers attempt to offset sluggish growth through increased government spending while tax receipts are falling. See the discussion in Chapter 7.

[4] The following account provides a very brief overview of the Turkish economy and the events leading up to the 2001 IMF program. For particulars of the 1999 program and the chronology of events in the lead-up to the 2001 crisis, see Van Rijkeghem and Ucer (2005).

[5] Many of the 1980 reforms were undertaken early in the year before the government approached the IMF for support. The 1980 crisis resolution framework was noteworthy because earlier policies of import-substitution were dismantled, and the exchange rate regime was altered to allow maintenance of the real exchange rate. Despite the failure of the program to bring about lasting macroeconomic stability, it did enable a period of rapid expansion of exports and a resulting structural shift in the economy. That shift, in turn, contributed significantly to the Turkish growth potential that was unleashed when macroeconomic stability was attained after 2001.

percent; an IMF-supported program was started, but quickly went off track, although the annual rate of inflation slowed somewhat to a range of 70–90 percent. After falling 5.5 percent in 1994, the real GDP growth rate was over 7 percent for the next three years, but then dropped to 3.1 percent in 1998. By 1999, the country was in crisis, with real GDP dropping 4.5 percent and inflation nonetheless remained over 50 percent in 1998 and 1999.[6]

With high inflation, most depositors in banks sought and received dollar-denominated accounts. The Turkish banks, however, did not cover their dollar liabilities and kept open positions. This was a significant factor undermining the banking system when adjustments had to be made (see the numbers below).

If one examined the Turkish budget, the fiscal deficit seemed small. However, since the early 1980s, the Turkish government had mandated that the state banks lend to a number of government-sponsored activities (such as a fund for financing of residential construction and funds to lend to state economic enterprises incurring losses). While the central government budget showed a primary surplus of 3.5 percent of GDP, funding by banks for government-sponsored enterprises was about 13 percent of GDP.[7] The state banks, in turn, were entering the market to borrow to roll over their borrowings and had to pay higher interest rates than those offered by private banks. They also relied heavily on the Central Bank's money market facilities.[8] After a devastating earthquake in August 1999, interest rates rose to 115 percent on rolled over debt (with inflation around 60 percent), and the authorities approached the government for an IMF-supported program of reforms.

As of the end of 2000, the open foreign exchange position of the Turkish banks was 3,300 percent of capital, the accumulated duty losses of the state banks were 3,400 percent of their capital, and the short-term liabilities of the state banks represented 4,100 percent of capital.[9]

---

[6] All data in this paragraph are from International Monetary Fund (2004).

[7] Van Rijckeghem and Ucer (2005, p. 15). The banks were in effect printing money for the government, while the government books superficially appeared to be relatively sound.

[8] "Duty losses" had been incurred and were financed since the early 1980s. In 1980, there had been a major financial crisis, and reforms had been undertaken including the adoption of a more realistic exchange rate (adjusted periodically for the inflation differential with the rest of the world), and a sharp reduction in the fiscal deficit incurred by the government. This spurred several years of high growth rates but the government began resorting to duty loss financing to enable desired expenditures on infrastructure and other items. See Krueger and Aktan (1992) for a description.

[9] Moghadam (2005, p. 54).

The 1999 IMF program's central objective was to reduce inflation and restore growth. This was to be achieved by adoption of a nominal anchor exchange rate which was to guide expectations as to future inflation rates and by a simultaneous tightening of the fiscal accounts.[10] That, in turn, was to be supported by a number of structural reforms, and a gradual restructuring of the banks and their supervision.[11]

The nominal anchor exchange rate, which set forth planned adjustments to the exchange rate to accommodate anticipated (falling) inflation, was chosen as the basic policy tool to bring down both inflationary expectations and nominal and real interest rates. This latter was seen as essential to avoid a rapid build-up of debt as rollovers were undertaken and new financing needed even with the stipulated reductions in fiscal targets.

For several months, the program appeared to be working. Interest rates fell from over 70 percent to around 40 percent, the government passed a budget entailing a significant reduction in the fiscal deficit, and the inflation rate fell from its peak of over 100 percent. However, while the inflation rate fell, it fell by significantly less than was envisaged in the program.

This built in a fundamental weakness. Not only was the real exchange rate appreciating (by the differential between the actual Turkish inflation rate and the planned rate relative to the world's) but the prospect of real appreciation led to a high rate of return to foreigners investing in Turkish lira. As long as the nominal anchor exchange rate policy was maintained and the inflation differential led to high real interest rates denominated in foreign exchange, foreign investors could expect a handsome return on their investments in Turkey.

Thus, for a short while after the IMF program had been launched in December 1999, things appeared superficially to be proceeding reasonably smoothly. But rapid expansion of credit, a widening current account deficit both because of the increasing overvaluation of the exchange rate and because of the rapidly rising price of oil, and loosening fiscal policy all set in. The global recession made things worse. Moreover, some of the program's targets (such as closing some of the extra budgetary funds and increases in some taxes) were missed, even when exogenous events had not contributed to

---

[10] See IMF Letter of Intent (1999) for a full description of the program.

[11] Banking supervision had been the responsibility of the Treasury, which resulted in a serious conflict of interest as Treasury officials were to roll over debt and supervise the banks. The situation was further complicated by connected lending both to politicians and to others. The 1999 program envisaged the formation of an independent banking supervisory authority, which did happen but which took time to be legislated and implemented.

their delay. The third review under the IMF program was not completed. Bank purchases of government paper continued, with one large bank (Demirbank) financing its purchases on the overnight market.

Until November 2000, the economy limped along. The inflation rate fell (and was 32.7 percent for the year as a whole for the wholesale price index), real GDP was at least growing slowly after a drop of 4.7 percent in 1999, and the average treasury bill rate had fallen from 95 percent in 1999 to 39 percent in 2000 (although it was rising toward the end of the year). However, the current account balance as a percentage of GDP went from a negative 0.7 percent in 1999 to minus 4.9 percent in 2000, and concerns about the position of the banks intensified.

Starting in November 2000, the situation deteriorated rapidly.[12] Privatization revenues had fallen well below program targets. First steps toward better supervision of banks led to closures, jailing of bankers, and greatly increased uncertainty as to the future of the system. In September 2000, a revised banking law strengthened aspects of supervision and regulation, including elements such as limiting connected lending, setting foreign currency exposure rules, and new accounting standards. In addition, the independent Banking Regulation and Supervision Agency (BRSA) was established (although it was obviously going to take time for these provisions to make a significant difference).

Despite the completion of the second and third reviews under the IMF program, the net domestic asset targets had to be breached to supply liquidity to the domestic banking system, and foreign exchange reserves fell by $8 billion in the last two months of 2000. An effort to restore credibility was made in December, with additional reform measures and new targets announced by Prime Minister Ecevit, and the approval by the IMF of an additional $10 billion loan through its Supplemental Reserve Facility (SRF). Among the reforms, which were enacted but did not have time to take effect, was a new banking law, which guaranteed deposits, made a number of loan provisions tax deductible, and contained other provisions designed to tide over the banks until reforms were effected.

Markets were calmed, whether because of the strengthened reforms or IMF support, and the large foreign exchange outflows that had taken place were almost entirely reversed by early January. Interest rates fell to the low 50 percent range, and the IMF came for its fifth review in mid-January, with approval by the Executive Board early in February. Even so, the banks were

---

[12] For a blow-by-blow account of events in the November–February period, see Van Rijckeghem and Ucer (2005), Chapters V and VI.

fragile: as already seen, foreign currency open positions of the banking system as of December 2000 were 3,300 percent of capital, accumulated duty losses in the state banks were 3,400 percent of capital, and short-term liabilities of the state banks were 4,100 percent of capital.

In February, a political eruption against the background of confusion as to the direction of economic policy resulted in a full-fledged crisis. During a long meeting of the critically-important National Security Council, an argument erupted between President Sezer and Prime Minister Ecevit in which it was reported that the President had thrown a book at the Prime Minister. Political uncertainty intensified, and with it, increased difficulty in rolling over debt, increasing dollarization and shifts of funds out of Turkish banks with associated foreign exchange reserve losses, and rising interest rates.[13] In late February, a two-day banking holiday was decreed, but the interest rate fell only to 700 percent and capital outflows continued. Finally, it was announced that the nominal anchor policy was being abandoned and the TL was allowed to float. The next morning, the TL depreciated from TL687,000 per U.S. dollar to TL960,000 per U.S. dollar. The IMF publicly supported the float. However, Turkish foreign debt was downgraded by the rating agencies and outflows continued. The Central Bank was caught between needing to fund the state banks and simultaneously to avoiding bank runs. Overnight borrowing by the state banks had risen to TL6.4 quadrillion in mid-March from TL2.4 quadrillion late in 2000.[14]

For purposes of this analysis, the causes of failure of the 1999–2000 IMF program are not at issue. Some would argue that the nominal anchor exchange rate policy was at fault (although an exit strategy was built in). Others would focus on the lack of credibility of Turkish policies in light of political issues and Turkey's past record. Still others would point to the weakness of the banking system, and rising Turkish debt. Certainly the long history of volatile macroeconomic policy and high inflation reinforced doubts as to the credibility of the government's commitments.

All of these factors, and others, contributed. Regardless of the relative contributions of each, as of early 2001, the Turkish economy was clearly in deep crisis, and the outlook was poor. The fact that inflation and fiscal deficits had been high for a long time did not provide confidence that the government could adhere to a sufficiently rigorous program. But even if the government

---

[13] The overnight interest rate reached 4500 percent simple. Van Rijckegham and Ucer (2005, p. 85).

[14] Van Rijckegnham and Ucer (2005, p.85).

was initially willing to adhere to such a program, political fragility (not only between the President and the Prime Minister but also between the parties in a coalition government) made the likelihood of serious changes even more unlikely.

The situation was indeed dire by February 2001. Inflation had accelerated and reached more than 100 percent. Turkish debt was rising alarmingly, as reflected among other things, in the downgrading by the rating agencies and the refusal of creditors to roll over debt. The fiscal deficit had fallen beginning with the 1999 program, and the primary surplus actually reached 3.0 percent of GDP in 2000, but net debt was rising and the government's net debt to GDP ratio reached 93.9 percent in 2001. With high interest rates (the average Treasury bill rate in 2001 was 96 percent), and GDP falling in 2001,[15] it was clear that debt was not sustainable without significant changes.

Although the coalition government remained in power, personnel were changed in March 2001, with Kemal Dervis as Minister for Economic Affairs and the Treasury leading the economics team. As a well-known World Bank official, he had much greater credibility than his predecessors.[16]

In May, a new reform program was set forth.[17] It focused on reducing inflation, achieving debt sustainability,[18] and restoring growth. The measures envisaged were far reaching. Fiscal adjustment was to go further. The Central Bank was to introduce inflation targeting gradually. Financial reforms went much further, with a restructuring of the state banks, a closure of the SDIF (duty loss) banks, increased capital requirements for private banks, and enhanced asset management regulations.[19]

From that program onward, major and far-reaching reforms continued through at least the middle of the decade. Not only was there an increase in

---

[15] Real GDP fell by 7.3 percent in 2001.

[16] See Boulton (2001).

[17] The Stand-By of December 1999 was followed by a Supplemental Reserve Facility Loan of December 2000, a Standby of February 2002 and a Standby of May 2005. This last program expired in May 2008 (See Annex I, p. 3 of IMF, 2010).

[18] See Klingen (2005) for an analysis of debt sustainability prior to and following the 2001 crisis.

[19] See Josefson and Marston (2005) for a detailed account. To give an idea of the extent of restructuring, the number of branches of two big state banks, Halk and Ziraat was reduced from 2,478 in March 2001 to 1,658 by December 2003, while the number of personnel was reduced fromn 59,831 to 29,787. One large state bank was closed. The government injected about 13 percent of GDP into the state banks (Josefson and Marston, p. 55). It is estimated that the total cost to the government of bank restructuring was 32 percent of GDP. Nonperforming loans as a percent of total loans in the private banks fell from 27.6 in 2001 to 6.5 in 2003.

the primary surplus which was then sustained until the global crisis of 2007, but tax reforms and changes in the fiscal system significantly improved the quality of government expenditures and revenues. Some large subsidy programs were reduced or abandoned, civil servants' compensation was restrained for several years, some infrastructure financing was shifted to public-private partnership (PPP) financing, and much more. The BRSA undertook the serious and needed reforms in regulation and supervision of the banking system, although not without political and court challenges. Monetary policy tightened, and after several years, inflation targeting could be adopted. A major program of privatization was undertaken, which significantly reduced the role of state economic enterprises in the economy.[20]

There is still much that needs to be reformed in Turkey, but the economy and economic structure have been truly transformed. As stated by the *Economist* (2010):

"...ten years on, Turkey stands transformed. The economy suffered badly in the global recession of 2009, but over the previous five years it had been unusually vigorous, and it has bounced back so quickly this year that it is likely to grow faster than...almost all other European countries....[Turkey] is on the verge of acquiring an investment-grade credit rating, inflation is in single figures, and the government has been able to dump the IMF" (p. 3).

For present purposes, what is significant is that while the reforms were drastic (and much needed), and the considerable uncertainty that they would succeed, they were immediately successful. Fiscal tightening did not lead to a drop in the rate of economic growth. Almost from the start there was an acceleration in the rate of economic growth, as real GDP grew by 7.8 percent in 2002, and an annual average of 6.5 percent in the following eight years — a rate much higher than had been realized in any period of equal length in the preceding three decades. Inflation began dropping with the rate of inflation in producer prices falling to 25 percent in 2003 and reaching a single-digit 5.9 percent in 2005. Nominal interest rates fell sharply with the nominal Treasury bill rate falling from 99 percent in 2001 to 44 percent by 2003 and continuing its decline thereafter. By 2008, the real interest rate on public debt had fallen to 2.8 percent. Meanwhile, the debt/GDP ratio fell from 91 percent of GDP in 2001 to 70 percent in 2003 and 37 percent of GDP by 2007.[21]

---

[20] See OECD (2006), Table 1.1, p. 23 for a concise list of 22 "main economic reforms".
[21] Data in this paragraph are from IMF (2004), IMF (2010) and Moghadam (2005).

As summarized by the OECD

"The recovery from the 2001 crisis has been impressive. Over the 2002–2005 period, output increased by a third...annual inflation fell steadily, reaching single digits in 2004 for the first time in three decades, while sound fiscal and monetary policies improved confidence and reduced risk premia..." (OECD, 2006, p. 11).

Although reforms lost momentum with the global financial crisis, until that time economic performance, and continuing reforms, were impressive. During the crisis, Turkey's banking system remained sound, debt indicators rose only gradually, and while the fiscal deficit increased, it did so within moderate limits.

Taking the first six years after the start of the 2001 reform program, Turkish performance was impressive by any standard. After dropping in 2001, real GDP grew by 6.2, 5.3, 9.4, 8.4 and 6.9 percent in the years from 2002 to 2006. Only in 2009 did real GDP fall (by 4.7 percent) during the financial crisis, despite the sharp drop in real GDP in Turkey's trading partners. The rebound was much more rapid than had been anticipated and, as already pointed out, Turkish growth accelerated quickly.

BRAZIL: CRISIS DEFUSED AND ACCELERATED GROWTH

While the reforms in Turkey were taken largely in response to the crisis and the outcome led to a marked improvement in fundamentals, sustainability of growth, and greater stability in macroeconomics, the Brazilian story is one which was very similar until 2002, but then in which crisis was imminent and averted in 2002 after fairly good adherence to a Fund program that started in 1999. Reforms were undertaken thereafter, but the main characteristic of change contrasted with earlier periods was the sustained adherence to more realistic macroeconomic policies. By the middle of the decade, growth had accelerated and appeared sustainable and the inflation rate and debt indicators had fallen markedly. Brazil represents a case of successful crisis prevention.

Brazil had a history of very high inflation until the early 1990s. A series of stop-go cycles had taken place prior to the 1990s, in all of which control of inflation (which had been triple and even quadriple digit) had been the primary objective. The usual pattern had been that a new set of reforms (the most recent had been a change in 1986 to the "Cruzado Plan") was announced and implemented initially with a drop in the inflation rate. Rapidly, however, the program was relaxed and the rate of price increase accelerated again. After the 1986 reforms, for example, the annual inflation rate fell from 229 percent in

1985 to 140 percent in 1986 and then accelerated again, reaching a high of 2,704 percent in 1990.[22]

The 1994 reforms were again aimed at greatly reducing the inflation rate, and were based on a "real plan" in which the intended rate of inflation would be announced, and the real depreciated only by a preannounced rate equal to the inflation target. This started after an initial devaluation to a level that was judged to be a realistic real exchange rate. The "nominal anchor" was followed, but actual inflation rates exceeded their preannounced target rates by significant amounts. The inflation rate fell significantly, from 2,075 percent in 1994 to 966 percent in l995, but then reached single digits. But Brazilian fiscal and current account deficits increased markedly while high interest rates induced capital inflows. Public debt was growing rapidly and increasingly linked to the exchange rate and the rate of interest. With the Asian crisis, doubts increased about the sustainability of the Brazilian monetary and fiscal policy, including the nominal anchor exchange rate. After President Cardoso was elected to a second term in October 1998, a set of measures was adopted including a reduction in the fiscal deficit, curbing the growth of public debt and a series of structural reforms, supported by an IMF program. The crawling peg exchange rate was, however, maintained.

For a variety of reasons (such as the failure of Congress to enact the fiscal measures), pressures on the currency again grew quickly. The crawling peg was abandoned early in 1999 after serious losses of reserves and a sharp depreciation of the currency. The IMF program was renegotiated and the fiscal targets for 1999 and 2000 were reached. Although public debt remained about the same relative to GDP after the new program, the share of debt linked to foreign exchange and the interest rate increased. But adherence to the IMF program and the implementation of reform policies (including, later in the year, inflation targeting and a clean float in the foreign exchange market) resulted in increased economic activity, and real GDP actually grew in 1999 (by 1 percent) and 2000 (by 4 percent), contrary to the expectations set forth in the Fund program. However, the real continued to depreciate (by 20 percent in nominal terms against the U.S. dollar in the first half of 2001), and the spread on Brazilian foreign currency bonds rose.

The IMF program was due to end at the end of 2001, and Presidential elections were scheduled for October 2002. The authorities were concerned about efforts to manage without a program or to renegotiate a program in the midst of a Presidential election, and chose to cancel the 2000 program and to replace it with a 15-month program that would last until the end of the government's term in December 2002. Although the program was

---

[22] Inflation rates are for wholesale prices as reported in IMF (1996, p. 109).

announced in August 2001, there was little positive effect, in significant part because of investors' doubts about the new election, and in part because the world economy and finance deteriorated after September 2001.

But the chief factor was the scheduled elections. Mr. Luis Inacio Lula da Silva of the Workers' Party, who had run for President in three previous elections and lost, was again a candidate and polls were showing increased support for him. He had earlier been associated with very left-wing policies, and investors feared a sharp shift in policies, perhaps even including repudiation of the public debt.[23] As Perez and Gerson (2008, p. 114–5) indicated in their analysis,

"In effect, Brazil was now suffering for policies that had not been implemented by a government that had not yet been elected....only an ex post implementation of strong policies would fully assuage investors' fears of policy reversal. What was needed was a device to signal investors that Mr. da Silva's commitment to policies aimed at financial stability was genuine". Without support and a means of assuaging investors, it was clear that Brazil would be in a full-blown financial crisis before and during the election.

There were major risks. Investors might not find an IMF program credible; a new government might not be able to maintain the needed macroeconomic policies; and the ongoing Argentine crisis was leading to investors' reassessment of all emerging markets. On the other hand, Brazilian policies (as set in the 2001 program) appeared to be sufficient to enable growth and reduced inflation if they continued to be implemented, and Mr. Lula did commit (as did the other two Presidential candidates) to continuing them if elected. A new program was negotiated covering the period until mid-2003. The target primary surplus was raised from the earlier 3.5 percent of GDP target to at least 3.75 percent. In the program, there was also a commitment to maintain inflation targeting, and arrangements for foreign exchange intervention (during the period when international markets were closed) and a floor on foreign exchange reserves were also set.

A major question was how much financing Brazil needed. On one hand, an "ordinary" level of financing might not be sufficient to restore investor confidence. On the other hand, it was desirable that the Brazilian authorities were seen as having sufficient resources so as to be able to meet their financial needs. Ultimately, the program was backed by a $30 billion loan, much above normal IMF financing.[24]

---

[23] Perez and Gerson (2008), p. 113.

[24] However, much of the loan could not be drawn upon until 2003, when the new government was in office, and when the IMF staff and board could be assured that the program targets were being met.

Prior to the program's public announcement on September 6, 2002, each of the major presidential candidates publicly endorsed the major targets of the program. Even so, many were skeptical that the program would succeed in cooling the crisis, and some forecast that the central bank would run out of reserves.[25] However, bond spreads peaked (at 2,500 basis points!) at the time of the first round of the Presidential elections, and the real depreciated to almost R$4 per U.S. dollar at the end of October.

After that, conditions in the international market gradually improved. President Lula continued publicly to maintain macroeconomic policies for stability as well as to focus on social issues. He appointed a strong economics team, and an increase in the primary surplus to 4.25 percent was announced soon after the new government had assumed office.

The crisis was defused. By April 2003, Brazil regained access to international capital markets; by mid-2004, the spreads had fallen to around 500 basis points. Program targets were met, and financial pressures abated. When the 2003 program ended, conditions were sufficiently improved so that the authorities chose to treat a successor program as precautionary. Brazilian economic growth accelerated, reaching 3.2 percent in 2005 and rising above 5 percent in 2008 before the global recession. By 2005, the inflation rate fell to 6.9 percent and the government debt/GDP ratio fell to 48 percent. The $30 billion loan from the Fund was fully repaid by 2005. By late 2010, the concern in Brazil was not focused on growth, but on the risk that the economy was overheating: the growth rate was expected to be the highest in South America.

LESSONS

Prior to the financial crisis, many observers were noting the relatively small volume of outstanding loans made by the Fund, the small number of the crises which had occurred to date, and claiming that the Fund had become "irrelevant". But, as the experiences with Turkey and Brazil show,[26] two major

---

[25] See, for example, Goldstein (2003).

[26] There are many other cases, of course. The Fund played a crucial role in supporting policy changes in the countries of the former Soviet Union; it supported moves to improve fiscal and monetary policy in many Subsaharan African countries with only modest success initially but which have contributed to Africa's acceleration of growth in recent years; it was instrumental in supporting Uruguay when the crisis in Argentina led to difficulties in that country; and many more.

economies were faring considerably better than they would have in the absence of international support. It is inestimable how much smaller Brazilian output would have been in the years following the 2002 election had the new President entered office confronted with a full-blown crisis. In the Turkish case, it is difficult to estimate how Turkey would have emerged from crisis without international support, and how much worse off the country would have been.

A first lesson is that the Fund has both prevented crises and enabled a much more rapid recovery than would otherwise have been possible. But, connected to that, in neither case was success at all assured when policy reforms were undertaken. Indeed, the first programs (in 1999) were not followed by sustained growth without further support. At the time that the Turkish program in 2001 and the Brazilian program in 2002 was announced, it was difficult to estimate how private investors would react to policy changes, and in particular whether they would find the Turkish reforms and the Brazilian Presidential commitments sufficiently credible to result in a resumption of functioning markets. For Turkey, a new government was elected shortly after the February 2001 crisis, and it was not possible to know what its economic policies would be. In Brazil, expectations with regard to the frontrunner in the Presidential election turned out to be unduly pessimistic.

A second lesson is that earlier reforms can enable a larger benefit from later reforms in cases where the earlier ones address some fundamental issues, even if they are not sufficiently far-reaching to put the economy on a sustainable growth path. In Turkey's case, the reforms of the 1980s, which opened up the trade regime and removed the high walls of protection that had surrounded the Turkish economy, enabled a much more rapid and a much greater response to the 2001 program than could otherwise have occurred. Had there been fewer firms with experience in and knowledge of the export market, there would have been a smaller response to the changed incentives; that smaller response would have meant a slower turnaround in economic activity, and doubts about the program, and political opposition to it, would surely have been greater. In Brazil's case, the reforms of the educational system, the earlier reduction in trade protection, and other measures undertaken during President Cardoso's tenure certainly contributed to the speed and strength of the recovery after President Lula was elected.

So reform programs may fall short of correcting enough policy shortcomings to enable rapid growth. They can nonetheless bring about benefits in the short run and bring about more benefits when another reform program is undertaken.

A third, and important, lesson is that in the context of inflationary pressures and rising indebtedness, fiscal consolidation and tightened fiscal and monetary policy need not bring about significant and drawn out periods of austerity. When there are policy reforms that increase prospective returns from some economic activities (such as moving toward a more realistic exchange rate or freeing up the labor market), some or all of the reduction in demand resulting from fiscal consolidation can be offset by the shift of resources into the newly more attractive lines of economic activity. Indeed, in order for a meaningful depreciation of the real exchange rate, for example, to take effect, it can be necessary for resources to be released from other lines of endeavor.

Finally, it should also be noted that observers who are critical of reform programs often contrast economic activity immediately after reforms with that immediately before. When a crisis comes about because ongoing levels of activity are unsustainable, this is not the appropriate comparison. The correct comparison, which is very difficult to estimate, is what would have happened had the government attempted to continue on the unsustainable course (or, even more difficult, what earlier rate of growth would have been sustainable). In cases where spreads on bonds are already sky high and rollover happens only very short term, the relevant question is what would have happened had the government budget been unaltered and efforts to fund deficits had continued. That the markets would have closed at some point to such governments is a foregone conclusion. One can only guess at the political and economic upheavals attendant upon a government unable to meet its payroll.[27] Probably the realistic alternative to reforms at a given time is reforms at a somewhat later date. In that event, the high spreads, the slowdown in economic activity during the crisis periods, the additional borrowing undertaken in a futile effort to sustain policies, are all part of the costs of delay. The relevant political choice is whether to continue to try to hold together an apparently unsustainable set of policies (presumably in the hope that some exogenous event will save them) for a further period of time or to begin reforms earlier. All the evidence indicates that delay raises the costs of reform when it finally takes place.

---

[27] When a country is running a primary deficit, it cannot maintain its current rate of expenditures and taxes without highly inflationary financing or financing from abroad (if reserves are already too low).

REFERENCES

Boulton, L (2001). Turkey gets Ready to Swallow the Medicine. *Financial Times*, March 28, p. 3.

Brau, E and I McDonald (2008). *Successes of the International Monetary Fund.* New York: Palgrave Macmillan.

Economist, October 23, (2010). A Special Report on Turkey.

Goldstein, M (2003). Debt Sustainability, Brazil, and the IMF. Peterson Institute for International Economics, February, Working Paper 03–1.

International Monetary Fund (1996). *International Financial Statistics Yearbook.* International Monetary Fund, Washington D. C.

International Monetary Fund (1999). Letter of Intent. http:/www.imf.org/external/np/loi/1999/09229.

International Monetary Fund (2004). *International Financial Statistics Yearbook.* International Monetary Fund, Washington D.C.

International Monetary Fund (2010). Staff Report for the Article IV Consultation and Post-Program Monitoring, July 13. Available from Fund Website.

Josefsson, M and D Marston (2005). Bank Restructuring and Financial Sector Reform. In *Turkey at the Crossroads: From Crisis Resolution to EU Accession*, R Moghadam, International Monetary Fund Occasional Paper 242, Wasgington D.C.

Klingen, C (2005). How Much Debt is Too Much? In *Turkey at the Crossroads: From Crisis Resolution to EU Accession*, International Monetary Fund Occasional Paper 242, Washington D.C.

Krueger, AO and OH Aktan (1992). *Swimming Against the Tide: Turkish Trade Reform in the 1980s*, International Center for Economic Growth, San Francisco.

Lapper, R (2002). Bailout Averts Financial Chaos. *Financial Times*, September 27.

Moghadam, R (2005). *Turkey at the Crossroads: From Crisis Resolution to EU Accession*, International Monetary Fund Occasional Paper 242, Washington D.C.

OECD (2006). *OECD Economic Surveys: Turkey.* OECD: Paris.

Perez, LL and P Gerson (2008). Brazil: Anchoring Policy Credibility in the Midst of Financial Crisis. In *Successes of the International Monetary Fund*, E Brau and I McDonald, pp. 106–119.

Van Rijckenham, C and M Ucer (2005). *Chronicle of the Turkish Financial Crises of 2000–2001*. Istanbul Bogazici University Press.

Part III

SOVEREIGN DEBT RESTRUCTURING

Chapter 9

A NEW APPROACH TO SOVEREIGN DEBT RESTRUCTURING

Greater integration of capital markets and the shift from syndicated bank loans to traded securities have had a profound impact on the way that emerging market sovereigns finance themselves. Sovereigns increasingly issue debt in a range of legal jurisdictions, using a variety of different instruments, to a diverse and diffuse group of creditors. Creditors often have different time horizons for their investment and will respond differently should the sovereign encounter a shock to its debt servicing capacity. This is a positive development: it expands sources of sovereign financing and diversifies risk.

But the greater diversity of claims and interests has also made it more difficult to secure collective action from creditors when a sovereign's debt service obligations exceed its payments capacity. This has reinforced the tendency for debtors to delay restructuring until the last possible moment, increasing the likelihood that the process will be associated with substantial uncertainty and loss of asset values, to the detriment of debtors and creditors alike.

During the past several years there has been extensive discussion inside and outside the IMF on the need to develop a new approach to sovereign debt restructuring. There is a growing consensus that the present process for restructuring the debts of a sovereign is more prolonged, more unpredictable and more damaging to the country and its creditors than would be desirable. Exploring ways to improve the sovereign debt restructuring process is a key part of the international community's efforts to strengthen the architecture of the global financial system.

The absence of a predictable, orderly, and rapid process for restructuring the debts of sovereigns that are implementing appropriate policies has a number of costs. It can lead a sovereign with unsustainable debts to delay seeking a restructuring, draining its reserves and leaving the debtor and the majority of its creditors worse off. Perhaps most crucially, the absence of a mechanism for majority voting on restructuring terms can complicate the process of working out an equitable debt restructuring that returns the country to sustainability. The risk that some creditors will be able to hold out for full payment may prolong the restructuring process, and even inhibit agreement on a needed restructuring. The absence of a predictable process creates additional uncertainty about recovery value.

This paper seeks to outline the broad features of an improved sovereign debt restructuring process that would address these shortcomings. A sovereign debt restructuring mechanism (SDRM) should aim to help preserve asset values and protect creditors' rights, while paving the way toward an agreement that helps the debtor return to viability and growth. It should strive to create incentives for a debtor with unsustainable debts to approach its creditors promptly — and preferably before it interrupts its payments. But it should also avoid creating incentives for countries with sustainable debts to suspend payments rather than make necessary adjustments to their economic policies. Debt restructuring should not become a measure of first resort. By the same token, however, when there is no feasible set of policy adjustments to resolve the crisis unless accompanied by a restructuring, it is in the interests of neither the debtor nor the majority of its creditors to delay the inevitable.

Of course, difficulty in securing collective action is only one of a number of factors that have made sovereigns extremely reluctant to restructure their debt. Even if mechanisms for debt restructuring are improved, concerns about economic dislocation, political upheaval and long-term loss of access to capital markets will make countries loath to default on their debt service obligations in all but the most extreme circumstances. As a result, it is very unlikely that alleviating the collective action problem somewhat would significantly weaken the credit culture or create moral hazard.

The paper begins by establishing the case for improving the present framework for sovereign debt restructuring and then sets out the core features that any new approach would need to include. It then discusses the relative roles that the International Monetary Fund and private creditors could play in an improved mechanism. Finally, before concluding, it discusses the circumstances when exchange controls may need to be relied upon in the context of the resolution of financial crises.

THE NEED FOR A SOVEREIGN DEBT RESTRUCTURING MECHANISM

The Objective

The objective of an SDRM is to facilitate the orderly, predictable, and rapid restructuring of unsustainable sovereign debt, while protecting asset values and creditors' rights. If appropriately designed and implemented, such a mechanism could help to reduce the costs of a restructuring for sovereign debtors and their creditors, and contribute to the efficiency of international capital markets more generally.

Use of the mechanism would be for the debtor country to request; and not for the IMF or creditors to impose. If the debtor and creditors were able to agree a restructuring between themselves, they would of course be free to do so without having to invoke the mechanism, Indeed, the intention is that the existence of a predictable legal mechanism will in itself help debtors and creditors to reach agreement without the need for formal activation.

It is envisaged that a sovereign debt restructuring mechanism would be invoked only in very limited circumstances. Specifically, when the debt burden is clearly unsustainable. In other words, the mechanism would be invoked where there is no feasible set of sustainable macroeconomic policies that would enable the debtor to resolve the immediate crisis and restore medium-term viability unless they were accompanied by a significant reduction in the net present value of the sovereign's debt. In such cases, the country concerned would probably already have been implementing corrective policies, but would have reached the point where financial viability could not be restored without a substantial adjustment in the debt burden. Countries that are judged to have sustainable sovereign debt burdens may on occasion need to approach their creditors for a reprofiling of scheduled obligations. But it is not intended that an SDRM should be used for such cases.

There are two key challenges to the successful design and implementation of an SDRM. The first is to create incentives for debtors with unsustainable debt burdens to address their problems promptly in a manner that preserves asset values and paves the way toward a restoration of sustainability and growth, while avoiding the creation of incentives for the misuse of the mechanism. The second is to design the mechanism so that, once activated, the relative roles assigned to the sovereign debtor and its creditors create incentives for all parties to reach rapid agreement on restructuring terms that are consistent with a return to sustainability and growth. The policies of the IMF regarding the availability of its resources before, during, and after a member seeks a restructuring of its debt currently play a critical role in shaping these incentives. This would remain the case under an SDRM, whatever shape it were to take.

If an SDRM were designed and implemented in a manner that achieved an appropriate balance of incentives, it would provide a number of benefits. Debtors would benefit from addressing their unsustainable debt burdens at an early stage, thereby avoiding the exhaustion of official reserves and unnecessarily severe economic dislocation. They would also benefit from a greater capacity to resolve collective action problems that might otherwise thwart a rapid and orderly restructuring. Most creditors would also gain if the debtor acted before it had dissipated its reserves and would benefit from the resolution of collective action problems that would otherwise impede a sustainable restructuring. Moreover, creditors would benefit from the creation of a predictable restructuring framework that provides assurances that the debtor will avoid actions that reduce the value of creditor claims, Finally, if an SDRM is sufficiently predictable, it will help creditors make better judgments regarding how any restructuring will take place and the recovery value of the debt. This should make sovereign debt more attractive as an asset class, increase the efficiency of international capital markets, and result in a better global allocation of capital.

The Problem

Developments in the composition of international sovereign borrowing over the past decade — notably the shift away from syndicated bank loans toward traded securities as the principal vehicle for the extension of financial credits to sovereigns—have improved the efficiency of international capital markets. In particular, they have broadened the investor base for financing to emerging market sovereigns and have facilitated the diversification of risk. But the increasingly diverse and diffuse creditor community poses coordination and collective action problems in cases in which a sovereign's scheduled debt service exceeds its payments capacity. This leads to considerable uncertainty among all participants as to how the restructuring process will unfold, and contributes to reluctance by the sovereign, its creditors, and the official sector to pursue a restructuring, other than in the most extreme circumstances. This, in turn, increases the likely magnitude of the loss of asset values, which is harmful to the interests of both debtors and creditors.

During the 1980s debt crisis, collective action problems were limited by the relatively small number of large creditors, the relative homogeneity of commercial bank creditors, the contractual provisions of syndicated loans,[1]

---

[1] Specifically, most syndicated loans contained sharing clauses that provided strong incentives for negotiated settlements rather than resort to litigation.

and, on occasion, moral suasion applied by supervisory authorities. Incentives for collective action were reinforced by banks' interest in maintaining good relations as a means of safeguarding future business. Discussions between the sovereign and its creditors generally took place within a collective framework, with the major creditors negotiating through a steering committee. During the negotiations, the committee performed a number of functions, including the resolution of intercreditor problems, the assessment of the acceptability of the offers made by the sovereign, and the preservation of confidentiality. Moreover, the provision of new financing was facilitated by an agreement between the committee and the debtor that any financing provided after a specified date would be excluded from any future restructuring. This provided a basis for banks both to extend medium-term credits and to provide normal trade financing.

The move away from commercial bank lending as a source of external finance for emerging market sovereigns has made the coordination of creditors much more difficult than it was in the 1980s. Many creditors have no ongoing business relationship with the debtor to protect and are not subject to suasion by the official sector. The number and diversity of creditors has increased, with an associated increase in the diversity of interests and appetite for risk. These changes have been accompanied by an increase in the complexity of creditor claims. These developments have made creditor organization more complicated. A sovereign restructuring may require coordination across many bond issues, as well as syndicated loans and trade financing. This organization problem has been exacerbated by the repackaging of creditor claims in ways that separate the interests between the primary lender (the lender of record) and the end-investor (the beneficiaries that hold the economic interest).

Sovereigns with unsustainable debt burdens and a diffuse group of creditors can face substantial difficulties getting creditors collectively to agree to a restructuring agreement that brings the sovereign's debt down to a sustainable level. In particular, it may be difficult to secure high participation by creditors in a debt restructuring that would be in the interest of creditors as a group, as individual creditors may consider that their best interests would be served by trying to free ride in the hope of ultimately receiving payments in line with their original contracts. Both fears of free riding and other issues of intercreditor equity may inhibit creditors from accepting a proposed debt restructuring, prolonging the restructuring process and making it less likely that a deal will achieve the objective of restoring sustainability.

The absence of a mechanism that provides for majority action among a diverse set of creditors is a primary source of difficulties with collective action. Currently, a sovereign that obtained the support of a qualified majority of its creditors for a restructuring that could restore sustainability would lack the ability to bind in a minority that may hope to free ride and continue to receive their contracted payments.

Ideally, a country with an unsustainable debt would be able to reach agreement with its creditors on a needed restructuring prior to suspending payments and defaulting. But, in the current environment, it may be particularly difficult to secure high participation from creditors as a group, as individual creditors may consider that their best interests would be served by trying to free ride in the hope of ultimately receiving payments in line with their original contracts. If more than a small proportion of creditors attempt to free ride, a restructuring would not succeed in bringing debt to a sustainable level, and a default may be unavoidable. These difficulties may be amplified by the prevalence of complex financial instruments, such as credit derivatives, which in some cases may provide investors with incentives to hold out in the hope of forcing a default (thereby triggering a payment under the derivative contract), rather than participating in a restructuring. Difficulties in securing agreement on a needed restructuring prior to a payments suspension also may undermine confidence in the domestic financial system (to the extent that domestic banks have significant holdings of government securities) and may even trigger an unmanageable deposit run.

If a restructuring cannot be achieved prior to a default, collective action problems may still arise as creditors may decide to hold out in hope of a more favorable settlement, possibly through resort to litigation. To date litigation against a sovereign has been relatively limited and there is inadequate evidence to suggest that the prospect of such litigation will invariably undermine the sovereign's ability to reach an agreement with a majority of its creditors. Litigation is not an attractive option for many creditors. It is costly and may give rise to concerns relating to reputation damage. Potential holdouts face significant uncertainty regarding whether the debtor would be willing to make a more attractive offer to non-participating creditors. Nevertheless, the evolution of legal strategies has increased the uncertainties of postdefault restructurings. For example, the recent legal action against Peru may make potentially cooperative creditors nervous about participating in a future restructuring agreement. They may be worried that a holdout will be able to extract full payment from a sovereign by, for example, threatening the interruption of payments on the restructured debt.

In addition to difficulties securing collective action, creditors have identified other factors that they consider hamper the prospects for rapid progress toward predictable and orderly restructuring agreements. In particular, concerns about intercreditor equity stemming from debtors' decisions to make payments to certain favored creditors after suspending payments on other creditors may introduce delays. Creditors have also pointed to the reluctance of debtors to participate in a collaborative dialogue to develop restructuring proposals. The design and implementation of more efficient mechanisms for resolving collective action could also catalyze the establishment of a more collaborative framework for debtor-creditor negotiations.

CORE FEATURES OF A SOVEREIGN DEBT RESTRUCTURING MECHANISM

What features of a legal framework would need to be in place in order to establish adequate incentives for debtors and creditors to agree upon a prompt, orderly, and predictable restructuring of unsustainable debt? As will be seen, although the features of existing domestic legislative models provide important guidance as to how to address collective action problems among creditors in the insolvency context, the applicability of these models is limited by the unique characteristics of a sovereign state.

Existing Rehabilitation Models and Their Limitations

When a financially distressed — but fundamentally viable — company finds that it can no longer service its debt, the company and its diverse creditors cannot generally turn to their domestic authorities for financing as a means of resolving the crisis. Instead, domestic insolvency legislation provides the necessary framework to overcome coordination problems as they work out restructuring terms. A court-administered reorganization chapter of an insolvency law provides the necessary incentives for a debt restructuring agreement (that often involves substantial debt reduction). To the extent that the insolvency system is well-developed, most restructurings take place "in the shadow" of the law, that is, without the need — and expense — of actually commencing formal court-administered proceedings. As is discussed in Box 1, most well-developed corporate rehabilitation laws include the following features:

  (i) a stay on creditor enforcement during the restructuring negotiations;
  (ii) measures that protect creditor interests during the period of the stay;

Box 1:   Corporate Reorganization Model

Although corporate insolvency laws vary among countries, considerable work has been done to identify "best practices" in core areas.[1] The following features of well-developed insolvency laws provide the key incentives for corporate restructuring:

- *First, upon commencement of reorganization proceedings, a stay is imposed on all legal actions by creditors, thereby protecting the debtor from dismemberment.* This stay is designed not only to protect the debtor, but also addresses the intercreditor collective action problem. In the absence of a stay, creditors would probably rush to enforce their claims out of a fear that others would do so.
- *Second, during the proceedings, legal constraints are imposed upon the activities of the debtor and a reorganization plan must normally be prepared within a specified time frame.* As a means of ensuring that the interests of creditors are protected during the proceedings, the debtor is precluded from entering into transactions that would prejudice creditors generally (for example, transferring assets to insiders or making payments to favored creditors). To ensure compliance, the laws of some countries also provide for a court-appointed administrator to oversee the activities of the debtor during this period.
- *Third, as a means of encouraging new financing, credit provided to the debtor after commencement of the proceeding must be given seniority over prior claims in any reorganization plan.* Normally, a creditor that provides financing during the proceedings would have the right to be repaid once the reorganization plan is approved.
- *Fourth, a debt restructuring plan approved by the requisite majority of creditors will be binding on all creditors.* The law normally provides for the establishment of a committee of creditors that takes the lead in negotiating the terms of the debt restructuring plan with the debtor. To ensure there is no fraud in the voting process, the court normally oversees the verification of creditors' claims.

---

[1] Including by the IMF, World Bank, and United Nations Commission on International Trade Law (UNCITRAL).

(*Continued*)

Box 1: (*Continued*)

A predictable insolvency system enables corporate restructuring to take place out-of-court but "in the shadow" of the formal insolvency system. Such an out-of-court process generally mimics certain features of the formal process. For example, creditors agree to a voluntary standstill in the knowledge that, if they refuse, the debtor can make a standstill mandatory by commencing formal proceedings. Similarly, potential holdout creditors realize that, if they are inflexible, the debtor and majority creditors can use the law to bind them to the terms of the restructuring agreement. In sum, each party negotiates, with a clear understanding of the type of leverage it — and the others — would have if the formal system were to be activated.

(iii) mechanisms that facilitate the provision of new financing during the proceedings; and
(iv) a provision that binds all relevant creditors to an agreement that has been accepted by a qualified majority.

All of these features serve to maximize the value of creditor claims by preserving the going concern value of the firm. As will be discussed below, these features are relevant to a discussion of the design of a sovereign debt restructuring mechanism. It should be noted, however, that the applicability of the corporate model to the sovereign context is limited in a number of important respects.

- First, and perhaps most importantly, corporate reorganization provisions operate within the context of the potential liquidation of the debtor, which could not apply to a sovereign state. In the event that a reorganization plan does not attract adequate support from its creditors and the company continues to be in a state of illiquidity, most laws will provide for the automatic liquidation of the company. Moreover, the potential liquidation of the enterprise also limits the terms of any restructuring proposal. Most modern laws provide that creditors cannot be forced to accept terms under a reorganization plan that would result in their receiving less than what they would have received in a liquidation.
- Second, since one of the purposes of a reorganization law is to enable creditors to maximize the value of their claims through the going

concern value of the enterprise, most modern laws allow for the creditors to commence proceedings unilaterally so as to acquire the company through a reorganization plan that includes a debt-for-equity conversion that, in some cases, may extinguish all ownership interests of the incumbent shareholders. Again, such a feature could not be applied to a sovereign state.

- Finally, it is difficult to envisage how the constraints that are applied to the activities of a corporate debtor to safeguard the interests of creditors during the proceedings could be made legally binding on a sovereign and enforced, particularly with respect to the exercise of its sovereign powers, including, for example, its fiscal powers. In the sovereign context, we must therefore rely on having the right incentives in place.

In many respects, Chapter 9 of the United States Bankruptcy Code, which applies to municipalities, is of greater relevance in the sovereign context because it applies to an entity that carries out governmental functions. Although it includes a number of the core features of a corporate reorganization law, it differs from the corporate model in a number of respects. For example, only the municipality (not its creditors) may commence proceedings and propose a reorganization plan. Moreover, the bankruptcy court may not interfere with any of the municipality's political or governmental powers, property or revenue or the municipality's use or enjoyment of any income-producing property. Finally, a Chapter 9 case cannot be converted into a liquidation case. All of these features could be appropriately integrated into a sovereign debt restructuring mechanism.

There are, however, important differences between a municipality and a sovereign state that would have implications on the design of any sovereign debt restructuring mechanisms. Unlike a sovereign state, a municipality is not independent. Chapter 9 legislation acknowledges — and does not impair — the power of the state within which the municipality exists to continue to control the exercise of the powers of the municipality, including expenditures. This lack of independence of municipalities is one of the reasons why many countries have not adopted insolvency legislation to address problems of financial distress confronted by local governments.

The Sovereign Context

Although the applicability of the above models to the sovereign context is necessarily limited, a number of their features — if appropriately adapted — provide useful guidance when contemplating the design of a sovereign debt restructuring mechanism. Bearing in mind the objective of the mechanism — to provide a framework for the orderly, predictable, and rapid restructuring of debt problems in a manner that preserves value for the benefit of both the debtor and its creditors — the core features of the mechanism could include the following.

- *Majority restructuring* — The creation of a mechanism that would enable the affirmative vote of a qualified majority of creditors to bind a dissenting minority to the terms of a restructuring agreement would be the most important element of any new restructuring framework. From the perspective of creditors, such a mechanism would provide confidence that any forbearance exercised by the majority when agreeing to a restructuring would not be abused by free riders who could otherwise press for full payment after an agreement was reached. For the majority of creditors, the disruptive behavior of free riders not only raises intercreditor equity issues, but also reduces the ability of the debtor to service the newly restructured debt. From the perspective of the sovereign, the resolution of these collective action issues will make it more likely that it will be able to reach early agreement with creditors on a debt restructuring. Moreover, it eliminates the threat of disruptive litigation by dissenting creditors after the restructuring takes place.

    Majority restructuring provisions form the central element of the collective action clauses that are found in some international sovereign bonds. However, these provisions only bind bondholders within the same issue. They have no effect on bondholders of other issuances, which may in any event be governed by different legal jurisdictions. Moreover, they do not apply to other types of indebtedness, such as bank claims and domestic debt. To address the collective action problems that arise from the very diverse private creditor community that currently exists, such a mechanism would need to apply to all forms of private credit to sovereigns. This feature of a sovereign debt restructuring mechanism would be similar to the majority restructuring provisions of domestic insolvency laws, which aggregate the claims of all eligible creditors (irrespective of the nature of the instrument) when determining whether there is adequate support by a majority to make an agreement binding on all creditors. Aggregation, however, would not result in the equalization of all claims for debt restructuring purposes. For example, as in the case of the domestic insolvency law, safeguards would need to be in place to ensure that the seniority of certain claims is protected.

Ideally, the debtor and its creditors would activate the majority restructuring provision described above prior to a default on the original claims. As borne out by experience, avoiding a default would help minimize economic disruption in the debtor country and preserve asset values, including the secondary market value of creditors' claims.

- *Stay on creditor enforcement* — In the event that an agreement had not been reached prior to a default, a temporary stay on creditor litigation after a suspension of payments but before a restructuring agreement is reached would support the effective operation of the majority restructuring provision. In the context of corporate insolvency, a stay on litigation is intended to enforce collective action by preventing a rush to the courthouse and a "grab race" that could undermine the ability of a company to continue functioning, to the detriment of the debtor and its creditors (the value of whose claims is maximized when the company remains a going concern). The risk of widespread creditor litigation may be less pronounced in the sovereign than in the corporate context, largely on account of the relative scarcity of assets under the jurisdiction of foreign courts that could be seized to satisfy creditors' claims. Nevertheless, there is a risk that litigation could inhibit progress in the negotiations. This risk could increase if, as a result of the introduction of a majority restructuring provision, the only opportunity to use legal enforcement as a source of leverage is before rather than after the reaching of an agreement. This is one of the reasons why collective action clauses in international sovereign bonds also contain provisions that effectively enable a majority of bondholders to block legal action by a minority before an agreement is reached. But, as in the case of majority restructuring provisions, these provisions only apply to bondholders within the same issuance.

- *Protecting creditor interests* — An SDRM would need to include safeguards that give creditors adequate assurances that their interests were being protected during the period of the stay. These safeguards would have two complementary elements. First, the sovereign debtor would be required not to make payments to nonpriority creditors. This would avoid the dissipation of resources that could be used to service the claims of relevant creditors in general. Second, there would have to be assurances that the debtor would conduct policies in a fashion that preserves asset values. If, throughout the stay, the member was implementing an IMF-supported program or was working closely with the IMF to elaborate policies that could be supported with the use of IMF resources, this would provide many of these assurances. Beyond the fiscal, monetary, and exchange rate policies that lay the basis for the resumption of debt service and a return to sustainability, creditors also have clear interests in other policies, including, for example, the nature and terms of any domestic bank restructuring, the continued operation of the domestic payments system, the country's bankruptcy regime and the nature of any exchange controls it imposes. Depending on the circumstances, the creditors of the sovereign may have a particular interest in the effective implementation of capital controls to prevent capital flight.

- *Priority financing* — A majority restructuring mechanism could also usefully be buttressed by a mechanism that would facilitate the provision of new money from private creditors during the period of the stay. It is in the collective interests of private creditors and the sovereign debtor that new money be provided in appropriate amounts. Such financing, when used in the context of good policies, can help limit the degree of economic dislocation and thereby help preserve the member's capacity to generate the resources for meeting debt-service obligations. In the sovereign context, new money could help cover the sovereign's need for trade credit and could also finance payments to priority creditors. Under the existing legal framework, however, individual creditors have no incentive to provide new money in such circumstances, as the resulting benefits of a return to debt servicing would be shared among creditors as a group, and there would be no assurance that the new financing would not also get caught up in the restructuring. An SDRM could induce new financing by providing an assurance that any financing in support of the member's program extended after the introduction of the stay would be senior to all preexisting private indebtedness. This assurance could be provided through a decision of a qualified majority of creditors.

As discussed further below, if this mechanism is to be both equitable and transparent for a broad range of creditors, it will have to be supported by independent arrangements for the verification of creditors' claims, the resolution of disputes, and the supervision of voting. For example, such arrangements would protect against fraud that may arise through the creation of debt between related parties.

Among the many issues that will need to be addressed is the coverage of offical creditors. Given the special role that the International Monetary Fund and multilateral development banks play in providing finance during crises, their status as preferred creditors has generally been accepted by the international community. These claims would not be subject to the mechanism. However, this leaves the question of how to treat bilateral official debt; debt that is now routinely restructured in the context of the Paris Club. We will

need to explore further whether it would be feasible to include bilateral official debt under an SDRM and, if so, how this would be done in a manner that
pays due regard to the special features of these claims.

Another set of issues that needs careful consideration concerns the treatment of domestic debt in the context of an SDRM. Sovereigns typically have
a wide range of debts to domestic residents. These may include marketable
securities (issued under either domestic or foreign laws), loans from banks,
and suppliers' credits. With the growing integration of international capital
markets, and the tendency for residents and nonresidents to hold similar
instruments, the distinction between domestic and nondomestic debt has
become increasingly blurred.

While the treatment of domestic debt will need to be considered on a
case-by-case basis, in practice it may be necessary to include domestic debt
within the scope of a restructuring that is intended to bring a sovereign's debt
to a sustainable level. In particular, the magnitude of debt to nonresidents in
relation to the scale of the required reduction in the overall debt burden may
necessitate the inclusion of domestic debt. Moreover, nonresident investors
may only be willing to agree to provide substantial debt reduction if they consider that adequate intercreditor equity has been achieved — they would be
unlikely to be willing to provide such relief if it was seen as enabling other private creditors to exit whole.

Nevertheless, the treatment of domestic debt under a restructuring needs
to weigh a number of factors that will have a bearing on the prospects for
restoring sustainable growth. (These factors would need to be considered by
both the debtor in the design of a restructuring proposal and by foreign creditors in their assessment of the adequacy of intercreditor equity.) First and
foremost there is a need to ensure that the domestic banking system should
remain solvent after a restructuring, in order that it can continue to serve as
an intermediary for domestic savings and foreign financing, for example,
trade credit. Second, it would be important to take account of the likely
impact of a restructuring for the future operation of domestic capital markets,
and, in particular, the possible tradeoff between the magnitude of debt reduction obtained through a restructuring, on the one hand, and the prospect that
the sovereign will be able to mobilize savings from domestic capital markets
in the aftermath of a restructuring — particularly in the period while access
to international capital markets will likely remain closed.

In providing a legal basis for the treatment of domestic debt under an
SDRM, a number of approaches could be considered. One would have the
statutory framework cover a broad range of debt, including domestic debt.
This would make the claims of all resident investors subject to the majority

restructuring and other features of the mechanism. This need not preclude flexibility in the treatment of domestic debt under individual restructuring proposals, subject to the ability of the sovereign to attract the necessary degree of support from creditors for the overall package. An alternative approach would exclude domestic debt from the scope of the statutory approach and rely instead on the existing governing legal frameworks to facilitate any restructurings of these claims that may be required. Of course, this approach would not reduce the need to achieve an acceptable degree of intercreditor equity in order to garner the necessary support of nonresident creditors. It would also raise practical issues concerning the definition of domestic debt. Would this be based on the residency of investors, or the characteristics of the instruments, possibly the governing law, currency (or location) of debt service payments?

All of the above features, when taken together, would establish a framework within which an orderly and rapid restructuring could take place. Most importantly, the framework would address collective action problems that have, to date, made the cost of restructuring excessively high for debtors and creditors alike. This could help creditors and debtors reach agreement on equitable restructuring terms more rapidly, and thus facilitate the country's recovery. As noted above, it may facilitate restructurings prior to defaults, thereby protecting asset values for the benefit of debtors and creditors alike. Moreover, if the framework were sufficiently predictable, it would create the incentive for debtors and creditors to reach an agreement without having to rely on its actual use. For example, the voting provisions would encourage early creditor organization, and thus lay the basis for negotiations between the debtor and its creditors. In addition, potential holdouts would realize that, unless they are sufficiently flexible, the debtor and the majority of creditors could use the mechanism to bind them to the terms of an agreement.

More generally, to the extent that the establishment of a sovereign debt restructuring framework serves to create a more structured negotiating framework between creditors and sovereign debtors, it may enhance the value of sovereign debt as an asset class. Over the past several years, a number of dedicated emerging market creditors have complained about the absence of a predictable and equitable process that guides sovereign debt restructuring negotiations. They have argued that this makes it more difficult to attract long-term capital to the emerging market asset class, thereby undermining the stability of the investor base. To provide greater structure to the negotiating process, consideration could be given to designing the mechanism in a manner that gives a creditors' committee an explicit role in the restructuring process, as is the case in most modern insolvency laws. Creditor committees played a major role during the sovereign debt restructuring process in the 1980s and further efforts could be made to facilitate their formation and operation, taking into consideration the profound changes that have taken place in capital markets over the past twenty years.

THE ROLE OF THE IMF

If appropriately designed and implemented, a sovereign debt restructuring framework would assist in achieving the IMF's purposes in a number of respects. First, if such a framework facilitates an early restructuring of unsustainable debt, balance of payments viability could more easily be attained in a manner that minimizes the resort to measures that are destructive to national or international prosperity. The achievement of this objective would in turn help the IMF safeguard its resources. Finally, to the extent that a predictable framework assists creditors in their assessment and pricing of risk, it will help to avert future crises, thereby enhancing the stability of the international financial system.

In light of the above, what role should the IMF play in the actual operation of the mechanism? The financial support that the IMF provides for an effective economic adjustment program already shapes incentives that surround the sovereign debt restructuring process and would continue to do so under an SDRM. This section addresses the critical question of whether, under an SDRM, the IMF's role could be limited to the exercise of its existing financial powers or whether it would need to exercise additional legal authority.

The Role of IMF Finance

In the present environment, decisions by the IMF regarding the availability of its resources already influence all stages of the sovereign debt restructuring process. Specifically:

- The judgment of the IMF about the scale of the financing it is willing to provide in the absence of a debt restructuring and the design of an economic program supported by the IMF both help determine the timing of a sovereign payment suspension. Before a member decides to seek a comprehensive debt restructuring, it typically approaches the IMF for financing (either in the context of an existing or future arrangement) with the aim of avoiding such a restructuring and the associated economic, social, and political disruption. On being approached, the IMF is required to make a judgment whether the member's debt burden is or is not sustainable. This judgment determines the availability and the appropriate scale of IMF financing. Consequently, decisions about the availability of IMF resources strongly influence a member's decision as to whether to suspend payments in order to conserve its remaining international reserves.

- After a member has suspended payments, it is currently expected to work with the IMF on the development of an appropriate economic policy framework, and to negotiate a debt restructuring with its creditors. Approval of an IMF-supported program often, but not always, precedes final agreement on restructuring terms with creditors. In this context, the IMF currently makes judgments about the good faith of the member in its negotiations with its creditors in determining whether to lend into arrears on payments to private creditors. The IMF-supported program will specify a fiscal and external adjustment path, which will determine, in broad terms, the amount of resources available for debt service by the sovereign during the program period.

- When deciding whether to support a member that is about to conclude a restructuring of its obligations to private creditors, the IMF currently makes two important judgments. First, it assesses the consistency of the restructuring agreement with the adjustment path in the member's economic program. The payments stream that emerges from the private debt restructuring should be consistent with the member's program. Second, it assesses whether the resulting medium-term payments profile is consistent with the requirements for debt sustainability.

Under an SDRM, the nature of the financing decisions that the IMF would need to make before, during, and after a debt restructuring would not change. Consistent with its mandate, the IMF would continue to ensure that its resources were being used to resolve the member's balance of payments problems without resorting to measures that were destructive of national and international prosperity. Moreover, the IMF would continue to need to ensure that there are adequate safeguards for the revolving character of its resources. Both of these imperatives would require it to continue to condition the availability of its resources on the adoption of appropriate policies and, where necessary, on a debt restructuring that laid the basis for a return to sustainability.

Operating the Framework

In light of the central role that IMF financing plays, one could envisage a framework that empowered the IMF to make key decisions regarding its operation. Bearing in mind the key features described in the previous section, these decisions would include the following:

- First, *activation of a stay on creditor action* would require a request by the sovereign debtor and IMF endorsement. Such endorsement would be based on the IMF's determination that the member's debt is unsustainable and that appropriate policies are being — or will soon be — implemented.
- Second, any *extension of the stay* would require a determination by the IMF not only that adequate policies continue to be implemented but also that the member is making progress in its negotiations with its creditors.
- Third, IMF *approval of a restructuring agreement* that had been accepted by the requisite majority of creditors would be a condition for its effectiveness. Such approval would be based on a determination that it provides for a sustainable debt profile.

While the IMF's involvement in the decision making process, as described above, would help ensure that the framework was not abused, a number of concerns have been expressed regarding the above approach. As a creditor and as an institution whose members include debtors and bilateral official creditors, there are concerns that the IMF would not be perceived as being entirely impartial in exercising this authority. More generally, it is unclear whether the international community would be willing to confer additional powers on the IMF.

In light of these concerns, the remainder of this section discusses the benefits of an approach that would limit the role of the IMF in the operation of the mechanism itself. Under this alternative approach, decisions under the SDRM would be left to the debtor and the majority of the creditors. Accordingly, the IMF would have no power to limit the enforcement of creditor rights. Rather, the IMF would rely on its existing financial powers to create the incentives for the relevant parties to use the mechanism appropriately. How such an approach could be implemented is discussed below for each of the main features of the mechanism.

- *Approval of the restructuring agreement* — It would be possible to rely exclusively on the approval of the requisite majority of the creditors as a means of making the agreement binding on all creditors, that is, IMF endorsement of such an agreement would not be a condition for its effectiveness. Such an approach would make this element of the mechanism consistent with the majority restructuring provisions found in collective action clauses. The key difference would be that, while majority restructuring provisions only apply to bondholders within the same issuance, an affirmative vote by the requisite creditors under the mechanism would bind the entire creditor body.

This approach carries a risk that the debtor and creditors would conclude an agreement that did not achieve a sustainable debt profile. However, this risk could be addressed, as it is in the present context, if subsequent IMF financial support is conditioned on a judgment that the payments stream in the proposed restructuring was consistent with the adjustment path in the member's economic program and the requirements for medium-term debt sustainability. If it did not meet these conditions, the IMF would be effectively prevented from lending until the member had taken further steps to ensure debt sustainability, possibly involving a further restructuring.

- *Activation of the stay* — As an alternative to activating the stay upon the IMF's endorsement of a request, one could envisage a stay that would be activated only upon a request of the member that had been approved by the requisite majority of creditors. Such an approach would mimic, to an extent, certain provisions of collective action clauses found in many international sovereign bonds. These provisions effectively enable a qualified majority of holders of a single bond issuance to restrict a minority of holders of the same bond issuance from enforcing their claims against the sovereign during the negotiations of a debt restructuring agreement.[2] Under this approach, however, the decision would be made a qualified majority of all of the member's creditors, that is, creditor claims would be aggregated across instruments for voting purposes. Reliance on such an approach would serve to highlight the extent to which the problem being addressed by the mechanism is that of collective action.

A shortcoming of this approach is that, even if the requisite majority of the creditors were amenable to approving a stay that would be binding upon the entire creditor body, it could take considerable time to put one in place. In the context of a single bond issue where provisions exist that enable the majority of creditors to prevent enforcement by a minority, the process of ascertaining the will of the majority is relatively straightforward,

---

[2] Upon an event of default, most international sovereign bonds provide that an acceleration (where the full amount owing becomes due and payable) may be blocked by a defined percentage of bondholders. In addition, international sovereign bonds issued under trust deeds (traditionally governed by English law) give the trustee the primary authority to initiate legal action, and the trustee is only permitted to do so if such action is supported by a threshold percentage of bondholders.

although even that takes time. In contrast, a vote by all creditors (all bond issuances, bank debt, trade credit, certain official claims) as envisaged under the mechanism would need to be preceded by a verification of claims process that might take several months to complete.

There are several different ways in which the above shortcoming could be addressed.

- First, the mechanism could enable the sovereign to activate the stay unilaterally and enjoy the resulting legal protection for a limited 90-day period. At the end of that period, claims would have been verified and creditors would vote as to whether the stay would be extended and, if so, for how long. Although the IMF would not have a legal veto, in most cases a member would likely only activate the mechanism in consultation with the IMF, that is, after the IMF had determined that the debt burden was unsustainable and that further financial assistance would not be forthcoming in the absence of a restructuring. But a key question would be whether the ability of the sovereign to activate the mechanism for a limited period unilaterally might be abused by members whose debt was not judged to be unsustainable.
- Second, IMF approval of the stay could be necessary for it to be effective for the initial 90-day period. Any extension of the stay beyond this limited period would require the consent of the majority of the creditors. This approach would be designed to protect against the possibility of debtors' abuse of a purely unilateral stay prior to a creditors' vote. It would, however, entail IMF involvement in the decision-making process, albeit in a limited manner.
- Third, one could accept that a stay would not be in place until an affirmative vote of the creditors had taken place and focus instead on ways to limit the delay between a member's request and the creditors' vote. For example, as a means of accelerating the verification of claims and voting process, a standing organization could be established whose role would include registering claims against the sovereign and facilitating the organization of creditors in the context of a restructuring.

It should be noted that a brief delay between the member's suspension of payments and the activation of the stay would not leave a sovereign helpless in the event that the suspension gave rise to capital flight. Under certain circumstances, capital controls to stem outflows might be a necessary — but temporary — feature of an IMF-supported program. This is discussed further below.

- *Maintenance of the stay* — Just as a qualified majority of creditors might be given the authority to activate a stay, the majority of creditors might be given the authority to determine whether to extend the stay beyond the initial 90-day period. By that time, the claims of creditors would have been verified, and creditors would be in a position to vote on the issue. If the member was already in a position to submit a restructuring plan for approval at the expiration of this initial period, the creditors would vote on the proposal, and an affirmative vote by the requisite majority would bind dissenting creditors. If, however, more time were needed for negotiation, creditors would decide (again by a vote of the requisite majority) whether the stay should be extended and, if so, for how long.

The IMF's decisions regarding the availability of its resources would have a major impact on whether an extension would be approved by creditors. Specifically, the requisite majority of creditors would normally only be willing to extend the stay beyond the initial period if they had some assurance that the member was adopting policies that were being supported by the IMF. When making a decision to extend the stay, the majority of creditors would be in a position to judge whether the member was negotiating with them in good faith and their interests were protected.

Would such an approach give creditors too much leverage in the process? The concept of a stay being imposed upon all creditors through a decision by a majority is roughly analogous to the majority enforcement provisions that are found in many international sovereign bonds. Such provisions limit the ability to initiate litigation without the support of a given percentage of the bond issue. But while such provisions bind the bond-holders within the same issuance, an affirmative vote by the majority under the proposed statutory framework would bind the entire creditor body.

There may be a risk that creditors would withhold an extension of the stay in the hope that the IMF would provide more financing or call on the member to make additional adjustment efforts. For example, even in circumstances where the member is implementing good policies and negotiating in good faith, creditors may refuse to extend the period of the stay as a means of persuading the member to turn to the IMF for financing that could enhance the terms of any restructuring. The creditors could threaten to lift the stay to force the debtor to agree to more adjustment than contemplated under the IMF-supported program. Such risks could be reduced, however, by the resolute application of the IMF's policy of lending into arrears, under which it signals its willingness to continue to support a program, even if the member has interrupted payments to its creditors.

- *Priority Financing* — As noted in the previous section, an SDRM could provide incentives for new financing by providing an assurance that any new financing in support of the members program extended after the introduction of the stay would be senior to pre-existing private indebtedness. This could be achieved by giving a qualified majority of private creditors the power to subordinate the claims of all private creditors to claims arising from financing provided after the effectiveness of the stay.

THE LEGAL BASIS FOR A SOVEREIGN DEBT RESTRUCTURING MECHANISM

As discussed above, there would be a number of benefits in designing a mechanism where the decision-making process resembles features of the collective action clauses found in international sovereign bonds. Decisions regarding both the terms of the restructuring and the activation and maintenance of the stay would be made by the requisite majority and would be binding on the dissenting minority. In light of the benefits of this approach, therefore, the question arises as to whether the essential objectives of the mechanism could be achieved through the progressive adoption of contractual provisions that address collective action problems. This section addresses this question and explains why, notwithstanding the benefits of collective action clauses, the most effective basis for the mechanism would be statutory. It also discusses a number of issues relating to the establishment of a statutory framework.

The Benefits and Limits of Contract

The inclusion of collective action clauses in all international sovereign bonds would represent an important improvement in the international financial architecture. As has been discussed in earlier sections of this paper, and has been demonstrated in recent cases, collective action clauses include two provisions that can facilitate an orderly restructuring of sovereign indebtedness: (i) a provision that enables a qualified majority of bondholders to bind all bondholders of the same issuance to the terms of a restructuring agreement and (ii) a provision that enables a qualified majority of bondholders to prevent all bondholders of the same issuance from enforcing their claims against the sovereign.

The insertion of collective action clauses in all future international sovereign bonds would not require wholesale statutory reform. For example, although such provisions are not typically found in international sovereign bonds governed by New York law, they could be introduced without any legislative changes.

Moreover, it should also be noted that, even if a sovereign debt restructuring mechanism was established through legislation, as discussed below, such clauses could still play an important role. For example, since a statutory mechanism would only apply in circumstances where the member's debt is unsustainable, collective action clauses could facilitate restructurings in circumstances where the problems facing the member arise from illiquidity.

However, relying exclusively on contract as the legal basis for a sovereign debt restructuring mechanism would limit the effectiveness of such a mechanism.

First, it would be difficult to establish a purely contract-based framwork.

There is, at the outset, the problem of incentives for the adoption of traditional collective action provisions in all new indebtedness, By definition, a contractual approach would require the sovereign and its creditors to agree to the inclusion of these provisions in all future international sovereign bonds, and also in other debt and debt-like instruments that the market developed. Recent experience demonstrates that sovereign debtors facing financial difficulties actually prefer to exclude such provisions as a way of demonstrating their firm intention to avoid a restructuring. Neither have creditors pressed for their inclusion, notwithstanding the fact that they may make an unavoidable restructuring more prompt and orderly. The advantage of giving the framework for sovereign debt restructuring a statutory basis is that the collective action provisions that it would contain would effectively override the restructuring and enforcement terms set forth in the underlying agreements, as is the case with the collective action provisions contained in domestic insolvency laws.

Another barrier to the establishment of such a framework is the transitional problem. Even if all new bonds make use of the needed contractual provisions, a large portion of outstanding bonds with long maturities, including bonds governed by New York law, do not contain such provisions.[3] While this problem could conceivably be addressed by a series of exchanges that retired existing bonds, it is not clear how debtors and creditors would be persuaded to take such-action. It is also possible that use could be made of existing provisions that allow for amendment of terms not related to payment

---

[3] In contrast, if the mechanism relies upon a statutory basis, a transitional problem is less likely to arise. Most countries recognize that the establishment of a new legislative framework that is specifically directed at the suspension of creditor claims, such as insolvency laws, can apply to existing indebtedness. If the approach discussed in the previous section is followed, an SDRM would suspend the enforcement of the original claims by a minority of creditors (either prior to or after an agreement) in circumstances where the debtor and a qualified majority of creditors have agreed to such a suspension.

to facilitate debt restructurings in the interim. For example, Ecuador recently made use of "exit consents," to overcome the problem of holdout creditors generated by the absence of provisions allowing a majority to amend payment terms in outstanding bonds governed by New York law. Under this technique, bondholders who accepted the exchange voted to amend non-payment terms in ways that made holding "old bonds" less attractive. However, this technique has been somewhat controversial and it may not be immune from legal challenge in the future.

Second, even if a contract-based framework could be established, it would not provide a comprehensive and durable solution to collective action problems.

Collective action clauses traditionally only bind bondholders of the same issue. In contrast, the collective action provisions of a statute would be designed to apply across a broad range of indebtedness (potentially including international and domestic debt, bank loans, trade credit and official claims, if applicable). This is one of the reasons why the collective action provisions of insolvency laws are so effective. To address issues arising from the relative seniority of certain indebtedness, insolvency laws often provide for the classification of debt for both voting and distribution purposes. As discussed earlier, similar safeguards would need to be established under the mechanism.

To address the above limitation, one could conceive of the introduction of contractual provisions that provide for the restructuring of the instrument in question on the basis of an affirmative vote of creditors holding a qualified majority of all private credit. While further study on the feasibility of developing such clauses should be encouraged, such an approach would raise its own set of issues.

- First, such a provision would exacerbate the incentive problem: if it is difficult to convince a sovereign and the purchasers of one bond issue to agree to the inclusion of a collective action clause in that issue, it would be even more difficult to persuade debtors and creditors to include such provisions in *all* forms of debt instruments in a uniform manner. Indeed, a sovereign facing financial difficulties would come under pressure from certain creditors to exclude such provisions as a means of giving such creditors effective seniority. Moreover, it can be expected that certain creditor groups would be particularly reluctant to agree voluntarily to an arrangement whereby, for voting purposes, their claims were aggregated with all other present or future creditors.
- Second, even if all debt instruments contained identical restructuring texts, which would be difficult to achieve, there would be no assurance of uniform interpretation and application unless they were governed by the

same law and subject to the same jurisdiction. In the present environment, emerging market countries that have borrowed heavily often have a variety of bond issuances outstanding which are governed by the laws of different jurisdictions.

- Third, it may not be feasible to establish a process by contract that would effectively guarantee the integrity of the voting procedure. Under the statutory framework that governs the domestic insolvency process, a court oversees this process, including the verification of claims, so as to guard against fraud. In the absence of an independent party to verify the true value of claims, a debtor could, for example, inflate its debt stock by establishing matching credit and debt positions with a related party. That entity — which could hold a qualified majority of all debt — could vote to reduce the value of all creditor claims.

- Fourth, it is not clear that such provisions would be consistent with the existing legislation of all members. The fact that traditional collective action clauses are not included in international sovereign bonds in some jurisdictions arises, in part, from the absence of a clear statutory basis that allows for the rights of a minority of creditors to be modified without their consent. This issue would be amplified if contractual provisions attempted to aggregate claims for voting purposes.

- Finally, and more generally, the financial markets have consistently demonstrated the ability to innovate. A statutory regime is therefore likely to provide a more stable background than contractual provisions even if it were feasible to overcome all of the other difficulties referred to above.

Implementing a Statutory Framework

If a statutory approach that creates the legal basis for majority action across all sovereign indebtedness offers the best method of achieving the objectives of a sovereign debt restructuring mechanism, the question arises as to how best to implement a change in the statutory regime.

There are a number of reasons why the statutory approach could be more effectively implemented through the establishment of universal treaty obligations rather than through the enactment of legislation in a limited number of jurisdictions.[4] First, it would prevent circumvention: if the statutory

---

[4] In many jurisdictions, an international treaty, once effective, automatically supercedes domestic legislation. In other jurisdictions, however, the domestic legislation must be modified to incorporate the terms of the treaty.

framework is only in place in a limited number of jurisdictions, creditors could ensure that future instruments enable them to enforce their claims in jurisdictions that have not adopted such jurisdictions but whose money judgments are recognized in key jurisdictions under treaties or local law.[5] Second, an international treaty would ensure both uniformity of text and (if there is an institution given interpretive authority) uniformity of interpretation. Third, it would address a potential "free rider" problem: without a treaty, countries would be reluctant to adopt legislation until they were assured other countries had also done so. (A treaty could be designed that would enter into force at the same time for all signatory countries.) Finally, the establishment of a treaty facilitates the establishment of a single international judicial entity that would have exclusive jurisdiction over all disputes that would arise between the debtor and its domestic and international creditors and among such creditors. Moreover, such an entity would also have responsibility for the administration of a unified voting process, including the verification of all creditor claims. If one relied exclusively on domestic legislation in a variety of jurisdictions, the process for dispute resolution and claims verification would be fragmented one, with different claims being subject to the jurisdiction of different courts, depending, inter alia, on the governing law of the instrument.

What would be the advantages of establishing the treaty framework through an amendment of the IMF's Articles? This would be a means of achieving universality in the absence of unanimity: an amendment of the Articles can be made binding upon the entire membership once it is accepted by three-fifths of the members, having 85 percent of the total voting power. Moreover, given the considerable benefits of IMF membership, it is very unlikely that a member would wish to opt out of IMF membership in order to avoid application of the SDRM. It should be emphasized that, if an amendment of the Articles were merely to provide the legal basis for the "majority action" decisions, as described in the previous section of the paper, it would not give the Executive Board any additional legal authority. Rather, it would give a majority of creditors the legal authority to bind a dissenting minority.

Notwithstanding the above, relying on the IMF's Articles as a means of providing the statutory basis for majority action decisions to be taken by sovereign debtors and their creditors will require the resolution of an important institutional issue. As noted above, a treaty framework will require the establishment of a verification of claims and dispute resolutions process. However,

---

[5] Overriding the recognition of such judgments could be achieved by uniform recourse to the "public policy" exception to these general rules.

the IMF's existing institutional infrastructure would not accommodate it playing such a role. Specifically, the IMF's Executive Board would not be perceived as impartial in this process since the IMF is a creditor and also represents the interest of the sovereign debtor and other bilateral creditors.

One way of addressing this institutional issue would be to rely on the same amendment of the Articles that would be used to establish the collective action framework, described above, as the basis for establishing a new judicial organ that would carry out these very limited functions. Clearly, a key question is whether there would be adequate safeguards to ensure that such an organ operated — and was perceived as operating—independently from the Executive Board and the Board of Governors.

As a legal matter, the independence of the organ could be established by the text of the amendment itself. The amendment would provide that decisions of the judicial organ would not be subject to review by any of the IMF's other organs and that, more generally, the judges appointed to this organ would not be subject to the interference or influence of the staff and management of the IMF, the Executive Board or any IMF member. The text of the amendment could also specify in some detail the qualifications of the judges to be selected and, to ensure security of tenure, the grounds for their dismissal. One way of ensuring that the judges serving on the organ maintain some distance from the staff and the Executive Board would be to appoint them for a limited but possibly renewable period. Moreover, a procedure could be established whereby the judges appointed by the Managing Director (or the Board) would be derived from a list of candidates that would have been selected by a qualified and independent panel.

It should be emphasized that the role of this judicial organ—wherever it is located — would be a limited one. Specifically, the organ would have no authority to challenge decisions made by the Executive Board regarding, inter alia, the adequacy of a member's policies or the sustainability of the member's debt.

Exchange Controls

In the context of financial crises, exchange controls may need to be relied upon in at least two circumstances. First, in circumstances where a sovereign defaults on its own indebtedness, it is likely that such a default will trigger capital flight, particularly where the restructuring will also embrace claims on the sovereign held by the domestic banking system and the member maintains an open capital account. Second, even where the external debt of the sovereign is not significant, a financial crisis can arise because of the over

indebtedness of the banking and corporate sectors which, when coupled with
a loss of creditor confidence, leads to a sudden depletion of foreign exchange
reserves. In these circumstances, there may be a case for the authorities to
impose exchange controls for a temporary period.

The possible resort to exchange controls raises a number of complex
issues that would need to be addressed on a case-by-case basis. Inevitably, difficult judgments will need to be made against the background of considerable
uncertainty regarding the ways in which events may unfold. Nevertheless,
two broad sets of issues would need to be considered: first the timing of the
imposition of controls, and second, their coverage across different types of
transactions.

As regards timing, there is a question of whether it would be appropriate
to impose controls at an early stage of capital flight with a view to stanching
the hemorrhage of reserves, thereby preserving the resources available to the
economy, including for debt service. This would have the effect of reducing
the difference in the ability of investors holding claims of various maturities
to exit early, and from this perspective permitting a broader degree of equity
in the treatment of various types of investors. It is worth noting, however,
that differences in the ability of investors to exit early stemming from the relative maturity of claims is presumably reflected in the market pricing of the
instruments concerned and compensates investors for the relative risks.
Moreover, a shift toward a presumption that exchange controls would be
imposed at an early stage of capital flight could reduce the ability of domestic banks to attract and intermediate domestic savings and foreign capital, as
residents would be more likely to hold savings abroad and foreign creditors
would raise the cost of short-term capital.

An alternative approach of waiting until resources are exhausted before
resort to controls would lean in the direction of respecting the contractual
rights of investors holding short-term claims. It would also keep open the
possibility that if confidence stabilizes resort to exchange controls could be
avoided. It has the drawback, however, that once controls are imposed the
resources available to the economy have been depleted, which will have
adverse effects on the pace of recovery and capacity to generate resources for
debt service.

A second question relates to the scope of the controls. In cases where a member has the institutional capacity to implement exchange controls, it may be
possible to arrest capital flight without an interruption in debt service and
other contractual obligations. But this will depend on the severity of the crisis and the institutional capacity of the member. In circumstances where it is
necessary to interrupt external debt service, it would be important for the

authorities to put in place a framework for the eventual normalization of creditor relations by nonsovereign debtors, in order to minimize the long-term impact on corporations' market access. Such a framework could include two key features. First, the facilitation of an out-of-court workout mechanism operating in the shadow of domestic bankruptcy. Second, a specification of the minimum terms under which foreign exchange would be made available to service restructured debts.

The question arises, however, as to whether an SDRM should be designed to provide limited legal protection (in the form of a stay) during the period of renegotiation to domestic enterprises that might otherwise be subject to litigation as a result of the default arising from the imposition of controls.

It should be noted at the outset that, even if the decision were made to exclude nonsovereign debt from the coverage of an SDRM, exchange controls would still provide considerable legal protection in at least two respects. First, any restrictions imposed on the ability of residents or nonresidents to make transfers abroad would still be enforceable within the territory of the sovereign. Second, in the event that the controls give rise to payments arrears, foreign creditors would be precluded from enforcing their claims against a resident debtor in the territory of the sovereign. The legal protection that may *not* be provided by the controls would be protection against the enforcement of claims by nonresidents with respect to a resident debtor's assets that are located overseas. It is this latter category of protection that an SDRM could be designed to provided.[6]

Among the complex issues that would arise if an SDRM were to apply to exchange controls is the feasibility of making a distinction between those debtors that, except for exchange controls, would be able to service their debt, and other debtors that are not healthy and need to be restructured. While it would be reasonable for the former category to enjoy some temporary legal protection under an SDRM, it would be preferable to make the latter category subject to the local insolvency law. A second difficulty relates to the protection of creditor interests. During the period of the stay on litigation, what measures could be put in place that would give creditors the assurance that the debtor is not using the stay as a means of facilitating asset stripping?

A final question relates to the role of the IMF. As discussed above, in the context of sovereign indebtedness, it is possible to design a framework where

---

[6] As interpreted by the courts of some IMF members, Article VIII, Section 2(b) of the IMF's Articles may be invoked to stay creditor enforcement against debtors unable to service their external payments because of exchange controls that are consistent with the IMF's Articles.

the key decisions are made by the majority of creditors rather than the IMF. However, in the context of exchange controls that gives rise to the default of a multitude of debtors (each with their own group of creditors), such an approach would not be feasible. In these circumstances, the legal authority to approve a temporary stay, if that were deemed an eventual feature of a new statutory mechanism, would need to reside with the IMF.

CONCLUSION

The absence of a robust legal framework for sovereign debt restructuring generates important costs. Sovereigns with unsustainable debts often wait too long before they seek a restructuring, leaving both their citizens and their creditors worse off. And when sovereigns finally do opt for restructuring, the process is more protracted than it needs to be and less predictable than creditors would like.

The international financial system lacks an established framework for restructuring that is equitable across all of the sovereign's creditors. There are few effective tools to address potential collective action problems that threaten to undermine restructuring agreements acceptable to the debtor and most of its creditors. Holdout creditors may be able to use the threat of litigation to seek to avoid concessions that the majority have agreed to make.

All this explains why it is important for the official community, sovereign debtors, and market participants to discuss how to improve the sovereign debt restructuring process.

This paper has laid out a possible approach. An international legal framework could be created to allow a qualified majority of the sovereign's creditors to approve a restructuring agreement, and to make that decision of the majority binding on a minority. The vote would need to include all the relevant creditors of the sovereign, not just the holders of a single debt instrument. Broadening the majority voting process beyond a single debt instrument vastly simplifies the process of creditor coordination, and would facilitate the negotiation of a deal that treats all creditors fairly. This approach draws on the principles of well-designed corporate bankruptcy regimes, and is similar in concept to the decision-making procedures among holders of a single bond issue that contains a majority restructuring clause.

Provisions for majority action would be most effective if supported by three other features, all of which protect the debtor's assets and capacity to pay while it works with its creditors to reach an agreement. The features are: a stay on creditor litigation after the suspension of payments; mechanisms that protect creditor interests during the stay; and the provision of seniority for fresh financing by private creditors. A single body would need to oversee the process of verifying claims and to resolve any disputes.

In such a framework, the decision whether to give legal protection for the sovereign and provide seniority for new private financing could to be left to the debtor and a qualified majority of its creditors. Similarly, the sovereign and a qualified majority of creditors would agree on the terms of the ultimate restructuring. The primary purpose of an amendment of the IMF's Articles would be to provide the statutory legal basis to make an agreement between the debtor and the requisite majority of creditors binding on all relevant creditors.

There are a number of questions that would need to be fleshed out before such an approach could be made operational. Perhaps most crucial, and also most difficult, is the scope of the debt to be included in the voting process. It will also be important to explore with debtors and market participants how best to protect general creditor interests during the negotiating process, as well as how to structure the dispute resolution process.

These questions will not be easy to answer. But it is important not to shy away from the challenge. There is now widespread agreement that a new approach is necessary, and that a fairer, more efficient process for sovereign debt restructurings would represent a substantial strengthening of the international financial system. We should press ahead to achieve it.

Chapter 10

SOVEREIGN WORKOUTS: AN IMF PERSPECTIVE*

I. INTRODUCTION

Over the past several years, the international community has devoted considerable attention to improving arrangements for resolving financial crises and,
in particular, for the restructuring of unsustainable sovereign debt. These
efforts have benefited from the active participation of sovereign debtors, market participants, workout professionals, lawyers, economists and the "official
sector," including the International Monetary Fund ("IMF"). As can be
expected, perspectives regarding the dimensions of the problem and the direction of reform have varied. Nevertheless, a consensus appears to have been
reached on two broad issues. First, there is a recognition that, in circumstances
where a sovereign's debt has become unsustainable, all stakeholders — the
sovereign debtor, its creditors, and the system more generally — will benefit
from a restructuring process that is more rapid, orderly, and predictable than
is currently the case. Second, it is generally accepted that enhancing the effectiveness of the legal framework is critical to the success of any meaningful
reform in this area.

Much of the discussion has focused on whether the necessary strengthening of the legal framework can be achieved exclusively through private
contract or, alternatively, requires official intervention, perhaps in the
form of the IMF's proposed "Sovereign Debt Restructuring Mechanism"

* This paper was jointly written with Sean Hagan and was published in the *Chicago
Journal of International Law*, Volume 6, No. 1, 2005, pp. 203–218.

("SDRM").[1] Market participants have expressed concern that any form of official intervention would undermine the operation of capital markets in this area and, in particular, the quality of emerging market debt as an asset class.[2] In contrast, the premise behind the SDRM has been that official intervention, if appropriately designed, would strengthen rather than weaken the operation of the international financial system. While recognizing the important limits of the analogy, supporters of official intervention have pointed to the critical role that domestic insolvency frameworks play in a market economy.[3]

While there has been considerable support for the SDRM within the official sector, efforts are currently underway to improve the restructuring process through market-based reform and, in particular, through a reliance on the collective action clauses that are found in international sovereign bonds. Whether the official sector turns its attention again to the SDRM will depend, at least in part, on whether these clauses are sufficiently robust to limit the severity of the costs that arise from the restructuring process.

This article provides a brief overview of the key economic, financial and legal issues that have been central to the discussions in this area. Section II identifies the problems faced by a sovereign and its creditors when the

---

[1] See, for example, Anne Krueger, IMF First Deputy Managing Director, *New Approaches to Sovereign Debt Restructuring: An Update on Our Thinking*, Remarks at the Institute for International Economics Conference on Sovereign Debt Workouts: Hopes and Hazards (Apr 1, 2002), transcript available online at <http://www.imf.org/external/np/speeches/2002/040102,htm> (visited March 24, 2005).

[2] See Michael M. Philips, *Support Builds for Plan to Ease Debt Loads of Developing Nations*, Wall St J A16 (Sept 17, 2002) (quoting Charles Dallara, Managing Director for the Institute of International Finance, as saying "at a time of extreme risk-aversion in emerging markets, when capital flows are falling . . . approaches such as [the SDRM] add further to uncertainty and investor anxiety").

[3] For an analysis of the relevance of corporate reorganization legislation to the restructuring of sovereign debt, see Steven L. Schwarcz, *Sovereign Debt Restructuring: A Bankruptcy Reorganization Approach*, 85 Cornell L. Rev 956 (2001); Patrick Bolton, *Toward a Statutory Approach to Sovereign Debt Restructuring: Lessons from Corporate Bankruptcy Practice Around the World*, 50 IMF Staff Papers 41 (2003), available online at <http://www.imf.org/External/Pubs/FT/staffp/2002/00-00/pdf/bolton.pdf> (visited Mar 24, 2005); Patrick Bolton and David A. Skeel, Jr., *Inside the Black Box: How Should a Sovereign Bankruptcy Framework Be Structured?* 53 Emory L. J 763, 773–74 (2004); Hal S. Scott, *A Bankruptcy Procedure for Sovereign Debtors?* 37 Intl L 103, 123–26 (2003); and Michelle J. White, *Sovereigns in Distress: Do They Need Bankruptcy?* (2002), Paper for the Brookings Panel on Economic Activity, available online at <http://www.brookings.edu/dybdocroot/es/commentary/journals/bpea_macro/papers/200204_white.pdf> (visited March 24, 2005).

restructuring of the sovereign's debt becomes inevitable and, in that context, discusses the assistance the IMF can — and cannot — provide in these situations. Section III sets forth a brief analysis of the two primary proposals for legal reform: collective action clauses and the SDRM. Section IV offers some concluding observations.

II. THE PROBLEM

While a sovereign debtor and its creditors share a common interest in an early and rapid restructuring of unsustainable sovereign debt, developments in the international financial system have conspired to make this a more complicated and time consuming process than it need be. In some respects, the problem is similar to the one confronted by a company and its creditors seeking to maximize value in an environment where debt structures are increasingly complex and creditor interests diverse. Of course, the corporate analogy only holds at a certain level of abstraction. There are a number of distinguishing features that have important effects on the process — most importantly, creditors and corporate debtors engage in the restructuring process in the shadow of liquidation.[4] The "liquidation" alternative shapes not only the debtor-creditor relationship, but also the intercreditor dynamic, given the fact that a liquidation law defines the relative priorities among creditors. Nevertheless, the experience in the corporate context reveals that, as with corporations, once a judgment is made that a sovereign debtor will not be able to service its claims without a reduction in the net present value of the claims, everyone has an interest in initiating the process earlier rather than later. Moreover, all will gain from a process that, once initiated, is rapid, orderly, and predictable.

---

[4] Although insolvency laws vary considerably among countries, over the past several years it has become increasingly possible to identify emerging "standards" and best practices in this area. Perhaps most significantly, the United Nations Commission on International Trade Law ("UNCITRAL") recently adopted the Legislative Guide on Insolvency Law, which provides detailed analysis and recommendations on all aspects of the design of an insolvency law. UNCITRAL, *UNCITRAL Legislative Guide on Insolvency Law* (2004), available online at <http://www.uncitral.org/english/texts/insolven/insoguide.pdf> (visited Mar 24, 2005). This work builds upon work that has been done by a variety of international organizations, including that of the IMF and the World Bank, See also IMF Legal Department, *Orderly & Effective Insolvency Procedures: Key Issues* (1999), available online at <http://www.imf.org/external/pubs/ft/orderly/> (visited Mar 24, 2005) and World Bank, *Principles and Guidelines for Effective Insolvency and Creditor Rights Systems* (2001), available online at <http://siteresources.worldbank.org/GILD/PrinciplesAnd Guidelines/20162797/Principles%20and%20Guidelines%20for%20Effective%20I nsolvency%20and%20Creditor%20Rights%20Systems.pdf> (visited on March 24, 2005).

A. Unsustainable Debt and its Implications

In the corporate context, a distinction is generally made between "illiquidity" and "insolvency." A company is considered "illiquid" when it is unable to pay its debts as they fall due, but is "insolvent" when the value of its liabilities exceeds the value of its assets.[5] While the former concept focuses on problems arising from the structure of the company's debts, the latter addresses problems relating to the size of the overall stock. This distinction has a number of implications in how the corporate restructuring process will proceed. In either case, however, some form of statutory protection will be needed since, even if the problem can be resolved by a reprofiling of maturities rather than a reduction of maturities, the inability of a company to make payments will result in an enforcement of legal claims and the dismemberment of the debtor.

The corporate analogy does not translate directly to the sovereign context. A sovereign has choices available to it that are normally unavailable to a company that is facing a liquidity crisis. Among other things, it has the IMF. There will always be circumstances where, as a result of changes in external circumstances (a sharp and unanticipated drop in the price of a key export, for example), a sovereign will find it difficult to service its debt under the original terms. In many cases, the adoption of strong economic policies will provide a sufficient basis for weathering the crisis: even if a reprofiling of maturities is necessary, the net present value of the debt will be maintained and the future debt-to-GDP ratio will stabilize or fall. In these circumstances, the IMF can play a critical "catalytic" role by providing its financial resources in support of strong economic adjustment policies, thereby assisting the country to regain market confidence.

There may be circumstances, however, where, under any reasonable set of circumstances or policies, the sovereign's debt relative to GDP will grow indefinitely. A sovereign will never be "insolvent" in the strict sense: by virtue of its fiscal powers, a sovereign's assets are — at least theoretically — inexhaustible.[6]

---

[5] In the corporate context, the illiquidity standard is also referred to as the "cash flow" or "cessation of payments" standard; see *UNCITRAL Legislative Guide on Insolvency Law* at 57 (cited in note 4). Regarding insolvency, as a general matter, the United States Bankruptcy Code defines a company as insolvent if "the sum of such entity's debts is greater than all of such entity's property, at a fair valuation." 11 USC § 101 (32)(A) (2000).

[6] A number of commentators have recognized the difficulty of determining when indebtedness is unsustainable in the sovereign context. See Richard N. Cooper, *Chapter 11 for Countries?* 81 Foreign Aff 90, 92 (2002); see also Nouriel Roubini, *Do We Need a New Bankruptcy Regime?* Brookings Papers on Econ Activity 321, 322 (2002), abstract available at <http://static.highbeam.com/b/brookingspapersoneconomicactivity/march222002/doweneedanewbankruptcyregime/> (visited March 24, 2005); Scott, 37 Intl L 103 (cited in note 3).

However, at a certain point, its debt will become "unsustainable". Specifically, as the ratio of debt-to-GDP mounts, real interest rates in the debtor country will rise. While the sovereign may try to increase taxes or take other measures to service its debt, all of these measures will be growth reducing. As growth falters, the debt-to-GDP ratio will rise further. Of course, judgments as to debt unsustainability must be made on a probabilistic basis. There is always the possibility, however remote, that new natural resources will be discovered or that the terms of trade will shift in a country's favor. However, as borrowing continues, the probability of the sovereign being able to continue to service its claims will continue to drop. As lenders see that debt sustainability is increasingly improbable, they will no longer be willing to provide financing — at any price.

In these circumstances, the IMF will not be able to help unless the sovereign takes steps to restructure its debt in a manner that reduces the debt's net present value to a level that assures medium term sustainability. According to its charter, the IMF may only make its resources available to member countries if it determines that its assistance will actually assist the member in the resolution of its balance of payments problems.[7] Moreover, as a financial institution with limited resources, the IMF must have adequate confidence that the member will be in a position to repay the Fund within the relatively short repayment period (normally 3–5 years) that applies to its financing.[8] But when the IMF has made a judgment that a member's debt is unsustainable, its financing will only serve to delay — and exacerbate — the resolution of the problem unless efforts are made by the sovereign to both restructure its debt and implement effective adjustment policies that provide for medium term sustainability, In addition, in the absence of a reduction in the net present value of the claims on the sovereign, the IMF will have little basis to conclude that it will get repaid.

From the perspective of the borrower, there comes a point where further delays in the initiation of the restructuring process only exacerbate the economic dislocation that occurs when the crisis arises. Since the debt restructuring process is always a painful one for a sovereign (both economically and

---

[7] See *Articles of Agreement* of the International Monetary Fund (1944), Art V, § 3(a), available online at <http://www.imf.org/external/pubs/ft/aa/aaO5.htm> (visited March 24, 2005) (hereinafter IMF Agreement) which states:

"The Fund shall adopt policies on the use of its general resources, including policies on stand-by or similar arrangements, and may adopt special policies for special balance of payments problems, that will assist members to solve their balance of payments problems in a manner consistent with the provisions of this Agreement and that will establish adequate safeguards for the temporary use of the general resources of the Fund."

[8] Id, art V, § 7(c).

politically), governments are often tempted to introduce whatever economic adjustment efforts they think necessary to avoid a restructuring; in other words, they try to "gamble for resurrection". But after a certain point, these steps only reduce the policy options that are available when the debt restructuring process begins. Moreover, a desperate wave of borrowing from domestic banks when all other sources of credit have dried up only leaves the domestic banking system insolvent when the net present value of the banks' claims on the government is reduced. The ensuing recapitalization of the banking system places an even greater strain on the sovereign's fiscal resources.

Finally, there is the perspective of the sovereign's creditors. Actions taken by the sovereign government to delay the restructuring process and "gamble for resurrection" ultimately reduce value of creditor claims. To the extent that these delays serve to exacerbate the economic dislocation, this will effectively reduce the amounts that are available to service restructured claims. Perhaps even more directly, additional borrowing from the IMF — which, by virtue of its preferred creditor status is excluded from the debt restructuring process — will only further dilute the claims of existing creditors.

B. The Barriers to Restructuring

There is usually a brief period between the point at which it is highly probable that a sovereign's debt is unsustainable and the outset of a full blown crisis. This period presents a window of opportunity in which it may be possible to reach an agreement on a restructuring that offers the prospect of restoring sustainability while limiting the scale of economic dislocation and preserving the value of creditor claims. At this point, the net present value of the debtor's primary fiscal surplus will be larger if the debt is restructured since the economy's growth prospects can increase and real interest rates can fall. In these circumstances, an orderly and prompt restructuring can create value for both creditors and the debtor. Moreover, at this juncture, the IMF can provide financing in support of the implementation of strong adjustment policies during the debt restructuring process. Experience demonstrates, however, that there are a number of reasons why the restructuring process, once initiated, is more costly than it need be for the sovereign debtor, its creditors and the system more generally. The two most important reasons are briefly discussed below.

1. *The policies of the sovereign debtor*

As noted earlier, once the restructuring process is initiated, it is critical that the sovereign formulate and implement a set of economic policies that will provide a basis for achieving medium-term balance of payments viability. In the absence of such policies, creditors will have no confidence in the country's payment capacity and, somewhat understandably, will be unwilling to engage in restructuring negotiations. In addition to these substantive economic policies, it is also critical for the sovereign to take steps to establish a collaborative debt restructuring process with its creditors. Unfortunately, there is a general perception among creditors that sovereign debtors will often eschew a collaborative process and, instead, will launch "take-it-or-leave-it" exchange offers without providing creditors with the information necessary to enable them to make informed decisions.[9] Even where such an approach is successful in attracting a critical mass of support, it risks undermining the operation of the international financial system generally, and the value of emerging market debt as an asset class more specifically. For example, while this approach may be of benefit to distressed debt purchasers (who buy the debt at a steep discount as uncertainty regarding the restructuring process drives down secondary market prices), it is very problematic for those investors who extended the credit in the first place and continue to hold the claims at face value.[10]

2. *Collective action problems*

Even where the sovereign is implementing appropriate policies and is intent on engaging with its creditors in a collaborative manner, its ability to attract a critical mass of support among creditors may be undermined by problems of collective action. Specifically, creditors who would otherwise be willing to reach an agreement with the debtor will hesitate to do so out of concern that other creditors will hold out and, after the agreement has been reached, press for full payment on the original terms. Increased uncertainty as to whether a critical mass of creditors will support the restructuring will, in turn, make a sovereign even more reluctant to initiate the process, leading to further delays and, accordingly, a further loss of economic value.

---

[9] The approach relied upon by Ecuador to restructure its Brady bonds and Eurobonds from 1999 to 2000 generated considerable criticism in that regard. For a discussion of investors' concerns regarding the process that was relied upon by Ecuador to restructure its bonds, see Felix Salmon and Jorge Gallardo, *The Buy Side Starts to Bite Back,* 384 Euromoney 46 (April 2001).

[10] For a discussion of potential implications of the strategy relied upon by Ecuador, see IMF Policy Development and Review and Legal Departments, *Involving the Private Sector in the Resolution of Financial Crisis — Restructuring International Sovereign Bonds* 7 (2001), available online at <http://www.imf.org/external/pubs/ft/series/03/ips.pdf> (visited Mar 24, 2005). Interestingly, although Pakistan had collective action clauses in its bonds, it decided not to use them when it restructured its debt in 2000. Id at 5.

The magnitude of collective action problems currently facing a sovereign have increased with the evolution of capital markets over the past twenty years. During the 1980s, the claims being restructured were largely held by commercial banks in the form of syndicated loans.[11] The debt restructuring process, while protracted, was relatively orderly, with negotiations being led by bank steering committees. Although these banks were not always cooperative, the official sector was generally successful in influencing their behavior through the subtle — and sometimes not so subtle — use of regulatory authority. Moreover, given the extensive business that these banks had with the debtor governments and their residents, they understood that aggressive tactics would only undermine these long term relationships.

Over the past fifteen years, however, emerging market sovereigns have been able to access capital markets directly though the issuance of international securities and, as a result the relative importance of the commercial bank loans as a source of financing has declined significantly. While the process of disintermediation has resulted in a very large source of external financing for these countries, it also presents considerable challenges if and when the unsustainability of a sovereign's debt necessitates a restructuring. A debtor is confronted with a relatively atomized creditor community, holding bonds issued in a number of different jurisdictions. Perhaps even more importantly, the interests of these creditors are often diverse. While retail investors and some institutional creditors may hold the instruments at face value, others have purchased the instruments at a steep discount. Many of these creditors are unregulated and few have the type of long term relationship with the sovereign that will guide their behavior. Rather, they pursue a strategy of maximizing the value of their claims.[12] In some circumstances, they may

---

[11] For a discussion of the debt crisis in the 1980s, see Lex Rieffel, *Restructuring Sovereign Debt: The Case for Ad Hoc Machinery* 149 (Brookings Institution, 2003); William R. Cline, *International Debt: Systematic Risk and Policy Response* (Intl Inst Econ, 1984); CM. Watson and K.P. Riegling, *History of the Debt Crisis — Current Legal Issues Affecting Central Banks* (IMF, 1984). With respect to the IMF's role during the crisis, see James M. Boughton, *Silent Revolution: The International Monetary Fund 1979–1989* (IMF, 2001); see also Sean Hagan, *Sovereign Debtors, Private Creditors and the IMF in International Monetary and Financial Law in the New Millennium* 49 (British Inst Intl & Comp L, 2002).

[12] For a discussion of the tactics and success rates of distressed debt purchasers, see Christopher C. Wheeler and Amir Attaran, *Declawing the Vulture Funds: Rehabilition of a Comity Defense in Sovereign Debt Litigation*, 39 Stan J Intl L 253, 268–70 (2003). For a general discussion, see Samuel E. Goldman, Comment, *Mavericks in the Market: The Emerging Problem of Holdouts in Sovereign Debt Restructuring*, 5 UCLA J Intl & Foreign Aff 159 (2001–02); G. Mitu Guiati and Kenneth N. Klee, *Sovereign Piracy*, 56 Bus Law 635 (2001).

determine that this strategy is best implemented by participating in the debt restructuring. In other circumstances, however, they may choose to hold out.

The nature of the holdout problem depends on whether the debt restructuring precedes or follows a default. There are good reasons why a sovereign may seek to restructure unsustainable debt prior to a default. A default can trigger a crisis that causes major economic dislocation. For example, where the banking system holds a considerable amount of sovereign debt, the plunge in the secondary market of these claims caused by a default may result in an insolvent banking system. Fear of such insolvency may also result in massive capital flight, which only exacerbates the problem. For all these reasons, creditors have a similar interest in engaging in a predefault restructuring. Not only does the avoidance of a full blown crisis limit the decline in the value of their claims, but it also increases the amount of resources available to the sovereign to service its claims once they are restructured. Having to recapitalize an insolvent banking system places an extraordinary amount of strain on the sovereign's fiscal position.

Notwithstanding the commonality of interests among the sovereign and its creditors, the holdout problem may be particularly acute in these circumstances; a creditor contemplating a holdout strategy may calculate that, as long as a critical mass of creditors accept the offer, the sovereign may be in a position to service the original claims of those creditors that did not participate in the restructuring — and may be tempted to do so as to avoid the reputation damage that a default may create. However, because of this possibility, creditors who otherwise would have been interested in engaging in the restructuring may decline to do so out of intercreditor equity considerations.

In the event that the restructuring process takes place after a default, the credibility of the holdout strategy — and the degree to which it will undermine the restructuring process — depends on the ability of the holdout to enforce its claims against a sovereign. Enforcing one's claim against a sovereign, however, is hardly a straightforward task. Although a sovereign borrowing in the international capital markets is no longer protected by the concept of "absolute sovereign immunity" — at least under the laws in those jurisdictions that typically govern international debt instruments: usually New York state law or English law — there are still considerable obstacles confronting a creditor that is seeking recourse through the court system.[13] In particular, while obtaining a

---

[13] For a discussion of the barriers confronting a creditor wishing to enforce its claim against a sovereign, see Sean Hagan, *Designing a Legal framework to Restructure Sovereign Debt*, 36 Georgetown *J Intl L* (2005) (manuscript at 11–15, on file with author).

judgment may be relatively easy, collecting on such a judgment has traditionally been very difficult. In circumstances where the government itself is the borrower, the assets of state-owned enterprises are normally not available for attachment. Similarly, the reserves of the central bank are normally also immune from attachment, provided that the central bank itself is not liable under the claim.

Confronted with the difficult task of finding assets of the sovereign to attach, judgment creditors have recently sought to extract a recovery from a sovereign by threatening to undermine the sovereign's relationship with its other creditors. Relying on a court's injunctive power, creditors have sought — and obtained — court orders that effectively preclude a debtor from servicing its claims on its restructured debt unless it makes simultaneous and ratable payments to the judgment creditor. This strategy was first used successfully by a distressed debt purchaser against the Republic of Peru and has now been replicated in other contexts.[14] There continues to be considerable uncertainty regarding the legal basis of this strategy, in large part because there is doubt as to whether the provision in the underlying agreement that has been used by the distressed debt purchasers to effect this strategy in most, but not all, of the cases — the *pari passu* clause — should, in fact, be interpreted to require simultaneous and ratable payments.[15] Nevertheless, this strategy has exacerbated the collective action problem facing a sovereign and its creditors in at least two respects. First, to the extent that holdouts have a credible postdefault holdout strategy, creditors who are otherwise willing to engage in the debt restructuring process may be more reluctant to do so because of concerns regarding intercreditor equity. Second, creditors contemplating whether to accept a restructuring offer will clearly be concerned that the holdout strategy may be used to interrupt payments to them once the debt has been restructured.

---

[14] Id at 12–15.

[15] For an analysis of why it would be unreasonable to interpret the *pari passu* provision as limiting payments, see Lee C. Buchheit and Jeremiah S. Pam, *The Pari Passu Clause in Sovereign Debt Instruments*, 53 Emory L J 869 (2004). See also Philip R. Wood, *Pari Passu Clauses — What Do They Mean?* Butterworths *J of Intl Bank &Fin L* (Nov 2003); Gulati and Klee, 56 Bus Law 635 (cited in note 12). The successful action taken by a distressed debt purchaser against Peru involved an order issued by a Belgian court against Euroclear. Belgium recently amended Article 9 of the law that implements European Directive 98/26/EC for the purpose of ensuring that future court orders do not prevent Euroclear from receiving and channeling payments on account of bondholders; see Belgian Law 11/19/204, Art 15.

III. REFORMING THE LEGAL FRAMEWORK

In recognition of the above problems, efforts have been made over the past several years to strengthen the legal frameworks to restructure sovereign debt. Two principal models have been pursued: one based on contract, the other on a treaty-based framework that could be established through an amendment to the IMF's Articles of Agreement. While there are important differences between these two approaches, they are similar in important respects. First, both place a priority on the resolution of collective action problems in a manner that does not shift the leverage from creditors to the sovereign. Rather, they are designed to shift the leverage from individual creditors to creditors as a group. Second, both frameworks seek to enhance the predictability and quality of the dialogue between the sovereign and its creditors during the restructuring process. Third, by seeking to make the process orderly, predictable and rapid, both frameworks are designed to enhance the quality of emerging market debt as an asset class. Finally, neither purports to be a panacea. In the final analysis, the success of any restructuring process will ultimately depend on the quality of the economic policies being pursued by the sovereign.

A. Collective Action Clauses

Notwithstanding the attention that collective action clauses have recently received over the past several years, they are hardly a novel feature of international sovereign bonds. Two types of provisions have been prevalent for many years.[16] The first is a provision that enables a qualified majority of bondholders (typically 75 percent) to bind bondholders within the same issuance to the payment term of the restructuring. This provision, normally referred to as "majority amendment provisions" is a common feature in bonds governed by the laws of England and Japan. Until recently, however, they have not been included in bonds governed by the laws of New York. The second type of provision, referred to as a "majority enforcement" provision, is designed to limit the ability of a minority of bondholders to disrupt the restructuring process by enforcing their claims after a default but prior to a

---

[16] For a comprehensive analysis of the origins of collective action clauses, see Lee C. Buchheit and G. Mitu Gulati, *Sovereign Bonds and the Collective Will*, 51 Emory L J 1317, 1318–32 (2002). The various features of collective action clauses are also analyzed in IMF Legal Department, *The Design and Effectiveness of Collective Action Clauses* (IMF 2002), available online at <http://www.imf.org/external/np/psi/2002/eng/060602.pdf> (visited March 24, 2005).

restructuring agreement. Elements of this provision can already be found in bonds governed by laws of New York and England. Although experience with restructuring sovereign bonds has been limited, the evidence suggests that collective action clauses can play a valuable role in facilitating the resolution of financial crises. They were successfully relied upon by the Ukraine in 1999 (in bonds governed by English law) and Uruguay in 2003 (in bonds governed by the laws of Japan).

Over the past nine years, most of the efforts of the official community in this area have been devoted to promoting the inclusion of majority amendment provisions in bonds governed by New York law, which continue to constitute the largest share of instruments used by emerging market sovereigns. Although there are no legal impediments to the introduction of majority amendment provisions in these bonds, there has been, until recently, very little appetite for them in the private sector.[17] The breakthrough came in early 2003, when Mexico included such a provision in its New York law-governed bonds. Since then, these provisions have become a standard feature of bonds issued under New York law. How does one explain this reversal? As has been observed by some commentators, market participants were finally willing to embrace collective action out of a recognition that, unless progress was made regarding the adoption of these clauses, the official sector was likely to press ahead with the SDRM.

While the inclusion of these clauses in bonds governed by New York law represents a major step forward, there is room for further progress. In a 2002 report issued by a working group formed by the G-10 ("G-10 Working Group Report"),[18] two recommendations were made regarding the design of collective action clauses that have yet to be fully implemented. While the first relates to the use of trust deeds, the second involves the introduction of "representation" provisions. With respect to the first recommendation, certain bonds governed by English law are issued under trust

---

[17] The US Trust Indenture Act of 1939 prohibits any impairment of a bondholder's right to receive payments due (or to recover the missed payments) without its consent, except that it allows a majority of bondholders with 75 percent of outstanding principal to postpone interest payments for up to three years. See 15 USC § 77 (2000). However, this limitation does not apply to sovereign bonds. For further discussion, see Buchheit and Gulati, 51 Emory L J at 1326–30 (cited in note 16).

[18] Group of Ten, *Report of the G-10 Working Group on Contractual Clauses* (Sept 26, 2002) available online at <http://www.oecd.org/dataoecd/62/51/2501714.pdf> (visited March 24, 2005).

deeds, which give the trustee the right to initiate legal proceedings on behalf of all bondholders.[19] The trustee is only required to act if, among other things, it is requested to do so by the requisite percentage of bondholders (typically more than 25 percent).[20] Moreover, any amounts recovered by the trustee must be distributed pro rata among all bondholders.[21] Such a de facto sharing provision creates an important disincentive for a minority of bondholders to initiate litigation, even if they control a sufficient amount of the bond issue to force the trustee to take action. Unfortunately, however, the use of trust structures in the sovereign context is still relatively uncommon for bonds governed by New York law.[22] The second recommendation — the adoption of the representation provision — is designed to facilitate an early dialogue between bondholders and the sovereign in the context of an emerging crisis.[23] Specifically, the provision would enable bondholders to elect a representative with the authority to enter into restructuring discussions. This representative would not have the authority to bind bondholders to the terms of a restructuring agreement, however.[24] To date, such "representation" provisions have yet to become a common feature of international sovereign bonds.

B. The SDRM

The SDRM proposal developed by the IMF during the period from November 2001 through April 2003 envisages the resolution of collective action problems through a treaty-based framework.[25] As with collective action clauses, the SDRM would enable a debtor and a qualified majority of its creditors to make decisions that would be binding on the minority, including decisions regarding the acceptance of the final restructuring terms.

---

[19] Id at 6.

[20] Id.

[21] Id.

[22] The bonds issued by Uruguay in the context of its recent debt restructuring represent a welcome exception to this rule. See Ben Maiden, *Uruguay Faces up to Challenges of Emerging Market Debt*, 22 *Intl Fin L Rev* 10 (May 2003).

[23] Group of Ten, *Report of the G-10 Working Group on Contractual Clauses* at 2 (cited in note 18).

[24] Id at 3.

[25] The details of the final SDRM proposal are set forth in the attachment to IMF, *Report of the Managing Director to the International Monetary and Financial Committee on a Statutory Sovereign Debt Restructuring Mechanism* (April 8, 2003), available online at<http://www.imf.org/external/np/omd/2003/040803.htm> (visited March 24, 2005).

Unlike collective action clauses, however, the SDRM envisages that, for voting purposes, claims would be "aggregated" across different instruments, even in the absence of a contractual framework that links these different instruments. Accordingly, the majority needed to effect a restructuring would be calculated on the basis of all of the claims that would be covered by the restructuring, subject to rules regarding classification. This approach draws on the design of corporate insolvency laws where claims are also aggregated for voting purposes. In an environment where a sovereign has issued a multiplicity of different debt instruments in a variety of different jurisdictions, aggregation prevents creditors from disrupting the restructuring process by, for example, establishing a controlling position in a single bond issuance.[26]

The SDRM would also establish a comprehensive framework designed to enhance the quality of dialogue during the restructuring process: both from the debtor-creditor and intercreditor perspective. During the restructuring negotiations, the sovereign debtor would be required to provide detailed information to its creditors regarding both nature of its indebtedness and how it intends to treat such indebtedness.[27] In addition, the SDRM envisages the creation of a representative creditors committee that would provide a focal point for such negotiations.[28]

The premise behind the SDRM proposal was that, to the extent its operation was sufficiently predictable, it would create incentives for debtors and creditors to reach an agreement without having to rely on its actual use. The aggregated voting provisions would encourage early creditor organization, thereby laying the foundation for structured negotiations. Potential holdouts would realize that, unless they were sufficiently flexible, the debtor and the majority of creditors could use the mechanism to bind them to the terms of an agreement. Ideally, the restructuring process would take place prior to a default, thereby protecting asset values for the benefit of both the sovereign debtor and its creditors. In both these respects, the SDRM could operate in a manner that is similar to the "prepackaged

---

[26] In terms of the resolution of collective action problems, the SDRM would also be more comprehensive than collective action clauses by virtue of the fact that it would bind judgment creditors: those creditors whose claims are no longer subject to the provisions of the underlying contract by virtue of the fact that they had received a judgment against the sovereign from a court of competent jurisdiction.

[27] IMF, *Report of the Managing Director to the International Monetary and Financial Committee on a Statutory Sovereign Debt Restructuring Mechanism*, § 5 (cited in note 25).

[28] Id at § 8.

bankruptcy proceedings" that are relied upon in the corporate context in the United States.[29]

C. The Role of the IMF

As the SDRM proposal was developed, a number of complex design issues were identified and, for the most part, resolved.[30] Among those issues that attracted the most attention were those that related to the role of the Fund in the operation of the SDRM.

From the outset of the discussions regarding the design of the SDRM, it was recognized that, given the central role the Fund currently plays in the resolution of financial crisis, the IMF would be involved at each stage of the SDRM's operation. A country facing debt service difficulties normally approaches the Fund for financing in order to avoid a debt restructuring and the associated economic, social and political disruption. As noted earlier, however, when the Fund determines that a member country's debt is unsustainable, it is precluded from providing financial support in the absence of adequate assurances that the member's debt will be restructured in a manner that provides for medium term sustainability. Consequently, the Fund's own decisions regarding the availability of its resources often have a significant impact on whether and when a member will initiate the restructuring process. To the extent that the SDRM was successful in reducing the costs associated with the debt restructuring process, it was recognized that establishing it would allow the Fund to more easily resist the pressure to provide financing in those cases where there was a very high likelihood that the member's debt was unsustainable.

Once the debt restructuring process begins, the negotiations between the debtor and its creditors often take place against the backdrop of an IMF-supported program. Depending on the circumstances, this program may shape the dialogue between the sovereign debtor and its creditors in two respects. In terms of "process," where the member has already defaulted on

---

[29] Under the US Bankruptcy Code, the votes for a plan may be solicited and obtained prior to the commencement of reorganization proceedings. 11 USC § 1126(b) (2000). For a discussion of prepackaged and prenegotiated plans under Chapter 11, see Stephen H. Case and Mitchell A. Harwood, *Current Issues in Prepackaged Chapter 11 Plans of Reorganization and Using the Federal Declaratory Judgment Act for Instant Reorganizations*, 1991 *Ann Surv Am L* 75.

[30] For a detailed discussion of the design of the SDRM proposal, see Hagan, *Designing a Legal Framework to Restructure Sovereign Debt* at 30–75 (cited in note 13).

its external obligations, the Fund's policy on "lending into arrears" requires it to make a determination, as a condition for future financing, that the member is making good faith efforts to reach an agreement with its creditors.[31] Regarding substance, the program supported by the Fund typically — but not always — specifies the fiscal and external adjustment path that provides the basis for medium term sustainability. This adjustment path determines, in rather broad terms, the amount of resources available for debt service during the program period. Accordingly, the terms of any debt restructuring would need to be consistent with these program assumptions.

As the SDRM proposal was developed, the question arose as to whether the central role that the Fund typically plays in the restructuring process should be effectively codified under the new legal framework. In particular, would a sovereign debtor's ability to activate the SDRM be made conditional upon the IMF's determination that the member's debt was, in fact, unsustainable? On the one hand, the need for some form of "gate keeper" was motivated out of a concern regarding debtor moral hazard. There was a perceived risk that the availability of an internationally sanctioned restructuring framework would increase the domestic political pressure on governments to utilize it, even where the member's debt was sustainable. On the other hand, concerns were expressed about any framework that would enhance the Fund's legal authority in this area. In the end, it was decided that IMF approval would not be a condition for commencement. The moral hazard risk arising from a country's ability to activate the SDRM on a unilateral basis was mitigated by the fact that, once activated, the SDRM would not necessarily enhance the debtor's leverage over its creditors. In particular, and unlike domestic insolvency laws, any stay on legal enforcement would require creditor support, consistent with the approach relied upon in collective action clauses.[32]

---

[31] Originally established in 1989, the lending into arrears policy enables the IMF to provide balance of payments support to countries that are implementing a strong economic adjustment program but have not yet reached agreement with their private creditors. As a condition for providing financing in these circumstances, the IMF must make a determination that the member is making a "good faith effort to reach a collaborative agreement with its creditors." See *Selected Decisions and Selected Documents of the International Monetary Fund*, 305–11 (2003).

[32] A separate issue regarding the role of the IMF under the SDRM proposal relates to the dispute resolution process. It was recognized from the outset that the aggregation of claims for voting purposes would necessitate the establishment of some centralized dispute resolution process that would oversee the implementation of the SDRM. As in the corporate context, it is inevitable that the disputes would arise between the debtor and its creditors — or among

CONCLUSIONS

Ever since the Mexican, Asian, and Russian crises in the mid 1990s, efforts have been underway to find means for more effective prevention of financial crises. Much has been achieved in this area: exchange rate flexibility is much greater than it was and there is increased transparency and improved oversight of the financial system. More generally, greater attention is paid to unsustainable policy stances. But no matter how much is done, crises will, on occasion, continue to occur. Moreover, these crises will always be painful for the sovereign, irrespective of the success of any reform efforts. Nevertheless, it has become clear that, as result of developments in the capital markets over the past twenty years, the restructuring process has become more painful than it need be. In particular, uncertainties created by problems of collective action give a sovereign with unsustainable debt an additional reason to delay the initiation of the debt restructuring process. However, such delays only exacerbate the economic dislocation that eventually occurs, while further eroding the value of creditor claims. Accordingly, the objective of any reform of the legal framework is to create incentives for a sovereign and its creditors to initiate the restructuring of unsustainable debt as early as possible. For the moment, the international community is focusing on solutions that are based on contract. Our experience with future crises will tell us whether more robust, statute-based reform, is necessary. Whichever approach is adopted, the success of any restructuring exercise will ultimately depend on the ability of sovereigns to formulate and implement effective economic policies during this difficult period. The IMF's role will continue to be that of providing timely financial support for such policies.

---

creditors — regarding the value or validity of claims being submitted. However, while the SDRM would be established through an amendment of the IMF's Articles of Agreement, there was a consensus that the existing organs of the IMF — and, in particular, the IMF's Executive Board — could not perform this function. It was agreed that a new, independent organ would be established to administer the SDRM, called the Dispute Resolution Forum ("DRF"). Drawing on the considerable precedent in the international law area, the members of the DRF would be selected through a process that relied upon external associations and institutions with demonstrated expertise in this area, thereby ensuring both their qualifications and independence. See IMF, *Report of the Managing Director to the International Monetary and Financial Committee on a Statutory Sovereign Debt Restructuring Mechanism*, § 8 (cited in note 25). See also Hagan, *Designing a Legal Framework to Restructure Sovereign Debt* (cited in note 13).

Part IV

MULTILATERALISM FOR THE TWENTY-FIRST CENTURY

Chapter 11

THE FOUNDING OF THE BRETTON WOODS INSTITUTIONS: A VIEW FROM THE 1990s*

The history of the founding of the Bretton Woods institutions presents something of a puzzle. As early as the lend-lease agreements, and continuing with the Atlantic Charter, Britain and the United States commited themselves to establishing a regime of free and open multilateral trade at the end of the Second World War. As Gardner (1956, p. 13) notes, "the best short description of the Administration's basic objective in international affairs would be "the reconstruction of a multilateral system of world trade". Cordell Hull, the Secretary of State, was powerful in the Administration and a firm believer in free trade.[1]

Yet, in 1944, delegates met at Bretton Woods and agreed upon the Articles for the International Monetary Fund and the World Bank. Congress approved the legislation for these organizations in 1945. By contrast, the *first* meeting of delegates to agree upon an international trade organization did not convene until November 1945, a charter was not negotiated until 1948, and, of course, it was never ratified.

The United States was not only first among equals: it was clearly dominant. With the American government commited to a multilateral trade organization, why did this not come about simultaneously with the Bretton Woods agreements? Why did the international financial institutions (IFIs) — the World Bank

---

* I am indebted to Evren Ergin for research assistance in preparation of this paper.
[1] It is arguable whether he believed in unilateral free trade or only reciprocal free trade. He certainly viewed the reciprocal trade agreements as a politically viable means of achieving free trade. Whether he would have advocated unilateral free trade in the absence of such agreements is more questionable. Hull was, of course, instrumental in the wording and drafting of the lend-lease agreements (1940) and the Atlantic Charter (1941). See Hull (1948).

and the International Monetary Fund (IMF) get established, apparently so readily, while the trade organization never came into being?

This is a political economy puzzle of some interest. Conventional wisdom regarding the founding of the Bretton Woods institutions is approximately the following. Because of wartime pressures, economists (especially Keynes) were free to develop the plan for the three postwar international economic institutions. It was only the curmudgeonly American Congress that partially thwarted the plan by failing to ratify the proposed Articles for the International Trade Organization. The world was therefore left with the IMF, the World Bank, and a small GATT — which was an "agreement" which did not require Congressional approval — which was all that could be done in support of an open multilateral trading system in light of Congress' refusal. Further, it is widely believed that the proposed ITO would have stood as a strong bulwark for free trade, while the weaker GATT in effect could only gradually assume the functions intended for the ITO.[2]

While this interpretation has substantial validity, the truth is significantly more complicated and somewhat different. There is no question but that whe International Monetary Fund was intended to provide an international monetary system that would support an open trading system. The political economy puzzle becomes all the more remarkable when it is recognized that the Fund and the World Bank both required far larger initial resources from the United States than the ITO would have.

The World Bank[3] was conceived as facilitating international capital flows, since it was believed that the events of the 1930s had effectively precluded any resumption of private long term capital flows on an adequate scale. But underlying both of these conceptions, as well as that of the ITO, was a perceived tension between the goals just stated and concerns about the future evolution of the world economy in light of Keynesian economics.

A reexamination of what happened, and why, is of interest not only in its own right, but also because of the light it sheds on certain issues in political economy. The founding of the postwar international economic institutions (including the failure to bring the ITO being) was considerably

---

[2] See, for example, Johnson (1965), pp.'36ff, for this interpretation.'
[3] The proposed institutions were the International Monetary Fund (IMF), the International Bank for Reconstruction and Development (now a part of the World Bank Group which includes the International Development Association, the International Finance Corporation and several other international economic agencies) and the International Trade Organization (ITO}. For simplicity I will refer to the IBRD as the World Bank unless the distinction between the various components of the World Bank group matter with regard to the point being made.

more complicated than the generally held view, and there are several points that are either erroneously reported or forgotten.

The purpose of this paper is to attempt, from the vantage point of the 1990s, to interpret what in fact was happening in the 1940s from the viewpoint of political economy. I shall argue that bureaucratic politics and personalities, the power of ideas, and even accidents all mattered. But within the power of ideas, the pressures and confusions of wartime precluded the carefully reasoned discussion and debate that might have taken place in calmer times over the Bretton Woods institutions, but also permitted their inauguration more readily than could have happened in peacetime.

A first section provides an outline of events that were significant in the evolution of the postwar international economic system. A second section then views these events in the light of the ideas that underlay them, focussing on the power of ideas in shaping the institutions. A third section, however, then examines the reasons for the demise of the ITO, contrasted with the relative ease with which the IBRD (now World Bank) and IMF were established. It will be argued that political power and personalities, especially in the American administration, made a significant difference in the outcome.

I. WHAT HAPPENED?

To set the stage for analysis, it is useful to start with a brief recounting of events. It is important to remember that World War II started when the economists and policy makers of the world were still in shock over the Great Depression. This had several important consequences: (1) there were many who believed that the world would revert to recession or depression at the end of the war[4] unless there was overt governmental action; (2) it was widely believed that "competitive devaluations" and other "beggar thy neighbor" policies, including the successive rounds of heightened tariffs and retaliation, had intensified the Great Depression greatly[5]; (3) the Depression had stimulated John Maynard Keynes to write his *General Theory* with its view that government intervention was essential to achieve a "good" equilibrium of full employment but with the corollary that free trade a la Ricardo and Smith was

---

[4] This was the "secular stagnation" doctrine, which held that the great investment opportunities of the nineteenth and early twentieth century had been exhausted, and that there was a chronic tendency for ex ante savings to exceed ex ante investment. Perhaps the name most closely associated with this view was that of Alvin Hansen, a professor at Harvard, although it was widely held. See Van der Wee (1983), p. 302.

[5] Eichengreen and Sachs (1985) have questioned the extent to which this belief was correct.

only desirable in a context where the good equilibrium had been achieved; and (4) many interpreted the lessons of the Great Depression to include the proposition that countries could not individually (or perhaps even bilaterally) avoid depressions and that international cooperation (and presumably international institutions) would be required.[6]

Proposals for all three international institutions had been underway during the war,[7] primarily between the British and the Americans.[8] John Maynard Keynes and James Meade were members of the British team which negotiated with the Americans and which met several times prior to Bretton Woods.[9] An American proposal for an organization supporting an open multilateral trading system was circulated in 1943, but there were significant differences between the Americans and the British on it (as discussed below).

Keynes' initial conception of the pillars of the postwar international economy consisted of four functional institutions. The fourth, which never came to fruition, was an organization to oversee and stabilize prices of primary commodities through the operation of buffer stocks. This plan was

---

[6] Van Der Wee (1986), p. 31 cites "a vague feeling of guilt" on the part of the American elite for U.S. isolationism in the interwar years. Isolationism (and failure to participate in the international institutions after World War I) was regarded as a major contributor to the disasters of the 1930s and U.S. support for postwar plans was based partly, if not largely, on the belief that an international economic system could prevent repetition. It is difficult with hindsight to recall that the predominant view was that the postwar problem would be one of the resumption of recession/depression.

[7] The Atlantic Charter, propounded in 1941, termed one objective of the war effort to be "to bring about the fullest collaboration between all nations in the economic field". Quoted in Diebold (1952, p. 2). The lend-lease agreements between Britain and the U.S. also contained provisions stipulating aspects of the postwar international economic organization.

[8] Representatives of other governments had been involved in the discussions to some degree. Both the French and the Canadians submitted alternative plans. Nonetheless, the dominance of Britain and the U.S. meant that the negotiations between representatives of those two governments were determinate of the outcome.

[9] Ikenberry (1993), pp. 164 ff. cites the emergence of a consensus in the "community of policy experts" during these talks, and believes that there was a consensus of views. And it is certainly clear that the British and American representatives had great leeway in devising the postwar architecture. However, a reading of such documents as the Moggridge (1992) diaries gives the flavor of considerably more disagreement between the British and the American policy makers, and considerably more decision-making under pressure than the Ikenberry account conveys. Moggridge (1992) reports great haste in drafting, noting that Keynes was unaware of some provisions (which had been opposed by the British and were not within his terms of reference as a British representative) in the IMF Articles until after the British delegation had returned to London.

gradually abandoned as the other three international institutions were negotiated, although the Havana Charter contained provisions for the International Trade Organization to undertake activities geared to commodity price stabilization.[10]

Events leading to the Bank and the Fund. Discussions for international monetary arrangements culminated in the Bretton Woods conference of 1944, with participation by representatives of 45 countries.[11]

Although it seems clear from all accounts that it was agreed that there would be three international institutions — to oversee trade arrangements,[12] the international monetary system, and to supplement private long term capital flows — only the International Monetary Fund and the IBRD Articles were drawn up and approved at Bretton Woods.

Proposals for the international monetary facility were considerably more controversial between the Americans and the British.[13] As is well known, Keynes initially proposed an international bank-money, called "bancor". The proposal focussed upon increasing world liquidity, and assumed that exchange controls and quantitative restrictions would persist in the international economy. The clearing union would be one in which members had virtually automatic drawing rights (like overdrafts), up to some specified limit. This proposal was firmly grounded in the Keynesian view of a world in which secular stagnation would be the chief problem and the solution would involve measures to stimulate demand. He therefore also initially proposed that a significant part of the adjustment of any payments imbalance be placed on the surplus country.[14]

---

[10] See Moggridge (1992, pp. 676ff).

[11] These "countries" included India as well as representatives of countries then under German rule. See James (1996), p. 48 for a listing.

[12] Agreements with regard to trading arrangements were a part of the lend-lease agreements, providing for recovery plans to include movement toward "the elimination of all forms of discriminatory treatment in international commerce; to the reduction of tariffs and any other trade barriers". Quoted in Diebold, 3.

[13] The atmosphere is best captured in the Meade-Robbins diaries. See Howson and Moggridge (1990). Skidelsky (1996, p. 101) describes the two negotiating sessions between the British (led by Keynes, Robbins and Meade) and American (led by Harry Dexter White) as being "mixtures of extraordinary eloquence, verbal as well as intellectual, and extraordinary rudeness to and about the Americans." After Bretton Woods, Keynes supported the Bretton Woods agreements wholeheartedly.

[14] Keynes is quoted in Horsefield (1969), 3:13, para 45, as stating: "It is widely held that the control of capital movements, both inward and outward, should be a permanent feature of the post-war system — at least as far as we (i.e., the British} are concerned. If control is to be effective, it probably involves the machinery of control for all transactions, even though an

The initial American proposal, by contrast, focussed on exchange rates as the key issue, and stabilization of rates as the chief purpose of the Fund. It was anticipated by all that the dollar would be a surplus currency. Changes in nominal exchange rates were regarded as inimical to private foreign investment and to trade.[15] Although White proposed a "unitas" unit, it was to be a bookkeeping unit of account and would be strictly limited in its issuance.

In fact, the key difference between the American and British plans focussed on the extent to which the future IMF would provide resources freely to its members. The British, anticipating deficits, wanted as much access with as few restrictions as possible; the United States, concerned that it would be the source of resources, wanted less access and more restricted access.[16] The U.S. plan placed no part of the burden of adjustment on creditor countries. There was also an issue over the extent of Fund control over changes in exchange rates. On that question, not surprisingly, the British wanted final control over the sterling exchange rate, while the American position would have required Fund consent for an exchange rate change. The final wording was, of course, a compromise, although it was much closer to the American plan than the British. As Skidelsky reports,

"The Bretton Woods Agreement, signed on 22 July 1944, after two difficult negotiating sessions in Washington, reflected American rather than British views. British and American conflicts on such matters as exchange-rate management, access to reserves, tariff policy, and responsibility for adjustment reflected national interests...Britain's negotiating achievements were limited to obtaining safeguards, postponements, and derogations within the framework of the American plan. The chief British success was to secure a 'scarce currency' clause which allowed debtor countries to discriminate...."[17] As will be argued below, it was over this issue that one of the fundamental problems with ideas at the time arose; the notion of a

---

open general license is given to all remittances in respect of current trade. But such control will be more difficult to work...by unilateral action than if movements of capital can be controlled at both ends. It would therefore be of great advantage if the United States and all other members of the Currency Union would adopt machinery similar to that which we have now gone a long way towards perfecting in this country..." The British dropped these plans in response to American opposition.

[15] Horsefield (1969), 3:46.

[16] Dam provides one quantification of the difference: the White Plan would, at one time during the negotiations, have cost the U.S. about $5 billion while the Keynes Plan would have cost the U.S. around $30 billion. See Dam (1982), p. 83.

[17] Skidelsky (1996), p. 101.

"fundamental disequilibrium" in the balance of payments has never been satisfactorily defined.

Negotiations over the Fund were carried out until 1943, when sufficient agreement was reached so that a joint British-American "Joint Statement by Experts on the Establishment of an International Monetary Fund" was released to other countries' capitals in the fall of that year. Although neither the American nor the British government at that time officially endorsed the text, it was in fact the basis for detailed negotiations that led to the IMF Articles.[18]

The IBRD Articles generated even less attention and disagreement than did the Fund's. The only real item at issue was the magnitude of the IBRD's resources, and the split over that issue was not dissimilar to that over the Fund's resources and scope.

At Bretton Woods, final issues were resolved and the negotiators initialled their assents.[19] Thereafter, the Articles were rapidly submitted to the U.S. Congress and other national legislatures for their ratification. In the case of the U.S., the Roosevelt administration submitted both sets of Articles to Congress in January 1945, with an appeal for speedy approval. While by that time the Allied forces were clearly winning the war, it was still wartime.

This fact is critically important in understanding what happened. The Bretton Woods conference was conducted during wartime, and while there was a definite mandate to the policy community concerned to provide for a postwar international economic order, the focus of public attention was clearly on winning the war. Even then, when the IMF and IBRD articles were debated before being ratified by the U.S. Congress, "the American Treasury set in motion a powerful publicity campaign to win support for the two instituitions."[20]

There was opposition to the Bank and Fund Articles. Senator Taft was a key opponent, claiming that... "in this case we are giving our money to a board which is controlled by the debtors, the very fellows who are going to borrow.... I do not think anybody has ever proposed to give away American money as this Fund proposes to give it away, to people who themselves will control its disposition."[21] There were also significant

---

[18] See Dam (1982) p. 84 ff. and references therein.

[19] There were many minor disagreements. For example, the United States held out for full-time resident Executive Directors, whereas Keynes strenuously opposed the idea, This, and other disagreements, are detailed in the Meade-Robbins diaries, Gardner (1956), and Moggridge (1990), among other sources.

[20] Gardner (1956), p. 129.

[21] Quoted in Gardner (1956), p. 130.

questions about the scarce currency clause, with concerns that American exports might be restricted.

By contrast, the U.S. Treasury overpromised. It stressed the extent to which the Fund's presence would support American exports. One Treasury official even testified that the Fund's establishment would result in a rapid end to *all* exchange controls. Even so, when Congress approved the Articles of Agreement, it stipulated that there should be another institution to prevent the replacement of controls over payments with controls over trade.

By July 1945, Congress had voted to approve the Bank and Fund articles. It had the support of most groups, and only a minority of Republicans (led by Senator Taft) continued to oppose the Bank and Fund.

Negotiations for a Trade Organization. As already mentioned, the commitment to an open multilateral trading system was already embedded in the lend-lease agreements and the Atlantic Charter. In both cases, the clauses were there at U.S. insistence, despite some resistance from the British who were simultaneously in a very weak bargaining position because of their need for American resources and committed to support their Commonwealth preferences.

Opposition to U.S. views was strong, and surfaced in early meetings between American and British officials over the possible outlines of a postwar institution.[22] While the Americans were advocating open multilateral trade, others (and especially the British) were concerned that their initial situations in the postwar period would require exchange controls; in addition, much more emphasis was placed on the necessity for maintaining domestic freedom of action when there was incipient recession or depression.[23]

Consequently, it was not until 1945 that the United States published and circulated "Proposals for Expansion of World Trade and Employment", its first published version of its proposals. This was put forward as a proposal prepared in consultation with the British, although in fact that "consultation" was negotiation over the Anglo-American loan of 1946 (in which the British sought $6 billion and finally achieved a loan of $2.75 billion). Thereafter, several draft charters were published after successive conferences in London, New York, Geneva, and finally Havana in 1948.[24]

---

[22] Dam (1970), Ch. 1, believes that, among other things, American insistence on enshrining principles in legal doctrine was a key flaw in the American proposals. He argues that this confused the role of the rule of law with substantive issues.

[23] It should be recalled that Keynes was apparently schizophrenic on the question of the desirability of free trade.

[24] Dam (1970), pp. 10–11 (footnote 2) provides a detailed acccount of the published documents and meetings that took place from 1945 to 1948.

As these discussions were proceeding, there was — at U.S. instigation — a first trade conference in Geneva in 1947 at which there had been multi-lateral tariff negotiations to reduce tariff levels. The General Agreement was drawn up as a mechanism to permit the agreed-upon tariff reductions to go forward without being in effect nullified by other trade measures.[25]

It was anticipated that there would be future reciprocal tariff negotiations, that they would take place under the auspices of the international trade organization then being negotiated, and that the General Agreement would be incorporated into the final Articles for the organization.

As Dam (1970) points out, the GATT essentially enshrines the U.S. position as earlier articulated by Cordell Hull[26] and other representatives of the U.S. The State Department was the lead agency in the negotiations. Essentially, all nontariff barriers should be eliminated, while tariffs should be reduced to the lowest possible levels on a multilateral basis. Effectively, after multilateral tariff negotiations, countries would "bind" their tariffs (until the next round of negotiations, although in practice that never happened and tariff concessions, once made, tended to be permanent, with the next negotiations starting from the lower tariffs negotiated in the previous round). They could not then increase them unless "injured", and then had to pay "compensation" in the form of alternative tariff reductions to countries whose exports were reduced due to findings of injury.

There were several bases of foreign opposition to an open multilateral trade organization which incorporated only the GATT principles. First, many policy makers in other countries were concerned that, especially in the immediate postwar period, they would be confronted with very high demands for imports relative to their export capabilities. This was certainly true of the British. Second, the belief that the world (and especially the U.S.) might revert to recession/depression led many to believe that free trade was a goal that should be subordinate to concerns with regard to domestic employment and income. Finally, as mentioned earlier, the British

---

[25] Otherwise, nations having cut tariffs could immediately have imposed quantitative restrictions on imports or taken other steps to maintain or even increase protection, and the tariff cuts would have been meaningless.

[26] Hull resigned as Secretary of State (because of ill health) in November 1944. He was succeeded by Edward Stettinius and then Dean Acheson. Acheson was Secretary of State at the time of the Havana Conference and seems to have supported the Hull position.

were desirous to maintain special relationships with Commonwealth countries, and also the imperial preferences.[27]

The GATT articles were therefore regarded as interim, to be incorporated into the ITO agreement, and it was clearly understood during the Geneva negotiations that the Havana conference would be held and the Articles augmented in ways that would address these concerns.

In the negotiations leading up to the Havana Charter, the U.S. gave ground on all three issues. Countries were to be entitled to use exchange controls and quantitative restrictions on imports for balance of payments reasons; countries were to be able to rescind their tariff concessions whenever there were domestic employment objectives with which they were inconsistent; and preferences were to be allowed.

There were entire chapters on exceptions arising from domestic economic concerns. There were chapters on "Employment and Economic Activity", "Economic Development and Reconstruction", "Restrictive Business Practices", and "Intergovernmental Commodity Agreements". These additions to the GATT articles in effect permitted countries to impose trade restrictions whenever deemed necessary to achieve domestic economic objectives, as well as procedural and organizational arrangements.

Once delegates had signed the Havana Charter, it had to be ratified. At that time (1948), European reconstruction needs were dominant, and the Truman Administration was proposing, and putting its efforts into achieving support for, the Marshall Plan. The Administration therefore did not even present the Articles to Congress in 1948. As reported by Diebold (1956, p. 6).

"As a result, the Charter was held over until the new Congress met in 1949. In April of that year President Truman sent the Charter to the Hill and asked for a joint resolution authorizing American participation. But by then Congress was busy with the North Atlantic Treaty, the Military Defense Assistance Program, and legislation for the second year of ECA [Economic Cooperation Administration — in charge of administering the Marshall Plan]. The Administration apparently agreed with Congressional leaders that it was

---

[27] Several U.S. actions led to increased opposition to the U.S. position abroad. On one hand, the U.S. negotiated a trade agreement with the Philippines in 1946 which provided for a twenty-year phaseout of the Philippines' special position with regard to tariffs; the Philippines were initially to maintain duty-free entry of their exports to the U.S. This led to charges that the U.S. was inconsistent in its demands for the end to British preferences. Second, President Truman enlarged the domain in which the escape clause could be applied. Third, just as the Geneva conference was starting, Congress passed a bill increasing the tariff on wool and setting high domestic price supports.

better not to press for quick action on the ITO since these other foreign affairs measures took precedence. The slight recession of mid-1949 brought on a series of complaints about employment allegedly traceable to imports, thus helping to create a sour atmosphere for the ITO. Not until April and May 1950 did the House committee on Foreign Affairs hold hearings on the joint resolution. The Committee did not report, and the matter never came to the floor of the House...."

In the meantime, British opposition to the International Trade Organization also arose. Of course, few nations would in any event have ratified the agreement if they knew the U.S. would not become a member of the organization. But Gardner (1956, p. 371) concludes that "It was doubtful that Britain would ratify the I.T.O., even if the United States should choose to do so..."

In 1950, of course, the Korean War began. Later that year, the Truman Administration announced that it would not again be asking for approval of the ITO, and it was in fact dead. The GATT Secretariat was gradually assuming some of the functions that an ITO would have undertaken, and over the years filled that role amazingly well.[28] And, not germaine to the present analysis, the success of the GATT, and the corresponding liberalization and expansion of world trade, finally led the members to negotiate a World Trade Organization in the early 1990s, which came into being in 1995, incorporating the GATT and considerably more.

2. THE ROLE OF IDEAS

In assessing the role of ideas, I focus primarily on the U.S. position. This is in part because the U.S. was the dominant country, and in part because it was U.S. support of the IFIs and failure to ratify the ITO charter that resulted in the birth of two, and not three, international organizations.

However, for the IMF and the ITO, British views were also important. They were important in part because the British negotiators were widely respected in the U.S. and therefore influential disproportionately to the U.K.'s power. They were also important because they gave rise to many of the chapters in the ITO charter that can be regarded as having been crucial in undermining the support of key constituencies for free trade in the United States.

---

[28] As Dam (1970, p. 16) commented in 1970, "In one of the happiest examples of ingenuity in the history of international organization, the GATT has risen above the legalistic confines of the text of the General Agreement and has improvised numerous procedures".

Underlying the conceptions of the three international institutions were strong legacies from the ideas that came out of the Great Depression. There is little doubt that the United States placed more emphasis on economic origins of the war than did the British, but in both countries the idea that prosperity would be conducive to maintaining the peace was generally accepted. It was widely believed that the beggar-thy-neighbor policies, and Smoot-Hawley tariffs had significantly intensified the depression. Cordell Hull's commitment to free trade had been important. Even during the Great Depression, he had been able to secure the passage of the Reciprocal Trade Agreements through Congress. Hull is widely quoted from the 1930s as having insisted on an open multilateral trading system not only as an economic goal, but as an essential element or prerequisite for peace. In his Memoirs (1948, Vol. 1, p. 9), he wrote:

"...unhampered trade dovetailed with peace; high tariffs, trade barriers, and unfair economic competition, with war. Though realizing that many other factors were involved, I reasoned that, if we could get a freer flow of trade...so that one country would not be deadly jealous of another and the living standards of all countries might rise, thereby eliminating the economic dissatisfaction that breeds war, we might have a reasonable chance of lasting peace". The American view seems clearly to have had "an exaggerated emphasis on economic policy"[29] as a lynchpin of the postwar system to guard the peace.

Following on the idea that a healthy international economy would be essential to preserve the peace was an insistence that this could best (if not only) be achieved by founding appropriate international organizations. They were clearly thought to be important and underpinned the Keynes Plan and in the U.S. proposals and planning for the postwar period.[30] For the U.S. administration, however, insistence on international organizations went further. Multilateralism was an essential element of policy.[31] This, too, implied reliance on international organizations but also a downplaying of any special relationships (such as that with Britain).

---

[29] Gardner (1956), p. 8.

[30] See Gardner (1956) pp. 6ff. for an array of quotes from influential people at the time, all of whom insisted that international *economic* organization would be essential for the postwar peace. Many blamed Hitler's rise on the economic difficulties of the earlier era, and they, in turn, were thought to have been caused in significant part by the absence of U.S. cooperation in the League of Nations.

[31] See Gardner (1956), p. 16 on this.

Thus, there was complete agreement that there should be international economic institutions, and both sides of the Atlantic agreed early on three institutions.[32] However, agreement stopped shortly after that point.

As already seen, with regard to the IMF (and World Bank), the disagreement focussed over the extent of resources to be available from the Fund and the conditions under which countries could be drawn upon. Britain, expecting to be a borrower, clearly wanted large resources and virtually unrestricted access.[33] The fact that the U.S. effectively held the pursestrings necessarily enabled resolution of this particular disagreement largely in accord with American preferences. This implied the imposition of conditions on lending from the IMF, which in turn was used to assure all but the Taft faction of the Republican Party that borrowing would not be "excessive".

With the American ideas holding sway, the focus of the IMF was to be on the exchange rate regime. Here, Keynes' ideas held sway. On one hand, he believed in fixed exchange rates — as did the U.S. On the other hand, he also believed that the British difficulties of the late 1920s had been a result of repegging sterling to gold at the "wrong" exchange rate in 1925.

A focus on "fixed but adjustable exchange rates", which was the Bretton Woods world from 1946 to 1973, was not entirely logically consistent. The insistence that exchange rate changes could be made only in cases of "fundamental disequilibrium",[34] without a definition of that term, left to a considerable degree an unresolved intellectual tension. It was also important that the compromise insisted that the Fund could not insist on any change in domestic policies *instead of* exchange rate changes when fundamental diseqiulibrium persisted.

The difficulties inherent in the notion of fundamental disequilibrium are obvious. Yet it is probably the case that use of the notion was what was able

---

[32] The commodity-stabilization provisions that Keynes initially proposed for a fourth institution were to be subsumed in the ITO.

[33] It is often forgotten how much relative economic power shifted between the late 1930s and the late 1940s. It is estimated that U.S. GNP in 1948 was 65 percent above that of 1938, while British GNP was only 6 percent higher. Van der Wee (1983), p. 30. While part of that shift was anticipated (especially by the British), it seems clear that Americans were less acutely aware of the economic difficulties facing Britain and the rest of Europe. See Skidelsky (1996), pp. 102 ff. See also the Meade-Robbins diaries for a series of entries commenting upon the differences in perception.

[34] See Gardner (1956), p. 114 for a description of Keynes' shift to the notion of fundamental disequilibrium when the proposals for a much larger and more automatic facility were rejected by the Americans.

to bring about coherence between the Keynesian ideas, on the one hand, and the principles that the Americans were willing to support, on the other.

With regard to the ITO, the situation differed. First, with the end of the war and the emergence of such nations as India from under colonial rule, the dialogue and discussions took place among a larger number of participants who could be effective in expressing their views. Virtually all, except the United States, were concerned that America might go into recession. The Keynesian theories had seemingly provided a case in which free trade might not be optimal from the viewpoint of an individual country (and perhaps the world): when resources were unemployed and a tariff might result in their utilization, imposition of a tariff would increase domestic output and employment and hence be desirable. Developing countries, of course, wanted to be able to protect newly-established industries in conformity with the idea that import substituting industrialization was necessary for development[35]; Europe wanted to be able to use protection during the period of reconstruction and was, in any event, less committed to free trade than was the U.S.

Consequently, when conferences were held regarding the ITO, American delegates were more "surrounded" by opposition than they had been in reaching agreement leading up to and at Bretton Woods. The GATT articles essentially already reflected American concerns; most of the additional chapters were the result of compromises between the American position and that of virtually all other countries.

Despite that, the United States delegation proceeded to negotiate an ITO charter at Havana. It reflected both the American commitment to open multilateral trade (in the GATT Articles which were incorporated in it) and the many exceptions insisted upon by the rests of the world. Unlike the IMF and World Bank negotiations, there were no American resources at stake that might have "persuaded" other countries to accept something closer to the American position.

Hence, whereas the IMF Articles reflected a compromise based on a fuzzy idea that papered over differences, the ITO document was really the result of two sets of ideas; and in the ITO charter, permitted exceptions could in fact be expected to offset most of the GATT principles much of the time.

3. BUREAUCRATIC POLITICS AND PERSONALITIES

There are several important aspects of bureaucratic structure and personalities that were important in determining the outcome.

---

[35] See Krueger (1997) for an analysis of these views in the context of the time.

It was obviously critical that President Roosevelt decided that the American Treasury, rather than the State Department be the lead agency in the monetary negotiations.[36] This was almost certainly the result of Roosevelt's much closer relationship to Henry Morgenthau than to Cordell Hull.[37] Once the Treasury had the lead responsibility, Harry Dexter White could assume a key role in formulating a proposal and in the negtiations.

The fact that the U.S. Treasury was the lead agency for the IMF and World Bank while the State Department was the lead agency for the ITO was also crucial in another way. That is, the State Department was largely over-whelmed by the pressing matters of dealing with allied countries during the war.[38] Despite Hull's commitment to the principle of free trade, because of his other commitments, he could not provide the active leadership for trade that the Treasury could for the IMF and World Bank. It is significant that, in Hull's almost 900 pages on the wartime years in his *Memoirs*, there is only one paragraph which mentions the IMF and World Bank, and not even a for-mal mention of their name.[39]

Although it is arguable that the clash of ideas over the ITO, along with the absence of desperately-needed resources to enforce American views, was responsible for its demise, it is also clear that the delay in bringing the ITO proposals forward until late 1945, with Havana not until 1948, was critical. During the war, attention was focussed elsewhere, and the Congress could ratify the Fund and Bank Articles with strong Treasury leadership and few other issues on which the Treasury was using "political capital" during the

---

[36] See Moggridge (1992), p. 722.

[37] Hull's biography repeatedly refers to Morgenthau's "meddling" in State Department business. See for example, Hull (1948), pp. 207–8, 1676.

[38] Hull in fact retired of exhaustion under doctors' orders late in 1944.

[39] "There is considerable discussion of postwar planning, but almost all of it refers to the United Nations. In the only paragraphs on the new economic organizations, Hull described a bit about them very briefly. Referring in the same description to the Food and Agriculture Conference, the Relief and Rehabilitation Conference, the International Labor Conference, and the Monetary and Financial Conference (at Bretton Woods), he wrote: "The State Department was not the leading department in these conferences, but we of necessity had to negotiate with other nations for their organization and operation, and many officials of the Department took part in them. The conducting of these conferences was in the hands of the chiefs of other departments...

These conferences arrived at valuable decisions on food supply, on relief, on the improve-ment of labor standards, and on the creation of an international monetary fund and an international bank. To us at the State Department they had the additional value of serving as a barometer of the degree of cooperation we could expect from the United Nations in the establishment of the postwar security organization." See Hull (1948, p. 1654).

war. Once the war had ended, the State Department's leadership was altered, the political agenda for the State Department was crowded, and, in any event, the clash of ideas that had underlay the ITO charter was considerably more fundamental than that which underlay the IMF and World Bank.

Keynes' personality was also an important determinant of the outcomes. Keynes himself was committed to the IMF and World Bank, even if they did not fully live up to his initial conception. He was much more schizophrenic regarding trade issues, as already seen. Keynes' influence was important in several ways. First, when it became evident that the U.S. would not accept British proposals, it was usually Keynes who proposed a compromise. Keynes was widely respected in Washington as well as in Britain, and he was probably therefore a more effective negotiator with the Americans than others might have been.[40] In addition, Keynes vigorously supported the proposed Bank and Fund Articles when they were under discussion in the United Kingdom.[41]

It is questionable whether Keynes, had he lived, would have been equally active in the discussions leading up to the ITO, or would have participated in the final negotiations. His role in bringing the Bretton Woods negotiations to closure cannot be disputed. But, in the case of the Bretton Woods institutions, he was supporting a scaled-down version of what he was committed to, and believed to be strongly in the interests of Britain. Although he initially proposed an organization for international trade, his schizophrenic views on free trade might have diminished his input in discussions, even had he lived. But, had he been as committed to an international trade organization as he was to the Bank and Fund, he could, quite clearly, have made a difference.

4. WHY DID THE BANK AND FUND EMERGE AND THE ITO DIE?

We now have the pieces to be put together. To the extent that the British (and others) disagreed with the American conception and formulation of the IMF and World Bank, it was because they wanted more of a good thing. Said

---

[40] However, that does not mean all went smoothly. Meade described the sessions in the following terms. "What absolute Bedlam these discussions are! Keynes and White sit next to each other, each flanked by a long row of his own supporters. Without any agenda or any prepared idea of what is going to be discussed they go for each other in a strident duet of discord which after a crescendo of abuse on either side leads up to a chaotic adjournment of the meeting..." Howson and Moggridge (1990), p. 127.

[41] Moggridge (1992), p. 730 ff.

another way, they agreed on the idea, but simply got less than they wanted. For the Americans, support was forthcoming because of the "vague feeling of guilt" and commitment to international organizations when the war was still in progress. Indeed, American negotiators had consistently had the necessity for Congressional approval in view, and had limited the extent of IMF and World Bank resources consistent with what they deemed could meet with Congressional approval.

There are two interesting questions. First, if Roosevelt had given the lead to the State Department, would the Bank and Fund articles have emerged in a form similar to that derived at Bretton Woods? The probable answer is "yes". There does not appear to have been significant difference with the State Department over the Bank and Fund articles, although the State Department might have tended to be more generous in initial funding for the IFIs. However, overburdened as the State Department was, there are significant questions as to whether it could have organized the Bretton Woods Conference in 1944 and whether it could have lobbied effectively for Congressional approval.

That, then, raises the second question. If the Bretton Woods conference had taken place a year later, and the results sent to Congress under peacetime conditions, would Congress have ratified the agreement? Here, the answer must be much more in doubt. The fact that it was wartime and that hopes for a future peace were high certainly helped gain Congressional approval. Once the Cold War had begun, and disillusionment set in with international organizations (especially the United Nations), it is arguable that passage by Congress would not have happened.

Turning to the ITO, several points are obvious. First, there was no consensus on the principles underlying the proposed organization. For that reason alone, support in both Britain and the United States was diluted. Second, and as emphasized by Diebold (1956) and to a lesser extent Ikenberry (1992), the document that emerged from Havana was therefore one that pleased no one. Protectionists did not want an international organization for open multilateral trade. Free traders did not want an organization with so many loopholes. While the American negotiators believed that they had beaten back demands for exceptions to the maximum extent possible, those supporting free trade (including the business community) were far more skeptical, although many finally gave lukewarm support. The absence of a strongly supportive pro-free trade group made opponents far more effective.

Finally, the ITO charter was not available for public discussion until late in 1948. By that time, disillusionment over the United Nations had increased. The cold war had become official and, with it, the hope that international organizations could keep the peace was substantially lessened.

5. CONCLUSIONS

Several themes in political economy are evident. Clearly, the power of ideas is important. Those ideas — at least in principle if not in well-aticulated detail — were present for the IMF and the World Bank. They were not as widely accepted in the case of the ITO.

Then, too, the notion that there are "windows of opportunity" during which new ideas of technocrats and policy makers can be implemented without quite the normal degree of political scrutiny certainly holds in the case of the contrasting fates of the three proposed international organizations. In 1944, there was such a window of opportunity, as the political focus was largely on the war effort. By 1948, it was much more "politics as usual" and the scope for reform was far more limited.

Finally, bureaucratic politics do matter. That the State Department had the lead in for the trade organization almost certainly meant that the window of opportunity was missed; as a corollary, it could not devote its political resources into supporting the ITO (because of commitments to the UN, the Marshall Plan, and other important agenda items).

In the end, however, the question must be: who got it right? The architects of the three charters, or the American political process? In light of recent economic history, it must be concluded that the American political process was closer to the truth. The "Bretton Woods System" served the world well for a quarter of a century despite the vagueness of some of the ideas; even after the move to floating exchange rates, the Bank and Fund have continued to play important roles in the world economy.

Likewise, the GATT served the world well; and, by the early 1990s, the need for an international organization was evident and acted upon. Although a stronger international trade organization might have achieved more, the ITO charter might also have been used in ways which thwarted some of the trade liberalization which did in fact take place under the GATT. Had all of the exceptions to the principles of open multilateral trade been enshrined in ratified ITO articles, that could well have retarded the process of trade liberalization in the postwar era, and hence, have dampened the very successful growth of the international economy.

REFERENCES

Dam, KW (1982). *The Rules of the Game*. Chicago: University of Chicago Press.

Eichengreen, B and J Sachs (1985). Exchange Rates and Economic Recovery in the 1930s. *Journal of Economic History*, 65, 925–46.

Diebold, W Jr. (1952). *The End of the I.T.O.* Essays in International Finance, No. 16. Princeton.

Gardner, R (1956). *Sterling-Dollar Diplomacy.*

Horsefield, JK (1969). *The International Monetary Fund 1945–1965.* International Monetary Fund, Washington, D.C.

Hull, C (1948). *The Memoirs of Cordell Hull*, Volumes 1 and 2. New York: MacMillan.

Ikenberry, GJ (1993). The Political Origins of Bretton Woods. In *A Retrospective on the Bretton Woods System*, MD Bordo and B Eichengreen (eds.), pp. 155–195. Chicago: University of Chicago Press.

James, H (1996). *International Monatary Cooperation since Bretton Woods.* New York and Oxford: International Monetary Fund and Oxford University Press.

Johnson, HG (1965). *The World Economy at the Crossroads.* Oxford: Clarendon Press.

Krueger, A (1997). Trade Policy and Economic Development: How We Learn. *American Economic Review*, March, 1–22.

Moggridge, D (1992). *Maynard Keynes. An Economist's Biography.* London and New York: Routledge.

Moggridge, D and S Howson (eds.) (1990). *The Wartime Diaries of Lionel Robbins and James Meade 1943–1945.*

Skidelsky, R (1996). *Keynes.* Oxford and New York: Oxford University Press.

Van der Wee, H (1983). *Prosperity and Upheaval: The World Economy 1945–80.* Berkeley: University of California Press.

Chapter 12

THE CLASH BETWEEN ECONOMICS AND POLITICS IN THE WORLD TRADE ORGANIZATION

I. INTRODUCTION

The collapse of the world trading system and global economy in the 1930s was a nightmare for all who lived through it. Economists and policy makers recognized the fact that each country, acting in its own self-interest, had achieved nothing and indeed made things worse. "Beggar-thy-neighbor" policies, as they came to be called, were put in place to devalue currencies and raise tariffs against the rest of the world in the hope that import substitution and greater export attractiveness at lower domestic prices would increase employment in the tariff-increasing and/or devaluing country. But since other countries' governments retaliated by raising their own walls of protection and devaluing, whatever was gained on the import-competing side was more than offset by losses of exports and higher costs of the import-competing goods.

At the end of the Second World War, technocratic policy makers, especially in the United States of America (USA) and United Kingdom (UK), were charged with designing a postwar international economic system designed to avoid a repetition of the disastrous 1930s. Because political attention was focused on the war and immediate postwar reconstruction, these policy makers — including John Maynard Keynes, Lionel Robbins and James Meade, among others — had much more latitude than is usually the case as they approached the international economic architecture for the postwar period.

The proposed postwar international economic institutions — the International Monetary Fund (IMF), the International Bank for Reconstruction and Development (now called the World Bank), and the International Trade Organization (ITO) — were designed with the experience of the 1930s vividly in mind. Thus, the IMF was intended to provide coordination on exchange rates so that there could be no more competitive devaluations: countries would maintain fixed exchange rates except in cases of "fundamental disequilibrium" and change to a new fixed exchange rate only with the agreement of the Fund. The World Bank was designed to permit capital to flow from low-return to high-return countries, as it was assumed that after the 1930s the world would not witness a resumption of long term private capital flows (which was at least partly correct until the 1990s) and that an efficient international economic allocation of capital would not result from private sector initiatives.

The ITO was intended to meet two objectives. On one hand, all recognized that an open multilateral international trading system was in everyone's interest and should be restored. On the other hand, in light of the experience of the 1930s, it was generally believed that full employment should be an objective of economic policy and could be achieved only by resort to government macroeconomic policies.

These two objectives were viewed as somewhat in conflict, as it was thought that a country might experience recession with high unemployment because of large imports and might be justified in imposing trade barriers in order to increase employment and output. Today, it is recognized that macroeconomic policies and conditions in labor markets are the determinants of the level of employment, and that conditions in the trade sector at most can have a short-run impact on employment. Countercyclical macroeconomic policies are obviously desirable, but do not include trade policy.

But that is ahead of the story. The charter for the proposed ITO sought to reconcile these two objectives by describing the appropriate policies that countries should follow in normal circumstances — these policies, when implemented, would result in something approaching the economist's ideal of an open multilateral trading system. The first half of the articles in the proposed charter in effect spelled out rules governing trade policy (tariffs, nontariff barriers, etc.) to be followed at full employment. The other part of the draft focused on exceptions countries might make in times of less than full employment. It was envisaged that countries might temporarily impose or heighten protectionist measures when trade flows were deemed to conflict with the full employment objective.[1]

This second part of the proposed Articles was much in keeping with the thinking of the times. However, it was rightly objected by many that the "full employment exceptions" in the second part were so all-encompassing that a country could do whatever it wanted in the name of achieving full employment. As such, there would be no international discipline to prevent a return to the "beggar-thy-neighbor" policies of the 1930s.

While these apparent contradictions were being debated in anticipation of a Havana Conference to finalize the text of the ITO articles, conditions in much of the world in the immediate postwar period were dire, especially in Europe and Japan. War-devastated countries were confronted with limited productive capacity and excess demand for imports, not only for food but also for capital goods to enable reconstruction. Because the USA had escaped all this, a "dollar shortage" was the order of the day. European countries (and many others) resorted to high levels of protection and quantitative restrictions on imports. In addition, there were bilateral clearing arrangements among the European countries under which imports were to balance exports country-by-country. These measures were appropriately viewed as an obstacle to the postwar reconstruction effort and certainly as a source of inefficiency in the world economy.

Opening up the trading system was therefore seen as of first order importance by many, including especially American policy makers.[2] To that end, they proposed a first round of trade negotiations for an open multilateral trading system prior to the Havana Conference and the passage of the ITO charter. To achieve this, most of the proposed articles that dealt with the desirable trading system, assuming no unemployment concerns, were to be

---

[1] It was recognized that a country might use exchange rate policy to maintain a rate which resulted in a current account surplus; the draft of the ITO articles and the GATT stipulated that the IMF should play a major role in judging the appropriateness of exchange rates and prevent the use of exchange rates for purposes of "beggaring neighbors". There was also a provision that a currency could be designated "scarce", in which case other countries could resort to protection against imports from the scarce currency country. The provision was never formally invoked. For a concise account of the ITO and GATT drafting, see Dam (1970, pp. 10–16).

[2] As is well known, the United States also adopted the Marshall Plan, under which it provided financial support for recipient countries. As a condition of receiving these resources, European countries were obliged to negotiate multilateral payments arrangements, first among themselves, and then more generally. Thus, most of Europe's bilateral clearing arrangements had expired by the mid 1950s.

implemented quickly, to be followed by a negotiating session to achieve some reciprocal reduction of tariffs.[3]

The General Agreement on Tariffs and Trade (the GATT) — the "liberal part" of the ITO proposal — was therefore inaugurated, in the case of the USA by executive decree, and other nations followed suit. The GATT, expected to be temporary, was provided with a small secretariat in Geneva to handle the necessary mechanics of a first round of trade negotiations.

As they say, "the rest is history". The ITO charter was never ratified, and the GATT continued, not as an international organization, but as an "agreement" until the 1990s when it was folded in to the World Trade Organization (WTO). But even in the WTO, the GATT articles remain as they were initially agreed: parts have been added on, but the basic trade structure remains.

The GATT was enormously successful. At the time of the first Geneva conference, it is estimated that the average tariff level among industrial countries on manufactured goods was above 45 percent, and, as already mentioned, there were also numerous nontariff barriers to trade. Services were virtually not traded, and agricultural commodities were in such short supply that importers were happy to get them. So the initial focus of the GATT was, naturally, on tariffs on manufactured goods. The average tariff rate imposed by developed countries on import manufactures fell to just over 3 percent by 2000.[4] Most of the nontariff barriers were completely eliminated so that, for manufactures, protection by 2000 consisted almost entirely of tariffs and was relatively low, especially among industrial countries. The growth of world trade has been a major stimulus to world economic growth which, over the past half century, has been more rapid than ever before over such a long period.

---

[3] The GATT was implemented by executive decree in the United States, since the President was unable to obtain Senate ratification of the Articles. The President's authority to negotiate reciprocal tariff reductions was scheduled to end prior to the Havana Conference, and the American authorities were anxious to use the authority to achieve some reduction in trade barriers prior to its expiry. It was anticipated that the ITO would later come into effect, including the GATT "liberal trade" part within its articles. See Chapter 11 for more details.

[4] Protection for agriculture was limited: in countries devastated by the war, efforts were made to increase agricultural production, but in the meantime, imports were vital and not initially highly protected. That changed over time, and, as protection against manufactured imports fell, that against agricultural goods increased (both by tariffs and by non-tariff barriers to trade and non-border measures) so that distortions in agricultural trade today far outweigh those remaining in manufactures. The USA, however, insisted upon "grandfathering" protection for agriculture in the GATT, so that it could continue with its support programs that had been developed in the 1930s. However, as noted by Dam (1970:257), "It would be difficult to conclude that the GATT's record in the sphere of temperate agricultural commodities is other than one of failure".

This phenomenal success has led to a host of new problems, At the same time, the very success of the GATT/WTO, along with technical changes enabling better and cheaper transport and communication, has led to a world with greatly increased awareness of globalization, and an inclination to blame that globalization for perceived economic ills in individual countries. One result has been weakened support for the open multilateral trading system and the WTO. That in turn has contributed to the failure, to date, of the Doha Round of trade negotiations to reach a satisfactory conclusion.

In this paper, I argue that a significant part of the problem is the clash between good economics and politics. A starting point is the GATT/WTO principles. Thereafter, the consistency of those principles and the acknowledged exceptions to them are evaluated. In that light, the paper ends with an assessment of the way forward for the world economy and the international trading system.

II. THE GATT/WTO PRINCIPLES

The GATT articles themselves consisted of the initial "rules of the game" such as nondiscrimination among trading partners, conditions under which there could be preferential trading arrangements, and the like. Subsequently, agreements have been reached on a number of issues (such as customs valuation and criteria for phytosanitary restrictions). The GATT was expected to do two things: first, to enforce the rules in the Articles (and also to enforce any subsequent agreements among members) and to adjudicate trade disputes arising out of negotiated agreements, and second, to provide the locus for negotiations for reductions in trade barriers.

As to the rules of the game, all signatories agreed to a set of principles by which they would abide. The principles of the GATT articles were relatively simple and straightforward. They were basically five: there was to be nondiscrimination among all countries so that if a country had a positive external tariff on a good, all its trading partners would be subject to the same protection. This might be called multilateralism, and is implied by the condition that each country have a "most-favored-nation" (MFN) clause in its trading agreements with all trading partners (who are signatories to the GATT, or, more recently, members of the WTO). Second, there were to be enforceable commitments — that is, once countries had agreed to a given rule or negotiated tariff reduction, failure to observe the rule would result in penalties. Third, there was to be transparency, which meant that the measures countries take to protect their domestic industries should be visible and readily ascertained. This meant, in particular, that protection should occur through tariffs and not through quantitative restrictions on imports or other measures where protection is not obvious.[5]

The fourth and fifth principles are less consistent with economists' understanding of the benefits of an open multilateral trading system. The fourth is the principle of reciprocity, by which was/is meant that countries reducing their protection should receive reciprocal reductions from their trading partners. The fifth is that there should be a safety valve, so that should a reduction in protection negotiated through GATT result in a sufficient increase in imports to cause severe dislocation, the importing country could take measures to limit imports to reduce the hardship.

The second, and quite different, role of the GATT/WTO was to serve as a forum in which members could bargain "reciprocally" for cuts in their protection levels (which, according to the principles, were to consist solely of tariffs). Members extended tariff "concessions" (i.e. reductions) to other countries in return for reduced tariffs confronting exporters on their goods of interest. Since all signatories were bound by MFN under the GATT, mechanisms had to be found to "balance" individual countries' concessions. Once an agreement was reached, countries "bound" their tariffs at least until the next round of negotiations (and unless the safeguard exception was invoked). Countries were free to lower their tariffs below the bound rates, but not to raise them above those levels.

Implicit in the GATT agreement was the dual role envisaged for the GATT. It was a negotiating forum and an enforcer. Enforcement was to be concerned not only with the provisions of the GATT articles, but also with the bound tariffs and negotiated rules.

III. ECONOMICS VERSUS POLITICS

It is the "concession" framework of the GATT/WTO negotiations that the first, and biggest, clash between economics and politics occurs. Economists

---

[5] There have been a number of GATT/WTO agreements and protocols over this. For example, countries were sometimes thought to use health and safety restrictions as an excuse to prevent or restrict imports of food, drugs, and other items. But a GATT understanding mandates that health and safety regulations (phytosanitary restrictions) must be based on scientific evidence: it is not adequate to say that imports of a particular fruit do not meet requirements: it must be demonstrated that there is a safety issue that scientists will attest. But many other non-tariff barriers to trade have lacked transparency: the famous Poitiers case comes to mind, in which the French authorities decreed that all televisions imported into France had to enter through the port of Poitiers and be individually inspected. Poitiers is a very small port and there was one customs inspector.

have shown that in most circumstances, countries that lower the protection they accord to their domestic industries benefit by so doing. Yet, in the GATT/WTO, lowering a trade barrier is regarded as something a country does because "it gets something in return", i.e. the reciprocal reduction in the trade barriers facing the country's exports. On the other hand, for political scientists, the genius of the GATT is that the trade negotiations bring exporters' interests to the process (as trade officials are bargaining for reduced tariffs abroad) as an offset to the pressure that import-competing producers are bound to exert to try to avoid any reduction in the protection which they receive. Having exporters pressuring for acceptance of a negotiated, multilateral reduction in trade barriers enables trade negotiators to resist much more of the pressure import-competing interests exert.

The clash between economics and politics has clouded discussions of a number of issues in the GATT/WTO from the outset and has come more and more to the fore over time. In the remainder of this paper, some of these issues are discussed. They include preferential trading arrangements, the "free ride" given to developing countries in early rounds of negotiations, the preferences given to developing countries' exports despite the GATT/WTO articles' commitment to nondiscrimination, and sectoral free trade agreements. The conflict also is a factor in the Doha Round and the role of agricultural protection.

Before turning directly to the issues, a background question must be addressed (even if an entirely satisfactory answer cannot be given). That is, why, if free trade is economically beneficial to the nation as a whole, does politics within countries prevent it? Economists have long puzzled over this. It is readily demonstrated that, in the absence of monopoly power in trade, there are always policies that can achieve desired objectives with more gain and lower cost to society than trade interventions.[6] For years, it was concluded that people simply "did not understand". But the persistence of protectionist pressures and measures suggests that the politics of trade are based on phenomena other than ignorance.

---

[6] Since most countries have little or no monopoly power in trade, and trade restrictions are seldom imposed on the grounds of taking advantage of monopoly power in trade, I leave aside the issue of monopoly power except to note that if all countries had, and tried to use, monopoly power in trade, the world would be worse off than if all removed their protection. Retaliation by trading partners would offset much, if not more than all, of any gain individual countries might achieve. Hence, for large countries, the GATT/WTO serves as a guarantor that there will not be a "trade war" in which large countries would try to use their monopoly power in trade and other countries retaliate. For small countries, the assurance of equal treatment may be equally, if not more, important.

Economists recognize that there will be losers from moves to free trade at least in the short run, but point out that the winners could always compensate the losers and still be better off than they are with protection. Within countries, it is certainly possible to establish policies so that the gainers could compensate the losers: trade adjustment assistance (whereby laid-off workers are supported while they enroll in technical training courses or given benefits additional to normal unemployment insurance) could be tailored to do the job.[7] But, in fact, opposition to reduction of trade barriers is strong, and stronger than one would expect given the overall gains to economies.[8]

One partial answer to the puzzle is that those who benefit from protection (producers of import-substituting goods) are concentrated, they know who they are, and can lobby effectively, while those who lose (consumers) are diffused and have difficulty knowing how to organize and may not find it worth their while given the small magnitudes of each individual consumer's gains. This was the answer given by Mancur Olson (1965) in his classic explanation of the puzzle.

While this obviously explains part of the puzzle, it overlooks the fact that when protection is greatly reduced, new economic enterprises will spring up to produce exportable goods, and existing exporting industries will expand. The gainers (including workers) will be concentrated in these new and expanded firms. It is not evident that these gainers will be any less concentrated than the losers. But since they are not already in firms or industries that will evidently benefit, they are not organized and cannot be organized (because identities are unknown) to support trade liberalization. The unemployed worker cannot know that if protection were reduced or eliminated, that exchange rate and other changes would render profitable expansion of a firm that might then hire him!

But the most frequently given answer for failure to adopt free trade has to do with time horizons: if a country removes its trade barriers, some will be

[7] There are, or should be, important questions concerning why citizens whose jobs were eliminated due to trade liberalization should be treated any differently than others whose jobs are lost. Even prior to that, however, is the equally important question as to how one might ascertain which jobs were lost due to trade liberalization, and which lost for other reasons (such as technical change and shifts in consumer preferences).

[8] There is also the question as to why "job losses" attributed to foreign competition are such a prominent and visible factor in some political discussions. Most estimates of job losses "due to trade" in the USA, for example, suggest that trade can account for at most 20 percent of those losses. Meanwhile, the "churn" in jobs in the USA makes those losses a very small fraction of total job turnover.

harmed in the short run. Many of the short-term losers can be expected to gain over the longer run, but they will nonetheless oppose lowering or removal of trade protection (and support increases in protection when they can). In part, this is a result of identity bias: all of those working in import-substitution industries believe that they are threatened with job loss or reduced income if protection were to be reduced even if in fact only a fraction of those dependent on the sector will be so affected; at the same time, those who will benefit from expansion of exports (and from establishment of new firms in the expanding exportable sector) do not know that they will so benefit. Hence, more will oppose tariff reductions than will in fact be hurt (even in the short run) while fewer will support trade liberalization than will in fact gain.[9] This, in a way, is an extension and elaboration of the "concentration" argument discussed above.

Another, and probably very important, part of the answer has to do with the existence of lobbies. Grossman and Helpman (2002) have shown how various groups will lobby politicians to gain favorable (protection for themselves or reduced protection of other industries depending on the group) treatment for their activities. Producers will support (and lobby) politicians who in turn will vote additional protection.

It is probably some variant of the Grossman–Helpman model that the framers of the GATT/WTO had in mind in the 1940s. For to speak in terms of "concessions" when a country reduces its tariffs is certainly not consistent with the proposition that free trade is the best policy for individual countries.[10] But, if in fact the political power of import-substituting producers is very strong and there is some asymmetry in information and identity bias, the political rationale for WTO negotiations makes eminent sense: once producers of exportables know that they will benefit by the opening of foreign markets if it is negotiated, they may exert counterpressure on politicians and lobby for tariff reductions.

It is on this political rationale that the reciprocity principle in the GATT/WTO makes sense. And, judging by the reductions in trade barriers since the founding of the GATT, it must be judged that the concession mechanism, at least initially, was highly effective. The more than fifty years after the founding of the GATT witnessed the most rapid rate of expansion of world trade in world economic history. That expansion of trade, in turn, was

---

[9] See Krueger (1990) and Fernandez and Rodrik (1991) for an elaboration of this argument.

[10] It is interesting, in this regard, to note that many of the developing countries that have grown most rapidly have not only adopted outer-oriented trade strategies, but have done so unilaterally and not in the context of a round of trade negotiations under the GATT/WTO.

associated with sustained economic growth at higher rates than the world had ever witnessed. As a rule of thumb, real world Gross Domestic Product (GDP) grew at twice the rate of growth of world trade and was certainly, for most countries, an engine of economic growth.

IV. ECONOMICS VERSUS POLITICS IN THE DOHA ROUND

But in light of the difficulties currently confronting the WTO and the failure to date to reach a conclusion in the Doha Round, it is worthwhile to ask whether the politically-wise concession approach may not have been a contributing factor. Consider first preferential trading arrangements (PTAs), such as the European Union (EU — a customs union) and North American Free Trade Agreement (NAFTA — a free trade area).[11] By definition, a PTA is discriminatory. Whereas an MFN tariff discriminates between domestic producers and those in the rest of the world, a PTA tariff discriminates between producers within the countries joining the agreement and the rest of the world. That forming such an agreement may constitute a move toward free trade (if the partners within the PTA are lower cost than producers outside it) and hence represent an improvement in welfare (at least for members) or away from free trade (if trade is diverted from low-cost nonmember countries to members) is well known.[12]

But if the political economy of "reciprocity" is correct, then PTAs are almost surely detrimental to further trade liberalization of the open multilateral trading system.[13] For once a PTA is formed, producers in each of the member states who expand their markets in the other states (behind the common external tariff in the case of customs unions and aided by the zero tariff between them in the case of FTAs) will have either an interest in

---

[11] A customs union entails a common external tariff with zero tariffs between members. A free trade area (FTA) has zero tariff rates between members, but each member retains its own external tariff (and rules of origin have to be established to avoid transshipment of goods within the FTA from lower tariff countries to higher tariff ones).

[12] For a survey of the literature on the welfare effects of PTAs, see Bhagwati, Krishna and Panagariya (1999).

[13] Article XXIV of the GATT permits preferential trading arrangements, both customs unions and free trade areas, provided that: (1) trade barriers are lowered to zero; (2) the agreement covers "substantially all" trade; and (3) that the signatories are to reach zero tariffs on a specified time table. See Dam (1970, 274 ff) for a discussion of the "fiasco" and imprecise nature (from a legal standpoint) of the Article XXIV provisions.

maintaining the status quo (because they are higher cost than producers out-side the arrangement) or less incentive to lobby for increased multilateral opening if they have already secured their market.[14]

Moreover, PTAs offer more scope for pressure from industry lobbyists than do multilateral negotiations, in large part because rules of origin (ROOs) can be very obscure and hide high levels of protection (Krueger, 1999). It is thought, for example, that USA automobile manufacturers lob-bied for ROOs in the NAFTA so that Japanese firms producing in Mexico would be disadvantaged because of the restrictions on the use of Japanese-made (imported) parts. Likewise in NAFTA, a "triple transformation" rule, whereby a PTA giving zero-tariff treatment to imports of apparel, meant that only when the raw material, the textile, and the fabrication into apparel were all undertaken within the NAFTA, would origin then be conferred. The equivalent levels of protection against imports from third countries for these ROOs have not been calculated, but are evidently significant and surely increased protection above and beyond that the external tariffs provided pre-NAFTA.[15]

A second area where WTO arrangements fly in the face of good trade pol-icy is the free ride given developing countries in negotiating rounds and preferential treatment of those countries. At least among industrial countries, tariffs are supposed to be lowered with reciprocity. For developing countries, Multilateral Trade Negotiations (MTNs) were negotiated among the indus-trial countries, and it was assumed that developing countries would benefit by being given a free ride — that is, they had to make no "concessions" in return. From the beginning, developing countries insisted upon, and increas-ingly received, "special and differential" (S&D) treatment under the GATT.

Two provisions in the GATT were important for policy toward developing countries. On one hand, protection of "infant industries" was to be permitted. On the other hand, all countries were entitled to resort to quantitative

---

[14] There are arguments that go in the other direction. For example, if those fearing multilat-eral trade opening learn from experience with a PTA that open trade is beneficial, it might change the political balance. And PTAs include provisions for opening services and liberaliz-ing capital accounts that may result in additional political pressures for further opening of trade.

[15] Customs unions resort to rules of origin less than free trade areas because of the common external tariff in a custom union, but the problem is not absent. In the case of the EU, for example, Japanese firms outsourced the final processing of some products to Europe after an anti-dumping tariff had been imposed, so that a very high fraction of the value added origi-nated in Japan. See Hoekman and Kostecki (2001, p. 166) for a description.

restrictions if needed "for balance of payments reasons."[16] In practice, developing countries used the balance of payments provision of the GATT articles, rather than the infant industry provision.[17]

To do this, they had to notify GATT/WTO annually that they had balance of payments difficulties and were maintaining quantitative restrictions for that reason.[18]

While economists recognize that there may be infant industries, experience has shown that it is difficult, if not impossible, to identify them in advance, and the very fact of protection may provide the wrong incentives for the development of a new industry. Bhagwati has suggested that infant industries became senescent industries without ever growing up in between! And, at any event, the infant industry exception was seldom used.[19]

And, whereas the infant industry argument might justify some form of assistance to new industries, economic efficiency is generally inconsistent with quantitative restrictions on imports for balance of payments reasons. Economic efficiency calls for the allocation of resources between exportables and import-competing goods in such a way that the marginal cost of earning a unit of foreign exchange equals the marginal cost of saving a unit of foreign exchange. In the face of balance of payments difficulties, therefore, the appropriate first-best policy advice is for a change in the exchange rate so that incentives for production both of exportables and of import-competing goods increase.

Save for the infant-industry and balance of payments provisions, however, nothing in the GATT articles provided for the "free ride" developing countries received in earlier GATT rounds. However, by the late 1950s, additional provisions were made so that developing countries could receive S&D treatment within the GATT. Thereafter, they received "preferences" in the form of lower (usually zero) tariffs on their exports to industrial countries than importers paid on goods from industrial countries.

---

[16] GATT Articles XII, XIII, XIV, XV and XVIII, part b all relate to balance of payments exceptions. These exceptions could be invoked when a country wished to forestall or stop a serious decline in reserves or to replenish seriously depleted reserves. The IMF was to be the arbiter on the need for invoking the clause. See Matsushita *et al.*, (2006, pp. 460–466) for a discussion.

[17] The infant industry provision was in Article XVIII and permitted protection (both tariffs and quantitative restrictions) by low income countries to foster new industries.

[18] India notified the GATT every year through 2001 that it needed quantitative restrictions for balance of payments reasons.

[19] See Baldwin (1969) for an excellent analysis of the difficulties with the infant industry argument.

Developing countries were beneficiaries of the rapid growth in world trade (and the reduction in tariff barriers in industrial countries that was one of the principal reasons for it); measures that accelerated the growth of trade, such as a greater reduction in trade barriers because of an MTN round, were highly beneficial to developing countries. Developing countries that opened up their economies and relied more on growth of exports as a development strategy benefited from the greater ease of entry into new markets that resulted from more rapid growth of the world economy and lower tariff barriers, but they usually lowered their tariffs and other trade barriers unilaterally.

Countries that maintained inner-oriented trade strategies nonetheless benefited from the rapidly growing international economy and from lower trade barriers. But the developing countries with inner-oriented trade strategies would have been even more successful in achieving their domestic goals of more rapid growth and rising living standards had they lowered their own trade barriers. That this was, and is, so is evident by the success of those countries that unilaterally liberalized their trade regimes and reduced trade barriers. Ironically, had they participated in MTNs, they might have reduced their trade barriers earlier to their own benefit, and confronted even lower import barriers in developed countries. The "concession" language of the GATT/WTO was certainly misleading, and "giving" the developing countries the right to maintain their trade barriers was no favor. Until the Doha Round, developing countries (including most emerging markets) did not participate very actively in the negotiations, but benefited from the tariff reductions negotiated primarily among industrial countries. Those countries moving to outer-oriented trade strategies, such as Korea, Singapore, and Chile, reduced their trade barriers and tariffs unilaterally.

The developing countries as a group not only believed that they benefited from leaving their high trade barriers intact, but also used their influence to receive the preferences, noted above, rather than reduced global tariffs. However, each industrial country, or group of countries, specified the goods eligible for preferential treatment and the conditions of that treatment. The USA, for example, imposed a ceiling on the amount of any given good that could be imported to the USA from a preference-receiving country duty-free.

The benefits of preferences were greatly exaggerated. Additional exports under preferences originated largely in the highest per capita income countries eligible for preferential treatment. The incentives for producers in preference-receiving countries were not entirely straightforward: on one hand, if exports of a product became too large, preferential access to the market in question might end; on the other hand, there was uncertainty as to how long preferences would last and whether the exporter in the preference-receiving country would

be able to compete once preferences were eliminated. Baldwin (1977) estimated that had developing countries successfully negotiated for a 1 percentage
point greater reduction in industrial countries' tariffs on textiles and apparel in
the Tokyo round (instead of preferences), the value to the preference-eligible
countries would have been greater than the value of preferences they actually
received. Most analysts have concluded that developing countries have placed
far too much weight on attempting to preserve or increase preferences relative
to their value, and far too little on MFN tariff reductions in those rounds.

To compound matters still further, some negotiators from preference-
receiving developing countries have expressed concern about multilateral
tariff reductions in the Doha Round, noting that any reduction in external
tariffs would reduce the value of preferences. Even the French President used
the erosion of the value of preferences as an argument against successful conclusion of the Doha Round!

It can certainly be argued that the rhetoric of "concessions", the granting
of S&D treatment to developing countries, and the tariff preferences they
received all delayed the time at which developing countries would lower their
tariff and nontariff barriers and open their economies to trade, to their detriment and that of the world economy as a whole.[20]

Questions can also be raised about sectoral trade agreements. The first
such major agreement was reached in the late 1990s, when forty countries
signed the Information Technology Agreement (ITA) under which they
agreed to keep current and future IT products duty-free. The agreement covered only the signatories, but other countries were welcome to sign in the
future. Signatories were predominantly industrial countries, most of whom
had export interests in IT products,[21] and the intent was clearly to prevent the
imposition of protection as new IT products were developed.

However, to the extent that the exporters had already achieved duty-free
entry into their major markets through the ITA, any pressure for achieving a
satisfactory outcome to the Doha Round that might have come from the IT
industry was lost: they already had achieved what they wanted! While the
economics of the ITA were good, the consequences for the politics of future
rounds were questionable.

---

[20] It is estimated that lowering of developing countries' tariffs would benefit other developing
countries significantly and result in considerable expansion in south–south trade.

[21] That there are difficulties with the commitment to keeping future new products duty-free
can be seen in the current dispute between the USA and Europe as the USA is claiming that
the EU is imposing duties on new IT products. The EU asserts that the agreement should
be renegotiated. See *Financial Times*, 9/18/08, p. 6, "Europe Wants IT Trade Pact Back
on the Table".

Turning lastly to agriculture, the politics of "concessions" may well have been a contributing factor to the inability of negotiators to bring the Doha Round to a satisfactory conclusion to date. Developing countries took the position that the major gains to them would originate in the dismantling of agricultural supports in industrial countries.[22] In fact, the major beneficiaries of the reduction in agricultural supports would be in the countries extending them: costs of price supports are high, and benefits go mostly to the larger farmers. The cost of providing income supports for small farmers would clearly be much lower. And, while negotiators had made progress in agreeing to end export subsidies, an important step, efforts to negotiate reduced over-all support (in the industrial countries) in return for reduced protection and a relatively high threshold before safeguards could be imposed because of "import surges" (in emerging markets and developing countries) failed.[23] Yet the biggest beneficiaries of the (beginning of) rationalization of agricultural production and trade would have been the countries that undertook ration-alization.[24] The politics of "concessions" and farm price supports for "small farmers" who by definition produce smaller quantities and therefore benefit less than large farmers, carried the day despite the economics.

V. THE FUTURE OF THE MULTILATERAL TRADING SYSTEM

Given the problems in the Doha Round, a major question is the future of the open multilateral trading system. On one hand, the very success of the GATT/WTO in providing a framework for tariff reductions and rules on

---

[22] It is worth noting that it was not until the concepts of aggregate measure of support and producer subsidy equivalent were developed (by technocrats) that there were meaningful negotiations centering on agriculture. Even then, agricultural negotiations take place separately from negotiations over other commodities (until the final stage) which makes cross–sector trade-offs difficult.

[23] The reported Indian position is perhaps indicative of the gap between rhetoric and economics. It was reported that the Indian negotiators refused to accept the lower "import surge" limit of 15 percent because of concerns about the incomes of "small farmers". But Indian prices of major grains are delinked from, and below, world prices and India is a net exporter of food grains. Imports have occurred only in years when harvests were poor and prices domestically were high. It is thus difficult to understand how small farmers would have benefited from the larger limit.

[24] It is also noteworthy that simultaneous rationalization (with, for example, reduction of farm supports in Japan, the USA, and Europe) with opening up of markets in developing countries would have made the needed adjustments less in each country than would be required if one country unilaterally removed its interventions.

other treatment of imports has left the remaining tasks more challenging. So, too, has the increased membership, On the other hand, the gains from the system have been so great that it is difficult to imagine that the system would break down.

A multilateral trading system has so many advantages that no substitute, based on bilateral or regional trading arrangements, seems possible. Equally, restarting from a zero base and devising an entirely new international economic organization seems infeasible, or worse yet, destined to reduce rather than increase global economic integration.

The way forward would therefore appear to be piecemeal changes that can improve the functioning of the system.[25] In the remainder of this paper, I consider some of these possible changes. They could either be undertaken individually, or they could be adopted as a package. If undertaken individually (or with a small number of changes at a time), there need not be any particular order. And none of the changes suggested here would, by themselves, constitute a major overhaul of the WTO, but cumulatively, the adoption of most, if not all of them, could improve the functioning of the system.

It is assumed that the Doha Round will be concluded within approximately two years. The discussion below does not focus on "how to conclude" Doha Round, although the measures suggested here could be undertaken concurrently with the conclusion of the round, or afterward.

There are a number of items, but they can be broadly grouped into three categories: changes in the WTO structure and decision-making processes, changes in WTO rules governing aspects of trade, and mechanisms for covering some of the "new issues".

VI. STRUCTURE AND DECISION-MAKING PROCESSES

Turning first to the WTO structure and decision-making processes, a number of concerns have been raised. Unanimity between more than 150 members is an incredibly high hurdle for achieving conclusions to negotiations. The Secretariat is small, underfunded, and weaker than it might be. Representation of each country in the monthly meetings of the General Council, without a relatively strong smaller group, raises questions. Enforcement sanctions or incentives could be strengthened.

---

[25] This is not to argue that there should not be another round of multilateral trade negotiations, but the possibilities discussed in this section could be undertaken independently of, and between, rounds.

Several suggestions have been made with regard to the need for unanimous agreement prior to conclusion of a Round. One possibility would be to require some sort of supermajority, with trade liberalization agreed and undertaken by the supermajority not extended to those not approving. Thus, if a significant supermajority of countries approved the proposed final agreement, but there were a few holdouts, the agreement could nonetheless proceed.

The advantage of such an arrangement is obvious: it would remove the possibility of one or a few countries vetoing the entire round. The disadvantage is also clear: it would require a very high threshold of countries trading in the product and reduce the incentive for other countries to follow suit. The ITA was an agreement signed under the WTO in which not all countries participated. But the agreement was reached only after countries representing 90 percent of trade in IT products had signed on. And countries not signatory to the agreement were "free riders" while products not of interest to the major actors were left out of the agreement. One negative effect was that producers of IT goods covered under the agreement were inactive in supporting the Doha Round (Hoekman and Kostecki, 2001, 231 ff). To make such a mechanism effective, some sort of inducement to the hold-outs to accept the agreement would be needed. One possibility would be not to require members of the supermajority to liberalize their trade with nonsignatories to the agreement. The obvious drawback is that it would require discrimination, going against the MFN principle, and would require relatively complex customs administration, probably inducing transshipment of goods through signatory countries.

But while achieving a supermajority agreement in a Round might prove difficult, a second and related major issue is representation at the WTO. Just as the IMF and the World Bank have been accused of underrepresenting some of their membership in their voting (where voting rights per country are based on a weighted formula including the size of a country's trade as well as of its GDP), the WTO can be accused of underrepresenting the very large trading nations with the one-country, one-vote (or requirement of unanimity) principle. This was relatively less important when the "quad" countries were first among equals in a small group of countries but as membership has increased, the awkwardness of decision-making has increased.

Moving to a voting formula for decisions such as accession of new membership, round agendas, and the like, which more accurately reflected the country's stake in the trading system would make sense. One possibility would be to weight countries' votes by some combination of their weight in international trade in goods and services and their population.

A related structural issue is the absence of an effective intermediate body between the full membership and the secretariat. If countries' votes were weighted (or even if they were not) it would be possible to have an Executive Council (similar to the World Bank and IMF) where the largest trading countries (presumably the USA, Europe, Japan, and China) held individual seats but where other representation had to be through a Council member representing a minimum number of votes. Countries would be free to choose their own partners in determining chairs. Other arrangements are possible but over the longer term, the functioning of the WTO would be greatly improved if such a body, regarded as legitimate, could function, issues such as agenda preparation could be addressed, and then sent to the entire Council, or to a Ministerial or member governments for final approval.

Another issue relates to the size and funding of the Secretariat. The WTO staff produces a very large volume of high quality work — Trade Policy Reviews (TPR), annual reports, trade data, and preparatory work for all meetings — but is very thinly stretched. Additional resources could be well used for the (very small) research staff, for support of trade facilitation and the TPR process, and improving information flows.

These, and other, ways to streamline and strengthen the functioning of the WTO could be done incrementally or as a package. The results of any individual reform would be positive, but the cumulative effect could be substantial.

A related, but separate, issue concerns dispute settlement procedures (DSP). Despite the improvements already made, dispute settlement procedures are still long and arduous, and large trading nations are at a great advantage relative to smaller ones in resorting to the DSP. It is clearly desirable to have procedures that give the differing parties incentives to resolve their disputes.

VII. CHANGES IN RULES GOVERNING TRADE

One of the serious challenges to the open multilateral trading system arises from the proliferation of PTAs, as discussed above. Each one has different provisions for rules of origin (200 pages, single spaced, in the NAFTA agreement), different timetables for tariff reduction, and different provisions for non-goods trade (such as agreements on treatment of foreign direct investment-FDI).

The discrimination inherent in these agreements flies seriously against the MFN principles, and, for reasons discussed above, can reduce support for further multilateral liberalization. One way to attempt to mitigate the discriminatory potential of PTAs would be to agree on a tighter set of rules governing them. One possibility would be to require PTAs to make all ROOs within a given agreement based on percentage of value added. One could go even further and require that the value added percentage should be the same across all goods. This would reduce, and perhaps even eliminate, some of the most egregious protectionist measures that can be embodied through ROOs in PTAs. Questions would arise, to be sure, as to the fate of already-negotiated PTAs. They could, of course, be grandfathered and left unaffected, or there could be a transition period during which existing PTA ROOs could be converted to a value added percentage.

Making the ROOs in all new PTAs a specified percentage of value added would also greatly increase their transparency. And if the percentage of value added specified were the same for all new PTAs entered into by all countries, negotiators could be assured that their PTA would not be "bested" by a lower percentage value added requirement in another one negotiated by their trading partners.

An alternative would be to have clauses in PTAs that specified that, if in future a country negotiated a PTA with a lower value added threshold for preferential treatment, that lower rate would extend to existing PTAs (this would be a sort of MFN among preferential trading partners). An advantage and difficulty with this, of course, is that it would increase opposition from industries benefiting from the protection of a higher value added requirement.

Yet another possibility, not inconsistent with the uniform ROO requirement, would be to adopt a rule that would require PTA signatories to admit any other country that would agree to the existing PTA rules. For example, if this rule had been in effect when NAFTA was negotiated, the Japanese could have signaled their willingness to abide by the rules and joined. Discrimination against their auto parts in Mexico would thereby have been thwarted.

These, and other, possibilities for achieving greater potential consistency of PTAs with the WTO's MFN principle would require careful thought. Issues would include how non-trade related aspects of PTAs would be treated[26] as well as the timing for phase-in of the new rules for agreements already under negotiation, new ones, and possibly even for existing ones.

---

[26] The non-trade aspects such as treatment of foreign direct investment could be resolved by splitting PTAs into two parts: one would consist of the trade-related issues where uniformity was mandated, while the other could consist of those provisions relating to non-trade measures (such as mutual recognition of phytosanity standards). But there are also some institutional issues that would require resolution, such as how dispute resolution bodies set up under a PTA between countries A and B would be affected when country C chose to join.

Other issues could also be addressed. Countries might negotiate a threshold below which tariff lines would go to zero — this could be two percent, three percent, or a larger percentage, but it could simplify customs administration. There could also be a higher *de minimis* standard for Antidamping (AD) — Countervailing Duty (CVD) filings, acceleration of the dispute resolution process (including possibly alternative procedures such as mediation or arbitration) to speed up resolution, and greater standardization of AD and CVD procedures across countries. Greater reliance on mutual recognition of standards is normally undertaken bilaterally. "Trade facilitation" — providing technical assistance to low-income countries in exchange for conforming with WTO agreements on procedures and mechanisms — could be strengthened.[27]

VIII. MECHANISMS COVERING NEW ISSUES

It has already been argued that agreements covering single sectors are problematic: those exporters benefiting may fail to support further multilateral negotiations. Furthermore, the ability to negotiate cross-sectorally will in general widen the range of possible mutually beneficial agreements.

But there are areas that are largely untouched where agreements on how to negotiate are probably a prerequisite for significant progress. Services is an area in which the potential gains from liberalization are very large, yet where the lack of a mechanism for quantification or comparability across sectors is a major obstacle to progress.[28] There are undoubtedly huge gains to be had: financial and other business services are a major source of high productivity in most industrial countries. Access to these services by low-income countries would carry large benefits. But other services, such as construction, could provide large employment and income opportunities for workers from low-income countries while enabling lower cost residential and commercial real estate services in industrial countries.[29] Perhaps the most

---

[27] This is an issue which could be negotiated jointly in a case where developing countries might otherwise be reluctant to agree (such as removal of tariffs below a certain threshold).

[28] An imperfect indication of the scope for gains is that services are estimated to comprise 25–30 percent of world trade in goods and services (and are growing rapidly) while they account for over two thirds of GDP in most countries. See Mattoo and Stern (2008) for an overview of services trade. See Maurer, Marcus, Magdeleine and d'Andrea (2008) for a discussion of the problems associated with gathering data on the value of services.

[29] Enabling construction workers from low-income countries to reside in high-income countries while engaged in construction activity would not necessarily entail migration: it would be possible for firms undertaking the construction to receive temporary work-residence permits while construction was in progress.

important is construction services, where there appear to be large potential gains from liberalization of trade, and at the same time, major problems arise in negotiations.

At present, there is no agreed-upon plausible way in which to value the "concessions" that industrial countries might make by permitting construction workers to have temporary work-and-residence; likewise, valuing the liberalization of financial, or of other, business services, has not been undertaken in a generally accepted way. Estimation of the height of protection received by domestic construction firms (by refusal to permit entry to foreign workers), or the value of reduction in protection to permit entry to a specified number of workers, has not yet been undertaken in a widely accepted manner. Yet if services liberalization is to be undertaken on a significant scale, a technique is needed for assessing these, and other, potential liberalizations. Only then could multilateral negotiation take place in the expectation that concessions would be "reciprocal".

That there are potentially major gains from the opening of business and financial services, construction, professional and personal services, and international transport is widely recognized. But the difficulties are large. The formation of the General Agreement on Trade in Services (GATS) in 1995 was a first step, and efforts to improve the measurement of services transactions are underway. But even when estimates of the volume and value of services trade are available, a metric for estimating the level of service trade restrictions will be needed. Just as the producer subsidy equivalent (PSE) and aggregate measure of support (AMS) framework enabled an advance in agricultural negotiations, a conceptual framework for estimating the barriers to trade in services would greatly increase the likelihood of fruitful negotiations across service sectors.

Some services (maritime shipping, construction, back office processing) seem to be ones in which developing countries may have a comparative advantage, while others (air transport, most professional services) seem to lie more in the range of activities where industrial countries are at lower cost. Major liberalization of services is therefore not likely unless cross-services negotiations can take place. And that is unlikely to happen until there is a framework for estimating the tariff equivalent of barriers.

Beyond services, there are other areas where major gains would result if multilateral agreement on liberalization could be achieved. One such area is the treatment of foreign investment. To date, a comprehensive investment agreement has escaped the international community, and bilateral agreements and treatment within PTAs are the main mechanisms for facilitating investment.[30] To reach a multilateral agreement within the WTO will require a great deal of effort and negotiations. It would most likely prove to be worthwhile to try to break apart the various components of such an agreement and dispute resolution.

A major issue which has been raised for several decades but upon which little has been achieved is competition policy. Clearly, large firms trading across borders could benefit substantially from the certainty that would arise if competition policy were uniform across countries. Given the very different economic structures of WTO members, however, it is unlikely that this is an issue upon which much progress can be made in the near future.

Perhaps the most difficult of the new issues, however, is that concerning trade and the environment. Environmental concerns are themselves a major focus of international attention, and there are numerous proposals to link environmental policies to trade. The issues are too complex to be addressed here. Unlike issues such as competition, however, it is very likely that policies with such links will be adopted within the WTO context, by a new international arrangement, or through various bilateral agreements. A challenge for the multilateral trading system will be to insure that these measures are least-cost and do not introduce hidden protection into the system.

CONCLUSIONS

A flawed rationale for trade liberalization ("concessions") was good politics and led to a good economic outcome. It is almost inconceivable that the 150-plus members of the WTO would agree to a new set of rules with a rationale more closely approximating good economics, and even if it could happen, it is questionable whether trade liberalization could proceed as rapidly as it has under the "concession" framework.

However, even if the Doha Round concludes, there will be a variety of important issues where the "reciprocity"–"concession" framework is unlikely to provide the impetus to good economic outcomes. These issues can perhaps best be dealt with in stand-alone negotiations apart from MTNs. Changing the decision-making processes within the WTO could be tackled on a stand-alone basis. Bringing developing countries more closely into the WTO discipline and taking them away from the S&D and preferential

---

[30] It will be recalled that, in the 1990s, an effort was made to hammer out a multilateral investment agreement under the auspices of the Organization for Economic Co-operation and Development (OECD). That effort failed, in significant part because the recipients of FDI in developing countries were not part of the negotiating forum.

framework would serve those countries and the world well, but is politically difficult. Finding rules that will render PTAs more consistent with an open, nondiscriminatory multilateral trading system may be possible, but it is not likely that the political logic of concessions and reciprocity in liberalization will be helpful. And agreement on improved rules for AD and CVD, investment, and new aspects of trade policy is unlikely to be achieved through the reciprocity/concession framework. Those arenas can therefore constitute a work agenda to be carried out outside the context of a new round of trade negotiations.[31]

For services trade, the biggest challenge is different: it is technocratic, and involves devising measurement tools for estimating the height of existing barriers. If that challenge can be met, it is possible that the reciprocity/ concession framework could then again provide the basis for a new round of trade negotiations. First, however, the Doha Round must be concluded. With that done, and some of the stand-alone agreements in place, a new round could be contemplated where once again the politics of the reciprocity framework can result in good economic outcomes. In the meantime, however, completion of the Doha round, and addressing some of the issues discussed above, can yield sizeable dividends to the international economy and preserve the open multilateral trading system which has served it so well.

REFERENCES

Baldwin, RE (1969). The Case Against Infant Industry Protection. *Journal of Political Economy*, 77(3).

Baldwin, RE (1977). MFN Tariff Reductions and Developing Country Trade Benefits Under GSP. *Economic Journal*, March.

Bhagwati, J, P Krishna and A Panagariya (1999). *Trading Blocs. Alternative Approaches to Analyzing Preferential Trading Agreements*. Cambridge, MA: MIT Press.

Dam, KW (1970). The *GATT: Law and the International Economic Organization*. Chicago: University of Chicago Press.

Fernandez, R and D Rodrik (1991). Resistance to Reform: Status Quo Bias in the Presence of Individual Specific Uncertainty. *American Economic Review* 81(5), 1146–1155.

---

[31] It is even conceivable that — even assuming that progress is made in completing the Doha Round — further progress in agricultural trade liberalization could take place without a full round of negotiations. After all, there has been little cross-sectoral trading between Non-Agriculture Market Access (NAMA) and agricultural issues to date.

Grossman, GM and E Helpman (2002). *Special Interest Politics*. Cambridge, MA: MIT Press.

Hoekman, BM and MM Kostecki (2001). *The Political Economy of the World Trading System*. Second edition. Oxford and New York: Oxford University Press.

Krueger, AO (1990). Asymmetries in Policy Between Exportables and Import-competing Goods. In *Political Economy of International Trade: Essays in Honor of Robert E. Baldwin*, RW Jones and AO Krueger (eds.), pp. 161–178. Oxford: Basil Blackwell.

Krueger, AO (1999). Free Trade Agreements as Protectionist Devices. In *Trade, Theory and Econometrics: Essays in Honor John S. Chipmann*, J Moore (ed.). London: Routledge.

Matsushita, M, TJ Schoenbaum and PC Mavroidis (2006). *The World Trade Organization. Law, Practice, and Policy*. Oxford International Law Library. Oxford University Press. Second edition.

Mattoo, A and RM Stern (2008). Overview. In *A Handbook of International Trade in Services*, A Mattoo, RM Stern and G Zanini (eds.), pp. 3–47. Oxford: Oxford University Press.

Mattoo, A, RM Stern and G Zanini (2008). *A Handbook of International Trade in Services*. Oxford: Oxford University Press.

Maurer, AYM, Y Marcus, J Magdeleine and B d'Andrea (2008). Measuring Trade in Services. In *A Handbook of International Trade in Services*. Oxford: Oxford University Press.

Olson, M (1965). *The Logic of Collective Action*. Cambridge, MA: Harvard University Press.

Rodrik, D and R Fernandez (1991). Resistance to Reform: Status quo bias in the Presence of Individual-Specific Uncertainty. *American Economic Review*, 81(5).

Chapter 13

AT THE SERVICE OF NATIONS: THE ROLE OF THE IMF IN THE MODERN GLOBAL ECONOMY

The IMF's role has changed greatly over its 60-year history, along with changes in the world economy. This adaptation has been essential for it to remain an important lynchpin for the international economy.

The Fund now serves 184 members, making its task in some ways rather more complicated than it was when the Bretton Woods Institutions were founded at the end of the Second World War: 29 countries originally signed the Bretton Woods agreement.

The Fund's principal responsibility remains unchanged, of course — a tribute to the vision of those who met at Bretton Woods in the 1940s. Now, as then, the mandate is for the maintenance of international financial stability; and now, as then, this is primarily a means to an end. Those who drew up the postwar economic framework at the Bretton Woods conference wanted to promote economic growth through the expansion of trade: and international financial stability is as crucial for those aims now as it was 60 years ago.

But as our members have grown in number, so they have grown more disparate. The world is no longer made up of rich countries and poor countries. Among our membership in the 21st century are the advanced industrial economies — richer and economically more sophisticated than most people could have envisaged in the 1940s. There are also emerging market economies: countries that, by and large, are growing rapidly and often facing enormous challenges as economic policies and structures struggle to keep pace with that growth. Then there are the so-called transition economies, although many of these are coming increasingly to resemble "normal" countries.

And there are what we now refer to as low income countries (LICs). In some cases, these are countries where growth has started to accelerate in recent

261

years, after years of poor performance, or worse. But even among these, many have lower incomes per capita than they had 50 years ago, and most are growing at too slow a pace to permit much in the way of poverty reduction. Most worrying of all, perhaps, is the group of low income countries that have yet to exhibit signs of economic growth; where poverty is increasing or at least stubbornly high; and where governments have yet to demonstrate an understanding of the policy requirements that can set these countries on a path to growth.

There has been a great deal of emphasis placed on the desperate plight of the millions of citizens in low income countries who live in poverty from which there seems little chance of escape. In this context, it is worth noting how rapid economic growth can transform the prospects of the poor: in China and India in the 1990s alone, some 200 million people were lifted out of poverty as a result of sustained and rapid growth in these countries.

The Millenium Development Goals (MDGs) were agreed in September 2000 precisely in order to address the plight of the world's poor. Much of the Fund's work on LICs is directed towards helping low income countries set in place the appropriate economic framework that can foster the sustained rapid growth that has already benefited citizens of so many countries in the postwar period.

The Fund continues to address the needs of all its members, rich, middle income, transition and poor. Globalization makes our task of maintaining international financial stability more important than ever. And it is a task which I believe we have discharged better than many realize. The absence of financial crises since the last global downturn in 2001–2002 is significant, though rarely remarked on.

Here, my main focus is on how the Fund discharges its responsibilities in the 21st century. We will examine how experience has shaped its work; and I will say something about the close links between financial sector health and macroeconomic stability.

Adaptability, and the readiness to learn from experience, have been key to the Fund's ability to discharge its task effectively over the years. The multilateral framework set up at Bretton Woods has underpinned the remarkable economic growth that the world has experienced since 1945. The wisdom and foresight of the Bretton Woods founders enabled dramatic rises in living standards across the globe; and, in the process, enabled many to escape from poverty.

A key element of the multilateral framework that the Bretton Woods founders designed was the principle of an open multilateral trading system. The expansion of world trade since 1945 has been a key driver of economic growth. World trade has consistently grown more rapidly than global GDP, and continues to do so. According to the WTO, the volume of world trade in 2000 was 22 times that of 1950. Merchandise exports have grown by 6 percent a year on average for the past 50 years. Last year, global growth was 5 percent; global trade grew by 8.5 percent.

The Fund's role in the maintenance of international financial stability has helped make possible rapid economic growth — and the Articles of Agreement make clear that was the intention of the founders of the Bretton Woods system. Providing a stable international framework that makes sustained and rapid growth possible has helped countries realize the benefits of globalization.

But how the Fund seeks to achieve financial stability has, of necessity, changed over time. The world economy is constantly evolving, and the Fund has to evolve with it. At the time of Bretton Woods, no one seriously believed that private capital flows would ever again be significant in size; for much of the postwar period, that assumption continued to hold. It was only in the 1990s that private capital flows started to assume the dominant role they have today, a development that has significant implications for the way the Fund operates.

In the early years of the postwar system, the fixed exchange rate regime established under Bretton Woods provided a stable environment that enabled the industrial countries to grow rapidly, at a pace that was at the time without historical precedent. America saw per capita income growth averaging 2.4 percent a year between 1950 and 1973; in Germany, per capita incomes grew on average by 5 percent a year, and in Japan by more than 8 percent.

By the 1960s, those rates of growth came to seem rather tame, as several developing countries started to experience even more rapid growth. South Korea achieved rapid growth over a remarkably sustained period, averaging real GDP growth of more than 8 percent a year for more than three decades. Other countries' growth rates also accelerated, in some instances markedly.

The period up to 1973 came to be known as a golden age, and many feared that the collapse of the Bretton Woods system of exchange rates in the early 1970s would bring that period of rapid growth to an end. In fact, the transition to floating exchange rates [triggered by the decision of the United States to close the gold window to which the fixed exchange rate system was pegged] was relatively smooth and timely: flexible exchange rate regimes helped economies adjust to the oil price shocks of the 1970s, disruptive though those rises undoubtedly were; and floating rates have facilitated smoother adjustment ever since.

But the 1970s marked an important turning point for the Fund in other ways. This marked the end of the period during which the industrial countries had been the Fund's largest borrowers. Britain in 1977 was the last major industrial country to borrow on a large scale from the Fund — indeed, the loan advanced to Britain that year was, at that time, the largest ever made by the Fund.[1]

The Fund had provided financial assistance to help developing countries adjust to higher oil prices. But the so-called third world debt crisis led to large-scale Fund lending to those countries in the 1980s. This crisis had its origin in the surplus revenues accumulated by the oil producers after the sharp rises in the oil price in the mid and late 1970s. These revenues had been "recycled" by the international banks who lent funds aggressively to developing economies, usually on floating rate terms. With hindsight, the result of this lending was predictable. Debt sustainability — regarded as a crucial element of macroeconomic policy today — was at the time an alien concept. As interest rates rose in the early 1980s, reflecting the efforts of industrial countries to reduce inflation, economic policy weaknesses were exposed and many developing country borrowers found themselves unable voluntarily to service their large debts. The Fund played a significant role in helping to resolve the problems developing countries faced, both in helping them make policy adjustments and in the provision of temporary financial support.

The experience of the 1980s brought a sharp reminder of the importance of economic policies in helping foster economic growth. This is now so widely accepted that it is hard to remember a time when it was less obvious. Policymakers in Asia implemented policies that created a growth-friendly environment — low inflation, outward oriented trade policies that enabled Asia to grow even though many countries were heavily dependent on oil imports. By contrast, in the 1980s many Latin American countries experienced soaring inflation, fuelled by inappropriate economic policies. In addition, higher barriers to trade hampered growth in Latin America over a long period. And oil exporting countries, in spite of their high oil revenues, experienced lower growth rates because of weak macroeconomic policies.

For the Fund, though, the 1990s brought the biggest challenges. In the early part of the decade, the Fund was heavily involved in assisting the countries of the former Soviet bloc to cope with a dramatic change in their circumstances. These countries needed Fund help both in the form of financial assistance but, more important in the long term, in managing the transition to become normally functioning market economies. This was an economic transformation of a kind that had never before been attempted and

---

[1] Until the Great Recession, it was generally assumed that the Fund's role as a lender to advanced countries had come to an end.

there was a steep and sometimes painful learning curve for those involved. Yet, most of these countries are increasingly regarded as normal, with normal problems: indeed, several are now members of the European Union.

A more far-reaching development for the Fund during this period, however, was the rise in private international capital flows. A series of financial crises during the 1990s, triggered by sharp changes in the direction of capital flows, underlined the extent to which sound economic policies both foster growth and help to prevent crises from occurring. It became clear, as the decade progressed, that these crises were fundamentally different from those to which we had grown accustomed.

There were crises in Mexico in 1994–5; in Asia in 1997–8; in Russia in 1998; and elsewhere. All were capital account crises, large in scale, and involving enormous upheaval for the countries involved.

Take the Asian crises as an example. Only a relatively small number of countries were directly affected: South Korea, Thailand and Indonesia were the worst hit. For those countries, years of spectacular growth ended in a dramatic series of national financial crises. But they had an impact well beyond the countries involved, in part because it was shocking to see economies that had experienced such rapid growth over such long periods suddenly appear so vulnerable and in part because there were, for a time, fears that the crises would spread further.

The proximate cause of the crises in Asia was the sharp reversal of capital flows to the region. Net inflows to the Asian crisis countries were over 6 percent of their GDP in 1995, and just under 6 percent in 1996. In 1997, net outflows were 2 percent of GDP, a figure which rose to 5 percent the following year. The economic dislocation caused by reversals of this magnitude was huge, and would have been so for any country.

But the turnaround in investor sentiment was not, as some have argued, wholly capricious. There had been a huge expansion of credit over a relatively short period of time. Rapid credit growth is almost always indiscriminate and, therefore, dangerous. The result had been a sharp rise in the number of bad loans. The rate of return on capital had fallen and, in consequence, nonperforming loans (NPLs) started to rise. As international creditors saw countries whose fundamentals were less sound than had previously appeared to be the case, a rapid reassessment of the creditworthiness of debtors and loan exposure was inevitable.

Several factors conspired to make the consequences of this shift in investor sentiment extremely painful. Fixed exchange rates prevented a more rapid adjustment to the shift in capital flows — and gave speculators the chance to make one-sided bets. Government assurances that exchange rate pegs would be maintained had left currency mismatches unrecognized until governments were forced to devalue. Banks had built up liabilities in one currency and assets in others. Devaluation then left financial institutions and businesses facing massive losses or insolvency. The weaknesses of domestic banking systems were revealed — as was the impact on economic performance.

The contraction in GDP that most crisis countries experienced made things even worse, of course, because the number, and size, of NPLs grew rapidly. The further weakening of the financial sector inevitably had adverse consequences for the economy as a whole. In short, the crisis economies found themselves in a vicious downward spiral.

The capital account crises in Asia and elsewhere had several common features: they occurred rapidly; they occurred because holders of a country's debt were concerned about the ability and/or willingness to service; and because there were doubts about underlying macroeconomic policies to service that debt.

The speed with which capital account crises erupted meant that financial support from the Fund for countries affected was often urgently needed — often in days rather than the weeks or months which the Fund programs for current account crises had usually taken to put together. In addition, the support needed was usually on a much larger scale than the Fund earlier provided because of the magnitude of the outflows experienced by crisis countries.

Fund programs with financial support were far-reaching. They included the commitment to rapid fiscal rebalancing; addressing underlying weaknesses in banking systems; a switch to floating rates or at least to more flexible exchange rate regimes; and programs of longer-term structural reforms aimed at removing structural rigidities and improving growth potential.

Much was learned from the experience of the 1990s. The importance of a sound macroeconomic framework was reemphasized. In a globalized world, economies must have in place monetary and fiscal policies that deliver falling or low inflation, budgetary prudence and sustainable debt levels. And analysis of the importance of debt sustainability and analysis of debt dynamics became a part of economists' toolkits.

There was also agreement that countries need an exchange rate regime that enables an economy to be sufficiently flexible to respond to shocks. Fixed exchange rates pose significant challenges because they require much greater reliance on fiscal, monetary and structural policies to provide the flexibility needed in an economy.

Another important lesson was the closeness of the link between the financial sector and economic stability and growth. Economic history teaches that growth in the real economy has gone hand in hand with the development of the financial sector. Even the most basic economies, when activity is confined to a few rudimentary activities in a small geographical area, use some medium of exchange. As economic activities expand and become more differentiated, demands on the financial system increase. Small, localized banks develop as mechanisms for more effectively enabling the owners of capital to lend it to those who can use it more productively. But to be effective in underpinning economic growth, banks, even small ones, must develop the ability to assess creditworthiness, risks, and returns. Without these skills, even in a relatively underdeveloped economy, the role of the banks as financial intermediaries is less than optimal and thus hampers growth. Resources need to be allocated according to productive potential and banks have an important role to play in directing resources to high-return investments — and reducing the resources wasted on low-return or unprofitable investments. But this, in turn, requires the capability to assess the likely returns to competing borrowers.

As economies grow, they become more complex and interdependent; and the demands placed on the financial sector grow commensurately. Banks grow bigger; they need to in order to meet the demand for investment capital. Economic complexity also means that banks must grow more complex, and become more diversified in terms of the risks they assume. Continued expansion brings increasing demands for geographical diversity — firms need banks that can serve their needs across national boundaries and they also need banks that provide specialized financial services.

But breadth and depth are important for the financial sector as a whole. Healthy and sustained growth of firms and economies requires the development of new financing modes for investment capital. The financial sector — in which I include banks, equity and bond markets, insurance providers and other financial intermediaries — has to meet the needs of the growing range of economic activity.

Experience has repeatedly shown that high growth rates are sustainable only as the financial sector develops in parallel with the economy as a whole. A weak financial sector can undermine growth. Resources are misallocated and average returns fall. We all knew that a healthy financial sector was an important ingredient of macroeconomic stability. But the role that weak financial sectors played in the crises of the 1990s made us appreciate even more than before quite how central the financial sector's role is. That, in turn had a profound impact on the Fund's work, which will be discussed next.

As noted earlier, the Fund's principal mandate remains the maintenance of international financial stability. The part of the Fund's work that attracts the most attention — crisis management and resolution — is important, but it is only a small part of it. Much of the work is aimed at preventing crises and at helping members to achieve sustained rapid growth through the implementation of sound macroeconomic and other economic policies.

Central to this is the Fund's surveillance. That consists of monitoring and assessing global and national economic developments and providing advice and guidance to member countries. Sometimes efforts are made to persuade members to modify policies to avert foreseeable trouble or to improve their growth prospects; sometimes Article IV, as surveillance reports are called, warn about risks to national or international financial and macroeconomic stability. Surveillance is carried out both at the global and at the national level. The World Economic Outlook is published twice a year and contains the Fund staff's latest projections for global and national growth and a series of other economic indicators. These projections are also qualified to reflect the potential risks that could undermine the central forecast.

Fund surveillance at the national level is conducted annually with each member, with occasional delays. Each country has assigned to it a team of Fund officials, and they conduct in-depth discussions with the authorities of that country. The team analyzes the country's economic prospects and policies. It cautions the authorities about potential risks to the outlook and of potential weaknesses in the economic policy framework, and discusses ways in which prospects could be improved. Fund staff also draw attention to policies that are effective in promoting growth and stability

The Fund's surveillance work gives the institution a unique cross-country perspective. It is, after all, the only institution that has such a broad membership and that has access to the relevant information about national economic policies. The surveillance work, and the work of the research department, permits comparative insights into economies and economic policies. Highlighting successful policies is actually as important a part of the Fund's work as sounding a note of caution when there are doubts about national economic policy choices.

Surveillance is important for all categories of the Fund's membership. The dialog with industrial country members focuses on issues that affect their prospects for growth and stability and that, because of the size of these economies, might also have implications for the world economy as a whole.

For several years, the Fund expressed concern in its surveillance consultations with Japan about that country's very slow or non-existent growth, and about the problem of deflation in the Japanese economy. Policy reforms there seem to have led to a significant and welcome improvement in Japan's growth performance in the middle of the decade.

The Fund is drawing attention to the economic and fiscal challenges posed by rapid demographic change, which will affect the industrial countries first.

In surveillance work with emerging market countries and most transition economies, the emphasis is on reducing vulnerabilities and raising potential long-term growth rates. The two go hand in hand, of course; the stronger the macroeconomic framework, the better the long-term growth performance of the economy will be. Low, or falling, inflation, sound fiscal and monetary policies, and sustainable debt levels are all important.

It is clear that macroeconomic stability is just as important for low-income countries. Most of those countries that have, often with Fund help and encouragement, put in place policies to reduce inflation and create the conditions for growth have experienced higher growth rates. Many low income countries also have hostile environments for business, property rights that are difficult to enforce and weak judicial systems that make contract enforcement in some cases virtually impossible.

During the past decade, the policy community came to realize that a sound macroeconomic framework needs to address institutional issues. Businesses are stifled and foreign investment discouraged if a country does not have an effective judiciary that makes contract enforcement possible and timely. Businesses simply relocate to somewhere that offers them greater legal protection. Similarly, countries that do not offer legally, and easily enforceable property rights will find it hard to attract and retain investment. Such shortcomings have always undermined business activity and, in consequence, economic growth: but as the world economy becomes more integrated, business has become more mobile and a climate hostile to business even more damaging. The Fund, in cooperation with the World Bank, works actively to promote institutional reform as a vital ingredient in promoting sustained and rapid economic growth. Institutional shortcomings are an issue in some emerging market economies; but they are far more serious and widespread in low income countries.

The Fund aims in its surveillance work to assess financial sector robustness in a variety of ways. Close attention is paid to banks' balance sheets, to the extent of NPLs and to risk in the financial system. The degree of competition and development within the banking system and the financial system as a whole is also examined. Competition improves the efficiency of credit allocation and can help diversify financial risk and cut borrowing costs. Issues such as the rate of credit expansion, regulation, and mis-matched exposures are also evaluated.

The breadth of financial instruments is important, as is the transparency of the system which enables more accurate assessments to be made of the asset and risk position of individual institutions. And a strong, effective regulatory regime, following international best practice, is vital.

Much of the financial sector surveillance is done through the Financial Sector Assessment Program, or FSAP, introduced in 1999. It is a voluntary program, and additional to Article IV consultations which also address financial sector issues. Member countries request an FSAP, at which point the Fund undertakes a detailed examination of the framework for financial regulation and supervision. The work carried out under an FSAP program involves a broad range of financial experts, many of them from outside the Fund.

The FSAP program (run jointly with the World Bank for low-income countries) aims to help member governments strengthen their financial systems by detecting vulnerabilities in financial supervision at an early stage, to identify where changes are needed; to set policy priorities; and to provide technical assistance when it is needed to strengthen supervisory and reporting frameworks. The end result is intended to ensure that the right processes and systems are in place for countries to make their own substantive assessments of individual institutions.

FSAPs do not examine the balance sheets of individual banks, or even the banking sector as a whole. Their purpose is to help countries ensure that an appropriate framework is in place so that domestic regulators and supervisors are able to make accurate judgments about the health of the banks and other financial institutions under their jurisdiction.

The Fund has also worked with the World Bank to develop a system of Standards and Codes — using internationally-recognized standards — that result in Reports on Standards and Codes (ROSCs). These cover 12 areas, including banking supervision, securities regulation, and insurance supervision. The financial sector ROSCs are an integral part of the FSAP and are published by agreement with member countries.

Surveillance of financial sector issues has identified many vulnerabilities in many countries that have subsequently been rectified. As a result, crises have been avoided and success in this area is best measured by the absence of crises. But some Fund research also suggests that there is another payoff — in the form of lower spreads — for countries where the Fund has undertaken ROSCs and where the reports have been published in full. The markets take a favorable view of this transparency which can translate into lower borrowing costs.

Another important element of the Fund's work with emerging market and low income countries is technical assistance, or TA. TA accounts for about a third of the Fund's activities. It is a vital part of the work done to help countries implement reforms that will strengthen their economies and raise their growth potential.

TA work covers a wide range of activities: from assistance in improving customs procedures or tax administration to the management of monetary policy. It can help countries increase the benefits of trade liberalization, both through customs reforms and through increasing other tax revenues through improved tax administration. Streamlining customs procedures can help governments create a more business-friendly environment and spur trade. The Fund helps countries to develop their foreign exchange markets and to improve public expenditure management — for poor countries keeping track of where the money goes can be as difficult as it is important.

TA can help countries make their public sectors more efficient. Helping countries to improve tax collection procedures, for example, can significantly raise the revenue stream from any given tax rate; lowering tax rates can also raise revenues by acting as a disincentive for people to participate in the informal sector of the economy. By providing help with pension reforms, TA can help countries manage fiscal policy more effectively, enabling them to free up resources for infrastructure and more targeted spending without increasing deficits.

The Fund has several TA centers around the world, including two in Africa. It also provides economists on long-term secondment to finance and other government agencies to work on particular issues, such as public expenditure issues and tax reforms.

The Fund is most visible in providing financial support to members. It can provide temporary assistance to deal with balance of payments crises, or to help countries avert them.[2] Such help is provided in Fund-supported programs, where the aim is to help countries undertake the reforms needed in response to a crisis. Mexico, Thailand, Indonesia, South Korea, Russia, Brazil, Turkey, Uruguay, and others have been in Fund-supported programs in recent years.[3]

While the Fund's programs have been most visible in emerging markets (and in Europe in 2010 and 2011), considerable support has been provided to low income countries, much of it on concessional terms.

All aspects of the Fund's work — surveillance, TA, and financial support — have a common goal. It is to enable member countries to ensure that they have in place policies that will deliver macroeconomic and financial stability and so lay the foundation for more rapid and sustained growth that is a prerequisite for sustained poverty reduction. The Fund's

---

[2] See Chapters 7 and 8 for an account of some Fund programs.
[3] This paper was presented in 2005. As is well known, some European countries confronted crises in 2010 and 2011 and entered into Fund-supported programs, as well.

unique cross-country perspective has significant advantages when helping countries address their economic policy needs.

The world economy has changed enormously over the past 60 years. Along the way, a great deal has been learned about how economies function and about how best to achieve sustained rapid growth, rising living standards, and poverty reduction. The Fund has been at the center of this evolutionary process.

The international economy will continue to evolve, though we do not know how. One of the few certain consequences of globalization is that the world is constantly changing. The Fund will continue to be at the center of these changes going forward. It has repeatedly demonstrated its capacity to learn and change as the international economy has evolved.

Chapter 14

AN ENDURING NEED: THE IMPORTANCE OF MULTILATERALISM IN THE TWENTY-FIRST CENTURY

Multilateralism has been the key to the huge economic successes of the past half century. The achievements of the multilateral economic system are increasingly underappreciated as it is ever more taken for granted, while the need for well-functioning multilateral international economic system is greater than ever as globalization proceeds. I shall argue that the multilateral financial institutions have performed remarkably well in underpinning economic success of unimagined proportions over the past sixty years. However, just as we take the air we breathe for granted, so, too, do many now take those successes and the multilateral system underpinning them for granted. They ignore the "public good" benefits that the multilateral system provides and focus instead on a narrow view of the short-term costs, often taking the benefits for granted.

On the face of it, there is wide support for the multilateral institutions and for the principle of multilateralism. But too often these days, that support is little more than lip service. On almost all issues, the cumulative impact of decisions that affect the strength and health of the institutions is usually underestimated, if it is recognized at all, and the "common good" is generally under-represented in global fora.

I start by considering some of the many reasons why multilateralism is so important. Then I want to remind us of some of the successes of the system over the past 60 years. Then I turn to some of the reasons why support for the system is not as strong as one would expect in light of its great accomplishments. Finally, I will examine some of the practical issues on which the common good seems to be underestimated relative to the particular concerns of individual countries or groups of countries.

THE ROLE OF MULTILATERALISM

To their enormous credit, the founders of the post-war international economic system knew, and understood, the importance of multilateralism. They knew it in theory, but they also knew it because they had all experienced the enormous cost of individual actions taken outside a multilateral framework in the 1930s. Then, governments, struggling to offset the impact of the Great Depression, undertook measures that, in effect, were designed to export their problems and that could only succeed if other countries did not take similar measures.

Competitive devaluations were designed to boost exports, but could have succeeded only if other countries did not respond in kind. But, of course, there were irresistible pressures on countries against which devaluation had been undertaken to follow suit and retaliate, and competitive devaluations worsened the situation.

Countries also raised their own tariff barriers, hoping to stimulate their own economic activity by reducing imports (again exporting both unemployment and reduced output to other countries). But, again, the fact that other countries were undertaking similar measures negated any beneficial effect. The volume of world trade shrank and high tariff barriers increased distortions and inefficiencies in the global economy. The American Smoot-Hawley tariff of 1930 was followed by such calamitous events that after the Second World War protectionism in much of the world was held at bay, if not defeated, for years by the mere mention of the name.

Interestingly, most European countries had learned the difficulties of negotiating tariff levels bilaterally (and therefore discriminating among countries) back in the 19th century. They had therefore adopted most favored nation (MFN) clauses in their trade treaties, insuring that imports of each commodity would be treated similarly regardless of country of origin. It was not, however, until the 1920s that the United States government recognized the drawbacks of bilateral trade treaties (at least as seen from an American perspective): the trading partner with which the United States was negotiating would have to lower its tariff for all its MFN partners, while the American tariffs were not extended to others. Most countries chose to offer more favorable tariffs to countries where they would receive larger reciprocal reductions (across other partners) in exchange. Thus, MFN countries could reduce tariffs with each other, leaving the US (and other countries that did not have MFN clauses) confronting the higher tariff rates. The United States was therefore in a position of bargaining with all MFN countries while being excluded from tariff reductions already undertaken among MFN members.

It was largely because of this manifestly unfavorable experience that, in the 1930s, Cordell Hull, the American Secretary of State, so enthusiastically supported "reciprocal tariff agreements" in an MFN context.

But the experience of competitive devaluations was equally compelling: an action taken by one country could be in its self-interest unless others followed, in which case all would be worse off. A multilateral framework to avoid this possible outcome seemed clearly warranted.

Correctly, the founders of the postwar international economic system recognized that multilateralism was desirable, not only to reduce and, they hoped, to eliminate the possibility of any recurrence of the 1930s, but also to promote nondiscrimination in international transactions. For my purposes today, I shall focus on the three key organizations: the International Monetary Fund, charged with maintaining international financial stability; the World Bank, responsible for the provision of development capital; and the World Trade Organization (earlier the General Agreement on Tariffs and Trade) supervising the world's multilateral trading system.

The founders of the postwar system recognized the benefits to be had from a resumption of international capital flows, but believed that the experience of the 1930s had destroyed prospects for a resumption of most private capital flows. They therefore were concerned with enabling official capital flows through the International Bank for Reconstruction and Development — now the World Bank — and did not focus on difficulties that might arise either from discriminatory treatment by source of private capital flows or from the lack of an agreed international framework governing treatment of foreign capital. Hence, the postwar international economic system and organization was assumed to be complete when, in addition to the GATT for multilateral trade relations and the World Bank for official capital flows, the IMF was charged with international financial and macroeconomic stability and rules governing current account transactions. The absence of a regime for private capital flows resulted from the assumption that these flows would be relatively unimportant.

What was enshrined in the Fund's Articles of Agreement was provision for convertibility of domestic currencies for current account transactions. By definition, if a currency is convertible without restrictions, it is multilateral and there can be no discrimination for current account transactions. Issues relating to discrimination on the capital account were not addressed, on the assumption that there were relatively few such transactions. Obviously, trade credits and perhaps some other short-term credits might enter international trade, but it was not thought that issues of discrimination would arise. Interestingly, this oversight led to problems even when private capital flows had resumed at very low levels: difficulties arose because of governments' terms for granting official export credit, aid tying, and related issues.

One of the most striking ways in which the world has changed has been the emergence of private capital flows as a major force in the world economy. I shall return to this issue later and argue that the absence of a multilateral, nondiscriminatory framework governing international capital flows (and exchange control mechanisms) is an important and potentially costly gap in the multilateral economic system.

The arguments for a level playing field in which all transactions with foreigners are subject to the same regime are straightforward, glaringly obvious, and hence very dull. Each country's citizens will be better off sourcing imports and finance from the cheapest available source; and selling goods and services and undertaking capital transactions where they can obtain the best terms. And, as I shall note later, efforts to discriminate by country of origin or destination also confront enormous practical problems that normally can be addressed, if at all, only with a highly complex, distortionary, and costly set of regulations.

While the arguments for multilateral regimes for trade, current account transactions, exchange regimes, and capital flows are profoundly correct, they do not provide a dramatic demonstration of the virtues of multilateralism. Experience with efforts to depart from multilateralism has provided more dramatic illustrations of the need for multilateral solutions to international economic policy issues.

Let me mention just three: efforts to impose trade sanctions bilaterally; American experience with so-called voluntary export restraints; and antidumping and countervailing duty administration.

Efforts to impose trade sanctions against a country or group of countries are of course an extreme form of trade discrimination. Yet experience shows that they are seldom very effective unless all countries participate or those imposing sanctions can prevent trade through a blockade or other means. Even in cases where "most countries" are supportive, even one open border (whether the authorities are openly permissive, simply turn a blind eye, or cannot enforce) has generally been sufficient to mitigate most of the potential impact of trade sanctions.

American experience with country-specific so-called "voluntary export restraints" (wherein country-specific levels of the good in question were to be permitted) illustrates the same point: VERs have been greatly reduced in their impact by third-country effects. Perhaps the most famous case concerned semi-conductors: the imposition by the US of a VER led to a major expansion of capacity in third countries and led many American companies to shift production activities using semi-conductors offshore. American semi-conductor producers gained little, if anything, while American consumers of semi-conductors (PC assemblers, etc.) suffered.

But the experience has been more general: when a particular country or group of countries is targeted, the existence of other suppliers (or consumers) of the product significantly reduces, if it does not totally prevent, the intended effect. European car producers were the big beneficiaries of the ill-fated effort by the U.S. to impose VERs on imports of Japanese cars, and Korea became a major auto producer more quickly than it otherwise would have.

Anti-dumping and countervailing duty measures are, by design, discriminatory against countries (and firms) that are found to be using "unfair" means to lower their selling price in the market to which they export. In many instances, firms have been able to shift production from a plant in the country against which the AD or CVD measures is applied to one elsewhere. But when that has not been the case, third country producers are often the big beneficiaries. A famous case was Polish golf carts; the full story is too long to recount, but the main effect of the American effort to impose a CVD on Polish imports was to induce entry of Spanish carts into the American market.

I hope I have said enough to indicate the crucial importance of multilateralism in a well-functioning international economic system. And, since there are occasions when individual countries can perceive it to be in their self interest to pursue discriminatory policies if it is believed that others will not do the same, an international economic regime underpinning and enforcing multilateralism in international transactions is vital. Third country effects; the temptation to retaliate; the fact that an open international economic system has many aspects of a "public good": all of these are arguments that underpinned the postwar international economic system.

But the experience of the postwar years, and the unquestionable success of the system, speak even more strongly as to its importance. In most discussions of globalization today, it seems to be forgotten exactly how far the world has come in the sixty years of the postwar international economic system.

Recall that the war-torn European and Asian economies were devastated and, in the aftermath of the war, had output levels significantly below those of the prewar years. Most had severe exchange controls, often with bilateral clearing arrangements, high tariffs and often quantitative restrictions on imports. The average European tariff on manufactured goods imports stood at over 40 percent, but that number understates the extent of trade restrictiveness as quantitative restrictions often kept imports below even the quantities demanded at those high tariff levels. Only 4 countries in the world had full currency convertibility. And, of course, many countries were still very poor, or underdeveloped, as they were then called, with very low per capita incomes and correspondingly poor indicators of health, nutrition, literacy, and other measures of well being.

But starting in the late 1940s, the global economy embarked upon a quarter-century-long period of rapid economic growth, greatly outperforming any prior period of comparable length in world economic history. European recovery accelerated rapidly, and most countries had re-attained their prewar output levels by the early 1950s. But they sustained their growth rates well into the 1960s and early 1970s. At the same time, Japan's economy began growing and by the 1960s was achieving rates of economic growth of 7–9 percent — well above anything that had earlier been thought possible.

Expanding world trade was the "engine of growth" in the postwar years. While real GDP was growing at rates far in excess of those realized in earlier eras, world trade was growing at almost twice the rate of real GDP growth. In part, the recovery from wartime conditions and growth of GDP spurred trade growth. But in addition, successive rounds of tariff reductions under GATT and other trade liberalizing measures spurred growth in trade and GDP. At the same time, bilateral trading agreements were gradually abandoned and then multilateral clearing of balances, and, finally, full current-account convertibility followed. It was a virtuous circle: reduction of trade barriers spurred economic growth; and economic growth enabled the further reduction of trade barriers. To leap ahead of my story, by the end of the 20th century, tariffs on manufactured goods among developed countries had fallen from over 40 percent in the late 1940s to an average of less than 5 percent, and quantitative restrictions on trade in manufactures were largely a thing of the past.

Several points about this phenomenal success deserve noting in connection with the role of multilateralism. Perhaps most important, the developing countries, with a few exceptions, failed to participate in trade liberalization in the quarter century after 1950. They mostly erected high trade barriers against imports of manufactures as it was believed that protectionism for "infant industries" was the appropriate policy to achieve more rapid economic growth.

Despite their failure to participate, however, developing countries grew at rates well above those that had been achieved in earlier eras. The fact that the world economy was growing rapidly enabled relatively favorable terms of trade and growth of export earnings (although their share of world trade declined as the industrial countries' trade liberalization led to even more rapid growth there). While the East Asian "tigers", whose policies included increasing integration with the international economy, were growing at spectacular rates, other developing countries benefited substantially from the rapid growth of the world economy, despite their failure to liberalize. In an important sense, those "inner-oriented" developing countries were "free riders" of the multilateral system: the rapid growth of trade benefited them even though they had not themselves liberalized their trade at that time. It enabled them to enter markets more readily than they otherwise would have done, and to increase their exports when domestic incentives were appropriate. That same growth enabled even greater benefits to accrue to them when they liberalized their own trade regimes in the 1980s and 1990s, encouraged by the examples of East Asian success. Trade barriers, both tariffs and quantitative restrictions, have been lowered dramatically in most of the economies now referred to as "emerging markets", thereby contributing to their further growth.

A second, and related, point, is that "globalization" was certainly occurring during the golden quarter century. Trade as a share of global GDP was rising, not only because of falling trade barriers but also because transport and communications costs were dropping sharply. It bears repeating that in 1931 a 3 minute phone call between London and New York had cost $293 in constant 1998 prices. By 2001, that same call cost $1; and today it costs at most just a few cents. Ocean shipping added about 30 percent to the f.o.b. value of exports in the late 1940s; that figure had fallen to 3 percent by the late 1990s. Air freight, a rarity in the immediate postwar years, now accounts for 40 percent of world trade in value terms. Those cost reductions meant that more and more goods were tradable; that many services were increasingly tradable; and hence that globalization was proceeding during the period.

In that connection, the tremendous advances in living standards around the world that accompanied rapid global growth should also be recognized. For example, life expectancy in India has risen from about 39 years in the early 1950s to over 60 years today. Similar dramatic increases have taken place in most developing countries. Since 1960, life expectancy in the developing countries has risen at roughly double the rate in the richest, with the result that the gap in life expectancy between rich and poor countries has shrunk from 30 years in the 1950s to around ten years today. Literacy rates have risen sharply, and other indicators of well being have improved dramatically in most countries.

But the main point is that the trade liberalization and globalization that took place during the first quarter century after 1945 was undertaken in a multilateral context. Bilateral trading agreements fell dramatically in importance; more and more countries adopted Article VIII convertibility; tariff and non-tariff barriers fell sharply.

Almost all of this took place in a multilateral system underpinned by the IMF, the World Bank and the then-GATT. But there was one exception to this generalization, and that exception may have contributed significantly to the current under-appreciation of multilateralism's importance. That was the establishment of the European Common Market, which has evolved into the European Union.

As is well known, intra-European trade barriers were reduced even more sharply than were Europe's external trade barriers. As the common market evolved, the European economies were increasingly integrated until now there is a common currency and Central Bank, a common agricultural policy, an internal customs union, and much more.

And the European economies were dramatically successful not only in recovering to their prewar level of economic performance, but in sustaining that growth over the next several decades. In truth, the European economies were benefiting from their global (multilateral) trade liberalization, increased integration which enhanced competition in each of them (in addition to other benefits) as well as from the worldwide expansion that was occurring. But, to many observers, Europe's stellar performance appeared (misleadingly) to be attributable to European integration. In fact, something like 90 percent of Europe's trade liberalization had been multilateral, and probably around an extra 10 percent had been extended preferentially within the continent.

The misperception that Europe's success has been largely attributable to its internal preferential arrangements has probably contributed to the failure to appreciate the importance of multilateralism, to the thrust toward preferential trading arrangements and to other bilateral and regional arrangements. As I shall argue later, this is highly dangerous for all members of the international economy, as preferential arrangements will achieve their intended purpose only in the context of a strengthening of the multilateral system.

To appreciate more fully why this is so, let us turn to the next thirty years after the Golden quarter century. The 1970s represented a major turning point. Perhaps most importantly, the "Bretton Woods system" of fixed exchange rates had to be abandoned, as major countries were unwilling or unable to follow the domestic economic policies that would have been necessary had it been decided to maintain fixed exchange rate regimes. It was probably fortunate for the international economy that that abandonment took place before the quadrupling of the oil price in 1973, as flexible exchange rates between the major currencies enabled the absorption of a significant portion of the shock with less economic dislocation than might have occurred had countries been trying to sustain their earlier, fixed exchange rates.

But several other, related, phenomena occurred. Worldwide inflation accelerated. Many oil-importing countries accessed private capital markets to borrow to finance their oil imports in the years immediately after the oil price increase, with the private capital markets in effect "recycling" the windfall gains from oil producers to the oil-importing developing countries. When, in the 1980s, industrial countries adopted anti-inflationary policies, the higher debt-servicing costs faced by developing countries, and other factors, led to the "debt crisis" of the 1980s.

The official international community — both the IMF and the World Bank — reacted, supporting adjustment efforts in many of the afflicted countries. By the late 1980s, growth in emerging markets was accelerating, and debt "overhangs" were addressed through the Brady plan and other measures. The Paris Club — another multilateral effort — found its role in the restructuring of official debt to official creditors greatly enhanced. I should note in passing that these efforts were necessarily in a multilateral context, as the debt which had to be restructured under the Brady Plan was held by a large number of industrial countries, and any country that had alone tried to enable a restructuring of developing country debt held by its nationals would have confronted the awkward fact that nationals from other creditor countries would benefit by its actions. Multilateralism was essential for the resolution of these difficulties.

Over this period, the IMF had adapted significantly to its new role. The Fund shifted toward greater emphasis on support and surveillance of economic policies in developing countries, and greater focus on the consistency of exchange rates with monetary and fiscal policies, largely in the context of current account issues.

But in the 1990s there was another sea change in the international economic system. The world economy was growing rapidly, fuelled by growth in world trade, in turn the result at least in part of further trade liberalization under the Uruguay Round. At the same time, the collapse of the Soviet Union led to major challenges in transforming those economies into functioning market economies. Again, bilateral efforts to support the transition would, by themselves, have been far clumsier. The existence of the GATT, subsequently the WTO, as a means of bringing trade regimes into the multilateral system, was essential. So, too, was the admission of economies in transition to the Fund and the Bank, enabling them to adopt the rules of the game for their exchange rate regimes and current account transactions.

Simultaneously, many of the developing countries whose economic performance in the 1980s had contrasted poorly with that of the successful East Asian economies began undertaking policy reforms, including shifting to a more open economy, in the hope and expectation that their economic performance could be improved. By the mid-1990s, China's rapid economic

growth was recognized by all, and India's economic reforms were beginning
to bring results.

Earlier, some of the East Asian economies had profitably utilized large
private capital inflows — in the case of Korea averaging almost 10 percent of
GDP during the high growth years — and had shown their creditworthiness.
This, combined with the improved prospects of many emerging markets, had
led private creditors to pay much more attention to emerging markets. As a
consequence, private capital flows to emerging markets mushroomed:
whereas in the early 1980s, less than half of capital flows to developing countries had originated from private sources, by the mid 1990s, private capital
flows predominated. And whereas a small number of developing countries
had been significant borrowers from private markets even in the 1980s, a
much larger number of countries, including economies in transition, were
able to access them by the mid 1990s.

At the same time, preferential trading arrangements, or PTAs, were pro-
liferating. Until the late 1980s, the European Union and the European Free
Trade Association (which consisted of some of the European countries that
had not joined the EU) had been the major PTAs in the world economy, and
the thrust of most changes in trade policies had been for intensification of
multilateral relations. There had been some efforts at PTAs among other
groups of countries, but most of them had been largely ineffective and, in
some cases, abandoned. But after the U.S.-Canada Free Trade Agreement,
which eventually became NAFTA, other PTAs abounded. To be sure, many
of them were between transition economies of Eastern Europe and the
European Union, but there were also many others. Today, there are very few
countries that are not members of one or more PTAs and many are members
of many!

From the beginning of the stampede toward PTAs, economists noted that
these could be either a "stepping stone" toward multilateral trading liberalization or a "stumbling block". If a PTA opens the way toward greater
multilateral trade liberalization and is consistent with a multilateral system, it
can improve the welfare of the countries involved in the arrangement, and
will not involve significant "trade diversion" from the rest of the world. If,
however, the main effect of a PTA is to divert trade from previous trading
partners towards members of the PTA, it will reduce the welfare of members
and also lead to increased resistance against, (or less support for) further multilateral opening. In addition, there is also the consideration that, when
countries' trade officials are focusing their attention on negotiating PTAs,
there are fewer resources — and perhaps less motivation — to support the
multilateral system.

While private capital flows were increasing in absolute and relative importance, and countries continued to liberalize, a series of events diverted attention from these trends. These were the crises in Mexico in 1994, Thailand, Indonesia, Korea and Malaysia in 1997–98, Russia in 1998, and Brazil in 1999. These crises, especially in the Asian countries, came as a major shock, in part because the rapid and sustained growth of those countries over such a long period had led most observers to believe they were invulnerable, and in part because of the rapidity and severity with which the crises erupted. These were different from earlier current account crises, in part because the capital account was more open and thus permitted more sizeable outflows relative to trade flows. It is not my intention here to analyze these episodes: for present purposes, the only point is to note that there was a great deal of learning to be done by all about the factors contributing to the crises and about the appropriate policy responses when crises did occur. Focus on those issues significantly distracted the international community from attention to the larger questions that arose in response to the emergence of such very large private capital flows and the drift away from multilateral international economic relations.

Lessons have been learned, and many countries' economic policies have changed in ways that make them less vulnerable to financial crises: there have been shifts to more flexible exchange rate regimes, attention has been paid to issues of debt sustainability, reserve levels are higher, and there is greater focus on the consistency of monetary and fiscal policy with exchange rate regimes. And, of course, the IFIs played an important role both in facilitating economic reform and disseminating the lessons learned: yet again something multilateralism was best equipped to do.

WHERE WE ARE TODAY

The international economy has prospered over the past few years. World real GDP has grown well in excess of 4 percent annually for four years running and is projected to sustain this pace into 2007. And all regions of the world are sharing in this growth. The world is a far more affluent place than it was a half century ago. Living standards, measured by indicators such as life expectancy, infant mortality, nutritional status, and literacy, have all improved. To be sure, some parts of the world have been more successful than others, and some have failed to share in the gains, and these problems need to be addressed.

Nonetheless, the broad brush picture is one of phenomenal economic success encompassing virtually the entire world, unparalleled by any period in economic history. And the multilateral system has underpinned much of that success. Countries undertaking reforms have realized gains far greater than they would have had the world economy been significantly less vibrant. And experience with reforms has been applied elsewhere, in part because the IFIs have enabled rapid transmission of lessons learned. The fact that trade and capital flows take place on a level multilateral playing field enhances efficiency, and increases competition in ways that are further growth-enhancing. On the surface, therefore, the outlook appears extremely promising.

But, beneath the surface, there are causes for concern. These arise in significant part because the multilateral system is so deeply embedded in today's international economy, and has been for such a long time, that it is largely and dangerously taken for granted. There are three major, related but not identical, factors that give rise to worry. One is the increased reliance on preferential arrangements, with their implied discrimination. The second is that private capital flows, despite their increased importance, do not yet fall into any coherent multilateral regime. The third is the tendency, probably increasing, for individual countries to place emphasis on their own position vis-à-vis the system, without regard to the extent to which their desired outcome may weaken the institutional underpinning of the very institutions they are trying to influence.

I shall close by considering each of these in turn.

I have already discussed the tendency for increasing proliferation of PTAs. By their very nature they are discriminatory, and each arrangement builds in some vested interests against multilateral liberalization. The best recent demonstration of this is the assertion that the reduction of barriers against imports of agricultural commodities by industrial countries would reduce the preferences that some developing countries receive. Yet the idea of preferences was to give developing countries a chance to develop their agricultural sectors over the medium term. So such an assertion for the longer term promises either a permanently inefficient pattern of production; or current investment in activities that will later have to be dismantled when preferences are removed.

It is not often asserted that the existence of preferential arrangements is a reason for failure to support, or opposition to, further multilateral liberalization. But the fact is that producers already exporting to PTA markets are either efficient and have already achieved the benefits (to them) of trade liberalization or they are inefficient and do not want multilateral competition. Either way, support for further multilateral liberalization has eroded. Many in the policy community have noted the absence of strong support from the US business community for the Doha Round, as compared to support for the earlier rounds of trade negotiations. It is not possible to prove that the absence of support for Doha is the result of PTAs (or the prospect of further PTAs) but it is certainly possible and even, I would argue, likely.

And, regardless of the causes, the multilateral trading system will inevitably be weakened should the Doha Round end without agreement. The failure to recognize the importance of open, non-discriminatory global trade is clearly a major factor in the current impasse. While the unraveling of the system would be a gradual prospect, it is nonetheless one that should be greeted with alarm by all who have shared in the rising living standards and global prosperity of the past six decades.

The second issue, the failure of the international economic system to have a coherent regime governing capital flows, is obviously more serious as private capital flows increase in size and importance in the global economy. Internationally-recognized rules for treatment of foreign assets and capital flows that provide for uniform treatment regardless of country or origin, and otherwise ensure a level playing field and efficient allocation of the world's capital resources, are clearly needed. The fact that most countries have to date extended uniform treatment to inflows and assets regardless of origin or ownership is heartening. But that may owe much to the traditions of the open multilateral trading system. Preferential trading arrangements permit the possibility of negotiations for favorable treatment for PTA partners and, hence, for discrimination among non-members. This should be cause for alarm and we should seek to head off such pressures before they gain currency. There would be less resistance now to developing protection for multilateral regimes for capital flows than could happen at a later date should preferential treatment become more prevalent.

Some may argue that a uniform regime is desirable for the treatment of foreign direct investment but unnecessary for other forms of capital flows. A major problem with this argument is that money is fungible: transforming one capital flow into another is relatively straightforward. Should investors in one particular country be able to transfer assets to another on preferential terms, it would not take them long to develop ways of using that favoritism to advance the cause of foreign investors from that second country. And, of course, such favoritism would have its flip side in discrimination against foreign investors from countries excluded from preferential treatment.

The third issue — the tendency of countries to place their own short-term interests ahead of their systemic interests in the multilateral system — is also cause for concern. More than one person has told me that his country has nothing to gain from the realignment of voice and representation in the Fund, indicating indifference, at best, to recent efforts. Yet that argument says that the country in question has no interest in the long-term health of the institution. The Fund will be strengthened by changes that better reflect the current relative positions in the international economy: and countries that do not gain shares will nonetheless gain from the healthier international economy that will result from stronger, better-functioning multilateral institutions.

Similarly, more than one major country has taken a position in the Fund supporting a program that violates Fund policies simply because the larger country politically favors the potential recipient of the program. Over the longer term, a weak program is likely to result in a less favorable outcome for the "protected" country. Quite aside from that, however, such behavior weakens the Fund itself, making it less valuable both to the members wanting favorable treatment for their favored clients and to the borrowing countries. There are similar problems with some diversity issues, where there are pressures for one country's national to be appointed or promoted on the grounds of diversity rather than merit. Cumulatively, the damage can be substantial, especially as other countries then argue that they should also be treated favorably, or advocate favorable treatment for their own nationals or a favored client country. Each successful intervention elicits still further interventions. It is a very slippery slope.

The proliferation of PTAs and the continuing absence of a multilateral regime governing capital flows are both glaring and dangerous departures from multilateral principles. The tendency to push narrow national interests is less obvious, and its impact if incremental: but it is no less dangerous a threat to multilateralism and one which we multilateralists ignore at our peril.

The very success of the multilateral system over the past six decades is both a cause for celebration and a strong argument for doing all we can to preserve both the system and the benefits it has brought. The international economy has been hugely successful over the past sixty years. Real rates of economic growth and, with them, poverty reduction, have surpassed what anyone thought possible at the end of the Second World War. There is still a great deal to be learned and done — not least to extend the benefits of economic growth to all citizens — but progress has already exceeded expectations by a wide margin.

The dramatic progress we have seen was made possible by the multilateral economic system and the liberalization that has come about through unilateral actions, through compliance with the conditions of membership of the multilateral institutions, and through multilateral negotiations. The fact that globalization has greatly intensified economic linkages and interdependence among countries increases the importance of open multilateralism.

In addressing the challenges we face, therefore, we must be careful to appreciate the continuing — even growing — importance of the multilateral system, and to strengthen it.

Of course, international institutions need to adapt to changes in the international economy. They have and they are. But as calls are made for them to achieve those objectives, the message should be clear that changing roles are in the context of a multilateral system: and that multilateralism has been a success that must be fought for and preserved.

Part V

LOOKING FORWARD

Chapter 15

POSTSCRIPT

Most of the material in this volume was first presented before the outbreak of the Great Recession of 2007–09. The successes of the international economy over the past 60 years should remain unchallenged. While the Great Recession certainly raised questions and underlined some weaknesses of the world economy, the lessons arising from the Great Recession strengthen the need for multilateral solutions. The issues previously underappreciated, some of which are discussed below, are almost all ones that individual countries would have difficulty solving.

Before discussing those, however, it is worth repeating that the contrast with living standards and measures of well-being 60 years ago remains. Despite the drops in real GDP in many countries and in the global economy, living standards in almost all countries are higher than they were a decade ago, and enormously higher than they were a half century ago. The emerging markets were badly hit by declining demand for their exports at the start of the Great Recession, but growth has resumed and living standards in most of them are already above their pre-Great Recession peaks.

It will be some time before the lessons of the Great Recession, or more accurately, the lessons arising from the factors that contributed to such a sharp downturn, are fully understood. But many of the contributing factors, if not precisely their exact roles and interactions, are reasonably well accepted.

Almost all of the lessons that have emerged call for multilateral solutions: many of the problems cannot be satisfactorily addressed by countries individually. This has been recognized, at least at some level, by the international community. Indeed, the G-20 began meeting regularly at the outset of the Great Recession and took leadership in pinpointing some of the international issues that required multilateral solutions. To date, however, less has been done about these issues than might have been hoped.

Most analysts agree that global imbalances and insufficient or improper financial regulation were two key factors contributing to the severity of the Great Recession. Both of these problems are crying out for multilateral solutions.

Turning to global imbalances first, many observers noted the unsustainability of the rising American current account deficits. But those deficits were the counterpart of rising current account surpluses which were realized by several countries, of which China's surplus was clearly the largest. By 2004, however, oil prices were increasing rapidly and current account surpluses of the oil exporters were also very high.

The surplus and deficit countries were mutual enablers. Had the Chinese been unwilling to realize such large surpluses, pressures (in the form of rising real interest rates and possibly of falling — or more slowly rising — levels of economic activity) would have mounted rapidly on the United States to undertake adjustments to increase savings relative to investment. Of course, the opposite is also true. Had the current account surplus countries undertaken policy measures to reduce their current account deficits, the Chinese terms of trade would have deteriorated and/or the Chinese would have grown more slowly.

What was needed for the global economy, of course, was that the U.S. take measures to raise its savings rate and reduce its current account deficits at the same time as the Chinese took measures to increase their domestic consumption, which would have reduced their savings and current account surpluses.

Real interest rates remained very low as economic activity was rising in the U.S. and elsewhere. Some argued that it was a "savings glut", but all agreed that real interest rates were abnormally low for that stage of a boom (in normal circumstances, domestic prices might have started increasing in the countries with rapid expansion of economic activity, but the large increases in levels of imports dampened inflationary pressures).

Residential and commercial real estate demand is highly sensitive to the real interest rate, as are some other investments with long expected lives (such as power and other utility investments). Low real interest rates enable people and businesses to borrow more, and hence spend more, on real estate, driving up their prices and inducing additional construction. While there might have been a boom in residential construction in the U.S., the U.K., Spain, and elsewhere, even if real interest rates had been higher, the boom would surely have been less frothy and probably have ended sooner than it did. A dampened boom, in turn, would have meant that the overhang of real estate would have been less and the negative impact on economic activity would have been smaller.

Low real interest rates also provide more incentives for "search for yield", which tempts more risk-taking and doubtful lending. While the rapid expansion of the financial sector might anyway have been excessive, higher real interest rates would, as with construction and real estate, have dampened that expansion at least somewhat.

Had the United States in, say, 2004 or 2005, undertaken policies to tighten fiscal and monetary policies sufficiently to reduce the current account imbalance significantly, with no action from the surplus countries, it is likely that worldwide recession would have resulted. Similarly, had the Chinese expanded their domestic demand enough to reduce their current account surpluses significantly, the likely outcome in the absence of offsetting policies in the U.S. and elsewhere would have been strengthened inflationary pressures.

Obviously, the desirable resolution would have been for there to be simultaneous but opposite adjustments for both deficit and surplus countries. But that did not happen.

A clear lesson for the international economy is the need to find a mechanism by which mutually enabling large countries can be induced to modify their macroeconomic stances when expansion becomes too rapid. The IMF, in its World Economic Outlooks and Global Financial Stability Reports, repeatedly called attention to global imbalances and the risks that were being incurred.[1] Under Managing Director Rodrigo de Rato, "multilateral consultations" were held between high-level representatives of the five groups of countries regarded as most involved: China, the ECB representing the euro area, Japan, the oil exporters, and the U.S.

While all participants in the multilateral consultations agreed there was a problem and that the issue should be addressed, the surplus countries generally insisted that it was the deficit countries that should adjust, and conversely. The result was agreement on the desired outcome, but no action.

With the onset of the Great Recession, the G-20 again raised the issue of global imbalances, and called for the IMF to carry out surveillance over macroeconomic policy of major countries to assess the global sustainability of plans. Termed the "Mutual Assessment Process", MAP, the process has just begun. The IMF has no legal basis on which to force countries to alter their behavior, and questions arise as to whether the MAP will achieve what the earlier multilateral consultations were unable to do.

But global imbalances were clearly an underlying factor in making the Great Recession as severe as it was, and it is evident that adjustment on the part of both deficit and surplus countries is called for. At the time of writing, imbalances are once again increasing, after having fallen for a while during the

---

[1] Raghuram Rajan, then Chief Economist and Head of the Research Department at the IMF, even gave a clear account of the risks and their likely outcome at the 2005 Federal Reserve Bank of Kansas City meeting at Jackson Hole. His warning met with anger and derision.

Great Recession. It is to be hoped that the MAP will be sufficient, under the auspices of the IMF, to induce deficit and surplus countries alike to undertake the appropriate adjustments. But whether the MAP is sufficient remains to be seen. If not, concerns must arise about the possibility of growing imbalances and a repeat of the difficulties in the years ahead. One has to hope that there will be sufficient multilateral action so that can be avoided. But it is clearly an issue for which multilateral action is required.

Financial regulation is another issue on which there seems to be agreement that faults contributed to excesses during the boom. It is clearly important that altered regulatory regimes are changed in ways that improve the functioning of the financial system and do not simply repress it. Assuming that to be the case, however, there are crucial issues best addressed multilaterally.

Financial instititutions in individual countries where tighter regulation is contemplated are naturally concerned that such measures as higher capital requirements and regulations calling for convertible subordinated debt will unduly handicap them in competing with institutions in other countries without similar regulations. Concern about a "race to the bottom", as the least regulated countries' institutions are able to outcompete others, is legitimate. Again, a multilateral solution is greatly to be desired. While this does not mean that regulation should everywhere be identical, it does imply that it is desirable to have a common framework where the parameters of regulation are such that there is a reasonably level international playing field.

Quite aside from the issues confronting policy makers with regard to the international monetary system, the Doha Round as discussed in Chapter 12 remains unfinished. The importance of the open multilateral trading system cannot be underestimated, and there are important issues requiring resolution, best addressed after the Doha Round is completed. Of these, a major one is finding a framework within which preferential trading arrangements can be more consistent within the WTO framework. But before work begins on new issues, the Doha Round must be finished. For reasons described throughout this volume, the open multilateral trading system is crucially important for the international economy.

As the Round drags on without resolution, the prestige and authority of the WTO is diminished, even as its importance for the international economy is increased.

The international economy has changed markedly since the authors of Bretton Woods transformed their vision of a prosperous international economy into the framework provided by the IMF, the World Bank, and the GATT/WTO. But the importance of an appropriate multilateral framework has increased. It is to be hoped that recognition of the tremendous progress of the world economy in the past half century, plus the lessons about the degree of interdependence arising from the Great Recession, will lead to greater appreciation of the importance of open multilateralism and a strengthening of the multilateral institutions in ways that encourage competition and an economic environment that will enable continued progress in sustained growth and rising living standards and welfare throughout the world.

AUTHOR INDEX

SUBJECT INDEX